MY LIFE IN PROPAGANDA

ALSO BY THE AUTHOR

Gramatyka mojego języka
(The Grammar of My Language). Poetry.

The Unspeakable: Narratives of Trauma.
Stroińska, M., Cecchetto, V. and K. Szymanski (eds)

The International Classroom: Challenging the Notion.
Cecchetto, V. and M. Stroińska, Eds.

Exile, Language and Identity
Stroińska M. & Cecchetto, V., Eds.

Relative Points of View
Linguistic Representation of Culture
Stroińska, M. Ed.

Stereotype im Fremdsprachen-unterricht
(Stereotypes in foreign language teaching)
Löschmann, M. & Stroińska, M. (eds)

Book Translation

Lingua Tertii Imperii, Notizbuch eines Philologen
Victor Klemperer (from German into Polish)

The Little Book: Story Reader for a Free Ukraine
Mykola Matwijszuk, Ed.
(From Ukrainian to English)

MY LIFE IN PROPAGANDA

LANGUAGE AND TOTALITARIAN REGIMES

MAGDA STROIŃSKA PHD

"Language is a guide to social reality."
Edward Sapir (1929)

Calgary, Alberta, Canada

Durvile & UpRoute Books
DURVILE IMPRINT OF DURVILE PUBLICATIONS LTD.

Calgary, Alberta, Canada
durvile.com

LIBRARY AND ARCHIVES CATALOGUING IN PUBLICATIONS DATA

My Life in Propaganda: Language and Totalitarian Regimes
Stroińska, Magda, author

1. Memoir | 2. Linguistics | 3. Political Science
4. Propaganda | 5. Poland

Durvile Reflections Series.
Series editor, Lorene Shyba

978-1-990735-33-2 (pbk)
978-1-990735-34-9 (ebook) | 978-1-990735-35-6 (audio)

Jacket design, Austin Andrews

Durvile Publications would like to acknowledge the financial support of the Government of Canada through the Canadian Heritage Canada Book Fund and the Government of Alberta, Alberta Media Fund.

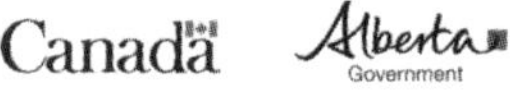

Printed in Canada. First edition. First printing. 2023.

Durvile Publication Ltd. is committed to reducing the consumption of nonrenewable resources in the production of our books. We make every effort to use materials that support a sustainable future.

We acknowledge the traditional land of the Treaty 7 Peoples of Southern Alberta: the Siksika, Piikani, and Kainai of the Niisitapi (Blackfoot) Confederacy; the Dene Tsuut'ina; and the Chiniki, Bearspaw, and Wesley Stoney Nakoda First Nations. We also acknowledge the Region 3 Métis Nation of Alberta.

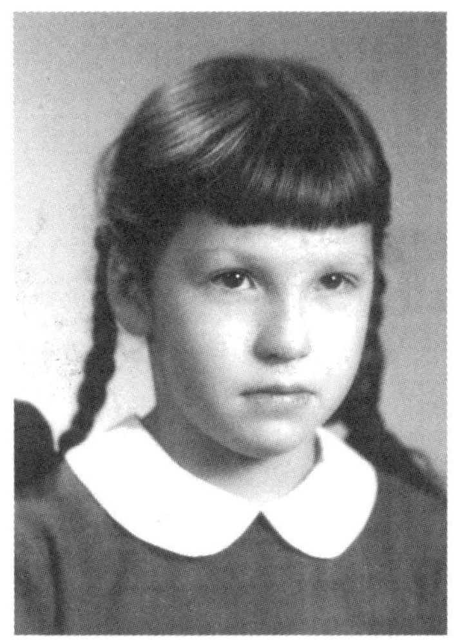

I dedicate this book
to my parents
who never lied to me
about important things
and to my children
so they understand
where I come from.

Little girls

for Kasia

we were two little girls
then barely ten
just two little girls

the one with blond piggy tails
was you
and I
with brown braided hair

we grew up
in big pre-war apartments
left to our own devices
by the busy parents

we learned about sex
by deciphering medical books
written in Fraktur
and translated them
with an old German dictionary

we played house
with one Barbie
and a few wooden dolls
one of them black

we did not have dolls that looked like boys…
so
instead of some happy families
we played JFK's and Martin Luther King's widows
the Barbie was Jackie

at an iron gate
we impersonated
Lenin in prison
flirting with Nadezdha

we tested each other
on difficult questions of history:
like who killed Polish officers in Katyń?
correct answers supported our friendship

and we were usually correct
as every night
we overheard our parents
listening to the white noise
known as the Voice of America
or Radio Free Europe

by grade four
we made plans to emigrate
and we did indeed, in our late twenties

who could have foreseen
where the turbulent waters
would wash us ashore?

we kept in touch
over the years
kept our friendship alive
only to reconnect
to write together
a book
on trauma

06/2018

CONTENTS

PREFACE

Which is to be Master?

"When I use a word," Humpty Dumpty said in rather a scornful tone,
"it means just what I choose it to mean—neither more nor less."
"The question is," said Alice, "whether you can make words
mean so many different things."
"The question is," said Humpty Dumpty, "which is to be master — that's all."

— Lewis Carroll, Through the Looking Glass, Chapter 6

THE ABOVE POPULAR FRAGMENT of the conversation between Alice and Humpty Dumpty is often quoted in linguistics textbooks. It illustrates the complexities of the concept of meaning, the relationship between speakers' intentions and hearers' interpretations, or the dilemma of the interdependency between language, thought, and reality. Lewis Carroll made a number of interesting observations about language in his two volumes of Alice's adventures, *Alice in Wonderland* and *Through the Looking Glass*, and some of his observations predate proper linguistic discoveries. The above conversation could be interpreted as pointing in the same direction as Ludwig Wittgenstein's breakthrough observation that the meaning of a word is defined by its use.

The distortion of the meaning of words is the essence of propaganda. However, in an authoritarian system, the process of twisting the meanings of words is, of course, not called distortion. Neither is it usually called propaganda. Except for Lenin and Goebbels, who proudly used the term to refer to their methods of information dissemination, governments, parties and individual politicians usually reserve the term 'propaganda' for the dishonest disinformation used by their opponents.

Instead, they choose to attest that what they themselves are doing when they distort the meanings of words is simply the process of defining the true significance of terms. If it is carried out without anyone noticing, this procedure can be very successful and may even be considered a natural process of language development. However, very little in the development of linguistic meaning is natural or accidental because language structure reflects mechanisms of human cognition and semantics reflects social reality.

It is here that the question "Which is to be master?" becomes important. In authoritarian regimes, the master or masters are easy to identify. They are the individual leaders or political parties who sociologist Stuart Hall labels as 'primary definers', i.e., those who have the power to set the agenda and define or determine what is discussed in the public arena, and how. Hall observed that the news media "translate into a public idiom the statements and viewpoints of the primary definers" (Hall, 1978, 59). In authoritarian countries, the total control of the government over the media makes this process very easy. In democratic societies, primary definers include not only the government, but also business and academic communities, the cultural elite, or other sufficiently influential individuals or groups of individuals.

It is an important historical task to describe how totalitarian regimes of the 20th century used propaganda in order to influence the behaviour of masses, however, from an individual person's point of view, an even more important objective is to find out how one can defend their inner freedoms and cognitive capacities in order to resist thought manipulation. In countries where propaganda is centrally planned and omnipresent, this means that one needs to understand how meanings are defined or redefined (manipulated and distorted) by primary definers and where deviations from truth or reality begin.

This means paying very close attention to the life of language and to the many separate lives of words. First and foremost, it means caution. A person who has experienced language manipulation, whether at a personal level, having been cheated or lied to in a vicious way, or at a societal level, as was the case in communist countries, will never be able to trust words again. Suspicion becomes second nature. It is an instinct, a self defence mechanism. This defence, however, may ultimately be counterproductive in everyday life. Suspicion may in fact help the distorters of meaning, piggybacking off the initial skepticism and developing into a firm belief that you can't trust anyone. In turn, this lack of trust hinders solidarity and promotes isolation of an individual. I had the impression that this lack of mutual trust was quite widespread in many communist countries but was not so much the case in Poland where communism was clearly perceived as a foreign import. A better and more efficient method of self defence is simply developing a critical attitude to official discourse.

The idea for this book was born in London, in July 2001 after I gave a talk at the London Institute of Economic Affairs at the kind invitation of Philip Booth, who became its Editorial and Programme Director in the following year. My talk was met with a very encouraging reception. To my greater surprise, when I mentioned the topic to Marion Berghahn from Berghahn Books, she was enthusiastic about publishing the ideas as a book. Needless to say, I was enthusiastic too.

My desire to study and write about propaganda, something I commonly refer to as linguistic manipulation in totalitarian countries, was somewhat of a personal mission of mine. And yet, despite the encouragement from Marion, it took me a very long time to find a format that would allow me to combine my academic interests in sociolinguistics and my personal experience of a life with propaganda.

In the years that followed, a book that had originated as an academic research project began to morph into something more closely resembling an academic memoir. My own project began to approximate one of the diary assignments I give to my students: observe the effects of advertisements of beauty products on your image of self…; Observe how you derive your understanding of social reality from the language the media use.

As I wrote this book, I was further reminded of other linguistic or philological memoirs I had read and admired.

Among those, first and foremost was *Lingua Tertii Imperii* ('Language of the Third Reich') by Victor Klemperer (published in 1946, based on the author's war time diaries and subtitled "From the notebook of a philologist") and Michał Głowiński's comments on words (*Nowomowa po polsku* ('Newspeak in Polish') 1990; *Marcowe gadanie: komentarze do słów* 1966-1971 ('March Chatter: Comments on Words 1966-1971') 1991; and *Peereliada: komentarze do słów* 1976-1981 (Polish People's Republic's (PRL) Carnival: Comments on Words 1976-1981) 1993).

The language of propaganda is a complex phenomenon. Its study involves grammar, semantics and the lexicon, i.e., the words. The words are not all alike: different parts of speech play different roles in propaganda discourse. We may in fact revisit what Humpty Dumpty had to say about that:

> They've a temper, some of them—particularly verbs, they're the proudest—adjectives you can do anything with, but not verbs—however, I can manage the whole lot of them! (Carroll 1971)

Verbs are indeed the proudest. They do not bend easily. This is why political slogans I remember were so often missing verbs or at least the inflected part of the predicate that would indicate the person, number, tense. Because of this vagueness, it was impossible to determine how to interpret slogans and therefore it was also usually impossible to say whether they were telling the truth. This strategy of verb omission, however, opens the door to many undesirable interpretations. One poster said *Naród z Partią—Partia z Narodem* (The Nation with the Party—the Party with the Nation) but it wasn't clear what they were doing together. My favourite example goes back to October Revolution posters and banners in Poland in the 1970s that read simply "Lenin in October." October was the month associated with the 1917 communist revolution and thus widely celebrated by Eastern European regimes. Some witty soul wrote underneath: "and cats in March"…

Yet, we do not need to look to communist times in order to find multiple examples of such ill-defined (on purpose) slogans. A popular Canadian road sign posted by the provincial government read "Working together for a better Ontario." Are we? Should we be? Who is or should be doing that? The government? The people? By leaving it to the audience to supply the missing verb and the intended subject, the authors of such slogans are making us their accomplices.

Verbs are also the proudest because it is difficult to break their so-called 'valency' requirements. Each verb naturally requires a certain number of necessary participants in order to form a complete utterance. The verb 'to love' naturally requires someone who is experiencing the feeling (the lover) and someone or something that is the object of that emotion. It is normally impossible to make the hearer forget or ignore the necessary participants in an action expressed by the verb. But politicians will try. When, in the 1970s, the Soviet Union broke off some arms reduction negotiations with the USA, Polish press used a rather convoluted construction: "Arms talks broken off at the fault of the USA." But the question "By whom?" could still be asked. For sure, had they been broken off by the Americans, the papers would have emphasized it. If the papers did not say by whom, it could only mean that the talks were broken off by the Soviet side.

If the necessary element of the verb valency has been left unspecified, we naturally look for the best available candidate to fill the empty slot. The best candidates are those that are easily available in the immediate context. In mid 1970s, there was a big banner on the sand mine in the little town of Płociczno, near the Wigry Lake: "We will distribute as much as we produce." Posted on the gate to the sand mine, it made it natural to think of distributing sand among Poles who were already feeling the consequences of the wrong economic management in the country and lacking most of the everyday products.

Those verbs that cannot have their meaning tampered with because their sense is too obvious and too well-defined can be replaced by other, more servile verbs. Thus, instead of 'killing' the enemy, our forces 'eliminate' and 'neutralize' him or her. Note that I said enemy, not enemies; singular form is important because there should be no suggestion whatsoever that there may be multiple enemies. That would be distracting and suspicious. If many of them are against us, they may have a reason. Also, the masculine gender of the word 'enemy' in many languages is very handy. Killing or eliminating feminine enemies could make one feel uncomfortable. The main reason such substitutes are used for the verb 'to kill' is to stop the hearer from associating the object of the action with living beings. To kill means to take away life from some person or other living creature. 'Eliminating' does not pose that problem. We eliminate obstacles or unpleasant odours. This is why euphemisms, not just in the domain of verbs but for all parts of speech, are very widespread in political discourse, especially at the time of war. And again, this is not restricted to the totalitarian regimes of the past. We can see this mechanism being used today by democratic countries. It makes a linguist wonder whether the presence of certain linguistic processes may be indicative of some deeper change in society.

It seems to me that paying attention to language change is not just useful or possibly rewarding in terms of understanding societal developments. I believe language can indeed serve as the best barometer of current or future social trends. When words come into being, it means that new phenomena are either already in existence or are being created through the introduction of new lexical items. In totalitarian regimes, it has always been easier to invent words than to create new things or to change the living conditions of the population. When the party declares that the production of refrigerators has been further increased, it makes one think that it had been increased in the past (so it must now be quite substantial) and, at the very least, it makes one assume that some refrigerators are being produced. This is simply a result of the presupposition force of the above statement. It makes sense within our logic to assume so but it does not have to be the case. To produce refrigerators is more costly than to say that they are being produced. I remember a several-month-long queue in a store in a remote part of Warsaw where my husband and I finally bought our first refrigerator. One of us had to go there once a week to make sure we stayed on the 'social queue list' (or was it a list of the social queue? *lista społeczna kolejki* or *lista kolejki społecznej*). Linguistic construction of social reality—or social fiction—was a powerful tool in both communism and German Nazism.

I believe that watching language used by a group of people tells us more about that group than almost anything. We could call it 'diagnostic' linguistics but it may in fact be part of what is established now as forensic linguistics. It can be entertaining when one looks at some more or less innocent language manipulation in advertising, like the omnipresent slogan, 'new and improved' (if anything, it is either 'or', not 'and'). It can be terrifying, if one looks at the use of hate speech and ethnic, racial, or religious stereotyping that often serves as a prelude to a war. Regardless, it is worth paying attention to.

This book became more personal than originally planned. I started to write it for an academic publisher as an account of totalitarian language abuse, but very soon came to think about that abuse at a very personal level because it was, in many ways, an account of my own life with propaganda. I spent more than 25 years growing up in a communist country and the next 40 years watching from a distance as Eastern Europe was changing and how, despite political and social reforms, its fundamental problems persisted. The era of communism I experienced was no longer the time of violent persecution of those who opposed the system. To tell the truth, I grew up in an environment where I had the right to assume that no one really supported the communist ideology. Some people were simply conforming—to various degrees—to political requirements for some immediate or long-term benefits. There were no communist books in the library in my parents' home and no one has ever made me read one, not even in school or at the university. Do I even have a right to write about communism?

I practiced what George Orwell called 'doublespeak' at school in those classes where I thought it necessary to use language that distorted or obscured the truth, but I tried not to practice 'doublethink'. Mine was a pretty typical childhood and life in the late stages of Eastern European communism. Perhaps it is worth documenting the effect propaganda had on an ordinary human being? How it changed people even when they thought they transcended it. How it made one struggle with words in order to get to the bottom of things and to determine which is to be master. This book is an attempt to document one life with propaganda. Mine.

What began as a mostly historical and somewhat autobiographical undertaking on my part, suddenly took on a new life when—after a short period of optimism following the fall of the Berlin Wall in 1989—new international and national conflicts and the surge of populism brought with them new variations of language manipulation. We know that every genocide starts with hate propaganda and dehumanization of social groups targeted as the enemy. It was clearly depicted by Gordon Allport (1954) as the pyramid of aggression. With the influence of the online communication and social media, everyone can spread disinformation. It seems to me that propaganda and thought manipulation have become some of the most important problems we face today: how do we know what is true and what is 'fake news'. As I have been asking myself this question for most of my life; I hope that my own struggles with language and its representation or creation of reality may be of some help to others.

Woodstock, Ontario, November 2022

CHAPTER 1

My Life in Propaganda

THIS BOOK is an attempt to bridge my personal preoccupation with language manipulation and my academic interest in linguistic representations of culture and society. As such, it is too personal to be seen as an academic book and may at times seem too academic to be considered a personal narrative or a memoir.

My naive curiosity about the mysterious and sometimes puzzling relationship between reality and its representation in everyday language and in the arts belongs to my earliest childhood memories. One such distinct early memory relates to Polish and Soviet post-war films that I watched and enjoyed as a child; but they often left me somewhat puzzled. My attention was particularly attracted by the fact that these black and white movies (maybe they were black and white as I watched most of them on a black and white TV?) often depicted picturesque cities, including my native Warsaw. What I found confusing was that the pictures on the screen differed considerably from my day-to-day experiences. In the early sixties, which is as far back as my recollections go, Warsaw was grey, poor, and the signs of destruction from the war were still visible everywhere. There were still some ruins, or nearly ruins, in the city centre and numerous (re)construction sites. Many buildings had been somewhat patched up to make them suitable for living. I do remember new apartment blocks, like the one into which my half-brother Renek had moved with his family, with tiny apartments and fake or minuscule balconies. I also remember the partly ruined or badly damaged but still-impressive prewar apartment buildings, like the one in Noakowskiego Street where my grandmother lived, with high ceilings, balconies with wrought iron railings and deep, well-like courtyards. The apartment building where I spent my childhood—built in the 1930s and never fully renovated until just a few years ago, more than 70 years after the end of the war—used to wear unhealed scars from fighting during WWII and destruction from the Warsaw Uprising of 1944.

Nothing that I saw around me looked like the happy, bright, and sunny cities in the movies, with their modern and clean houses, wide and festive looking streets, and new and shiny street cars or buses. And yet, I still recall my deep conviction that what I saw on the screen was the proper reality, the one that must have really existed, albeit not in my immediate surroundings. At least it was the reality that should have existed. The world around me was, I thought, an impoverished reality—perhaps the same, but worn down by time and abuse. Even people in the movies looked different. They smiled showing white and healthy teeth, and they looked happy, unlike the grey and subdued crowd on real life streetcars or buses.

The feature movie I remember from my childhood better than any other—perhaps because I must have dragged my mother to see it more than two or three times—was a Soviet production for children, *Timur i jego drużyna (Timur and His Team)*, based on a book by Arkady Gaidar. I first saw it at the annual International Children's Day celebration organized for kids at my mother's work place, the University of Agriculture (SGGW), where she was the deputy head librarian. Oh, how I wished to have a friend like Timur! He was handsome, full of mischief but also selfless, noble and even heroic in his efforts to help others. The action of that movie was set in a small town during *a* war—some men left for the front and the village boys were particularly concerned about helping anonymously those women whose husbands were fighting 'the enemy'.

What war was that? It seemed natural to me, at the age of six or seven, that the war in the movie must have been World War II and the enemy was the German army. For a small child in post-war Poland, that was *the* war. It was only relatively recently that a conversation with Inga Dolinina, my Russian colleague at McMaster University, made me revisit those memories and find out more about my favourite childhood movie and the book it was based on.

The story of *Timur and His Team*, written in 1940 and using the name of Gaidar's son for the protagonist, is considered Gaidar's most lasting contribution to Soviet literature. The online biographical Encyclopaedia of Soviet Writers provides a detailed tale of Gaidar's life and literary work. Timur's story, it says, "was part of the curriculum in every Soviet school even up into the 1990s." According to Soviet sources, at the very beginning of what in Russia is called "the Great Patriotic War," Gaidar was commissioned to write another story, *Klyatva Timura (Timur's Vow)*, as a screenplay for a patriotic film. 'The Great Patriotic War' is a Soviet propaganda term used to describe the period immediately following German Operation Barbarossa, i.e., the German invasion of the Soviet Union, which commenced on June 22, 1941. Until then, Nazi Germany and the Soviet Union were allies. The only 'war' that the Soviet Union was fighting in 1940, when the book was written, i.e., before the beginning of the conflict with Hitler's Third Reich, was the occupation of the former Polish territories which started on September 17, 1939 and the invasion of Finland which started on November 30, 1939. Was my childhood hero Timur helping families of those who fought against Poland? Or was it Finland? Whichever one it was, it changed the whole story and profoundly reduced my admiration for the film.

Gaidar apparently wrote the new screenplay in 12 days (having been given 15) and, immediately after finishing his work, volunteered to join the Red Army in order to be sent to the front. His request was refused and he went to war as a correspondent for the paper *Komsomolskaya Pravda*. He was killed in a battle in Ukraine on October 26, 1941. Apparently, the detachment he was with was surrounded by Germans, but Gaidar refused to retreat and continued to fight. That, at least, is the official story. The online Encyclopaedia of Soviet Writers alleges that, in 1979, Soviet journalist Viktor Glushchenko discovered a woman, who claimed that Gaidar and another comrade had escaped the encirclement, spent the winter hiding out in her home, and left only in the spring of 1942. Nothing about that has been officially confirmed but the journalist who publicized his discovery had been 'actively discouraged' by the Soviet authorities from pursuing it any further and he was 'sensible' enough to obey (for more details see the Gaidar entry). So, not only is the story itself somewhat suspect—my Russian friend maintains that the war in the book was just a generic war and, indeed, no details of *the enemy* are ever mentioned—but "the most celebrated children's author in the Soviet Union" may have died not at the time and place specified by Soviet encyclopaedias either, although this may only be a conspiracy theory. I am not convinced that this conspiracy theory is true as Gaidar's grandson, Egor Timurovich Gaidar, a Russian economist and pro-reform deputy Prime Minister in Boris Yeltsin's government, would have likely mentioned the controversy in his memoirs (Gaidar 1999).

I was not aware of those double interpretations and ambiguities when I was in love with Timur, but I think it was that film that has marked the beginning of my life in the realm created by propaganda. My parents were visibly not impressed with my admiration for the socialist realist art. My other favourite childhood movie was Disney's *Lady and the Tramp* (released in 1955) and I saw that one several times too. My childhood sense of beauty was strongly affected by this animated classic, and my sense of a romantic dinner was for ever set by the scene where Lady and Tramp share spaghetti and meatballs at an Italian restaurant. I am sure that my poor mother much preferred to watch *Lady and the Tramp* with me than *Timur.*

Even though Poland was definitely a poor country, I do not remember any significant economic hardship or even queues from my childhood. Of course, I had no comparison to any other reality. I have always had the feeling of plenty. Queues became part of my reality much later, around the age of eighteen. When I was little, shops were still relatively well supplied (for communist standards) and food was perhaps not sophisticated but plentiful. At Christmas, the family of my father's first wife from Łętownia, a small village in the southeast corner of Poland used to send us parcels with walnuts, wheat, poppy seeds, and honey—all we needed to make our traditional (Eastern Polish and Ukrainian) Christmas food dish—*kutia.*

I do not recall my parents ever instructing me that what I would be taught at school may not always be true and that different things may be said at school than what can be said at home. Somehow it was obvious, never questioned and never even seen as a problem. The world I grew up in was black and white, just like the news on TV only everything was "the other way around" than what TV or the papers were telling people. I understood in my childish way and simply took for granted that what was praised by the TV news announcer was not really good or not true and people who were portrayed as bad were actually good. I vividly recall my grandmother sitting on a chair close to the TV set, watching daily news and throwing invectives at the speaker. She was the only one in my family who, for some masochistic reasons, watched communist news on TV. She had to be close to the TV so that the volume could be set on low as no one else wanted to listen. She was repeatedly asking the same rhetorical question: "How can they be lying so blatantly?" (*Jak można tak kłamać w żywe oczy?*). She was particularly upset by the long speeches by Władysław Gomułka, the then 1st Secretary of the Communist Party. It was telling to find a very similar childhood account in the memoir by Vesna Goldsworthy (*Chernobyl Strawberries*, 2007) who too recalls her grandfather swearing at TV news. I remember my mother swearing at the TV in the year before she passed away, in 2006. Interestingly, I catch myself swearing when I watch today's news from Poland. I watch news online now rather than on TV but my reaction is just the same.

I guess, the assumption that the news was propaganda (I probably called it *lies*, not propaganda then) was a given to me, even though I did not understand the reasons for its untruthfulness. This led to some amusing situations when I constructed my own conspiracy theories based on the conviction that there was a widespread persecution of the innocent by the authorities. When I heard my aunt Wanda asking my mother whether she had seen Kafka's *Process*, I immediately assumed that it was some political process and was shocked to see posters for it with the logo of, I think, *Teatr Narodowy* (National Theatre) in Warsaw. A political process in a theatre! What will they do next?

However, the idea of a process in a theatre is not that unique. Mikhail Bulgakov uses it in his novel *Master and Margarita*. A more personal example was my husband's uncle, Jerzy Kazimierski, who was sentenced to death in 1945 for his participation in the Home Army's struggle after the end of WWII. His show trial was literally staged in a movie theatre in Łódź. The death sentence was later commuted to life, then 15 years of prison and he was released only after Stalin's death in 1953. At 22 years of age at the time of his trial, he was the youngest officer of the Home Army to be officially sentenced to death (many were killed without a trail). The note in the Warsaw daily newspaper *Życie Warszawy* (October 5, 1945) referred to him and those sentenced in the same trial as a "band of terrorists." The sentence was annulled and he was fully rehabilitated only in 1998. It seems my wacky conspiracy theories were not a complete nonsense.

I learned most about the recent history of my country from my family's history. I am sure that most Polish families could say the same. We used to visit family graves at two Warsaw cemeteries regularly when I was little and I actually enjoyed those outings, especially to the Powązki Cemetery which was full of old, moss-covered monuments and crumbling tombstones, many of them more than a hundred years old. We always visited the grave of Olga Zienkiewicz (maiden name Łozińska), my father's first mother-in-law and the symbolic grave of his first wife. "Died on July 7, 1941 in the USSR" it said on the tombstone. I knew that story by heart.

My father's family all came from the East. He was born in 1900 in Czortków (now Chortkiv, in Western Ukraine, east of Lviv), studied medicine at Lwów University and worked as deputy director of a public hospital in Czortków. He married a somewhat younger fellow doctor, Wanda Zienkiewicz, from a wealthy Lwów family, Polish but possibly with some Tatar or Armenian background. They had two sons. My father and his family moved to Warsaw in 1935 where my father started to work for the Social Security Institution.

In the summer of 1939, Dr. Wanda Zienkiewicz-Piotrowska, together with her two sons, Renek and Andrzej, then 8 and 7, was spending the summer visiting her parents in Lwów (now Lviv, Ukraine) and enjoying her newly acquired summer holiday place in Rudniki, some 50 km south of the city. My father, a medical doctor, was in Poland, participating in military exercises as a reserve officer and expecting mobilization for the war seemed imminent. When

Germany declared the war against Poland on September 1, 1939, my two half-brothers and their mother did not return to Warsaw but decided to stay in Lwów with the grandparents, in Miączyńskiego Street. On September 17, Eastern Poland was invaded by the Soviet Union, according to the secret Ribbentropp-Molotov agreement signed earlier in 1939. My father, recalled from reserve to active duty in the Polish Army, was captured by the Soviets and miraculously escaped their POW camp (and likely death) thanks to the help of his Jewish colleagues. Those brave men recognized my father and asked the Soviets for permission to call on him to consult on some serious medical problem of someone among the Soviet camp authorities. They gave my father civilian clothing and helped him escape from prison and flee. He went to Lwów, to his inlaws, not even knowing that his wife and sons were still there. I assume that many of those who were captured with my father were later found shot dead in mass graves of Katyń, Kharkov, or Miednoje.

Despite my father's efforts to bring his wife and the children back to Warsaw (he managed to return to Warsaw and sent her papers that would allow her to cross the border that divided Soviet occupied territory from the German occupied part of Poland), she decided to stay in Lwów. Maybe she did not want to leave her mother alone, after her father passed away in the winter of 1939. Sadly, she was deported on June 29, 1940 (third deportation), with the boys, to a small settlement of Panino, in Voronezh region of Russia. The journey on a crowded goods train took nine days. After months of hard physical labour, she was eventually allowed to work at the local field hospital—after all, she was a medical doctor, an ophthalmologist, the only physician for miles around. While this improved their living conditions for a while, she contracted typhoid and died on July 7, 1941, just a couple of weeks after Germany declared war against the Soviet Union.

My two half-brothers survived the war. Andrzej Piotrowski was evacuated with the Polish army formed in the USSR after Hitler attacked Stalin. He travelled with the army and the refugees from the Soviet camps to Scotland, via Persia. Renek Piotrowski stayed in the Soviet Union, adopted by a local Russian family who did not have children. This in itself is another sad story. Renek got Polio while in the deportation camp. His mother used all connections she could to get him transported to a 'proper' hospital where he actually recovered and, after some time, was sent back to Panino. By then, however, his mother was dead and Andrzej had left Panino with the newly formed Polish army. Some good people took Renek into their home and took care of him until the end of the war.

I believe that my half-brothers' entire lives have been profoundly shaped by this childhood trauma. Renek, a scientist, rarely spoke about it. Andrzej, a humanist, often recalled memories from that time in his poems, as poetry allowed him a degree of freedom that would not be possible in another form of expression. An attempt to put those memories into a prose account was his first book, *Prośba o Annę (Asking for Anna)* (Piotrowski 1962) but even its subtitle, *a story in sixteen dreams*, seems a gesture of self-censorship. As if the author were saying: it is all fiction. I only saw it in my dreams. Only in 1999 was he able to publish in Poland a memoir of his exile, describing the deportation, life in the little village of Panino, the death of his beloved mother, and many other ordeals he and his brother endured (Czcibor-Piotrowski 1999). What, in my view, is astounding about this book is that it is a memoir of love and life, not hatred and death. Written from the perspective of the little boy he was then, Andrzej recalls the horrors of war as a background for his childhood and early youth: playing with other children, Polish, Ukrainian, Jewish, and Russian, his first love, and the overwhelming power and beauty of nature. There was no need for pathos or any form of value judgment. It would have sounded false in the mouth of a child narrator. Neither was it necessary to spell out the accusations. What could be good about a system that sends mothers with children into the wilderness, that orders a female eye doctor to work cutting trees, that lets her die away from her family, leaving her sons at the mercy of strangers in a foreign land? And yet, Andrzej simply recalls the beauty and wisdom of his mother and the goodness of other women who took care of him. This makes his message much more powerful than if he spoke of the evil of communism. From my own childhood, I particularly remember Andrzej's story of Polish orphans in Persia who were issued milk of magnesia by some British or American charitable organization and who immediately consumed it and were all sick afterwards. Andrzej describes this in his second war-time memoir, *Cud w Esfachanie* (A Miracle in Isfahan')(Czcibor-Piotrowski 2001, 14).

The milk of magnesia story sounds a bit like the story reported by Alexandr Solzhenitsyn (1973) about Soviet prisoners who discovered the bodies of some prehistoric amphibians preserved in permafrost in Kolyma, in the far North of the Soviet Empire. I actually seem to remember a mention of that event (without any reference to prisoners, of course) in a children's magazine in Poland. The story was that the meat was so well preserved in ice that those present at the discovery of the animal carcasses immediately proceeded to grill their meat over a fire and consume it. The underlying horror of hunger can only be understood by those who know the context of both events. Who, in their right mind, would venture to eat millennia-old meat unless they were starving?

This part of my family history was non-existent in my school history textbooks. In communist Poland, the Molotov-Ribbentrop Pact was as secret in the 1960s or 1970s as it was in 1939. Deportations of Poles to Siberia or Kazakhstan never happened; it was a mystery why my father's first wife died in the middle of nowhere. And it was Nazi Germans who killed Polish officers and buried them in the mass graves in Katyń, I was told in school. It didn't bother me at that time that I had to learn history in two versions—an official version for school purposes and the real one, for everywhere else. In Grade 3 or 4, I became friends with Kasia Michałowska, a girl from my class whose parents, also medical doctors, asked mine if the two of us could have private English lessons together. The responsibility for the Katyń massacre of Polish officers was her test to determine whether I was a suitable company for her. We were walking home from school, nine or ten years old, hopping from one stone post to another in a low fence along Niemcewicza Street, when Kasia suddenly asked me in an age-appropriate provocative manner: "So tell me, who killed Polish soldiers in Katyń?" "Russians," I said, surprised by the seriousness of her tone. She said okay and we became friends. I passed the test.

Experiences like that do leave traces in our personalities. They make you realize that there may be different versions of every story we are told. And they introduce you to the concepts—and practice—of

Orwellian 'doublethink' and 'doublespeak' at a very early age. When my own children were little in Canada, we had a rule that whatever toys or fast-food deals were advertised on Canadian or American TV were not really worth buying. It worked better than constant arguments. One time I gave in and bought a toy both children wanted because it looked great in a TV commercial. It broke down almost immediately and the rule was never challenged again.

Despite daily problems with reality and language when I was young, my first serious personal encounter with *doublespeak* occurred only after the communist government in Poland imposed martial law in December 1981. I was then working as a junior assistant in the German Department at Warsaw University. Two developments had a significant impact on my perception of the events between December 1981 and August 1984, when I left Poland.

The first one was related to my volunteer work for the Committee of Assistance for Political Prisoners and Their Families, opened at St. Marcin's church in Piwna Street after December 13, 1981. I was introduced there by a friend, Piotr Świstak in the spring of 1982. I worked one or two afternoons a week in the Information Intake Section. We had a table and a few shoe boxes with used computer punch cards. On those cards, we recorded—by hand—information about arrests and other forms of harassment experienced by ordinary people. We asked friends and family of the people who had been arrested, when, where, what were the charges and where they were taken to. The card set kept growing and some names and incarceration places became familiar. Many people were coming to the Committee because they cherished the knowledge that someone kept records on the arrests and harassment they or their friends and loved ones experienced. This may have given them the reassurance that their suffering was not anonymous even if there were thousands of them and even if there was no mention of this in the media. One of my favourite visitors was the father of Solidarność (Solidarity) activist from Wrocław, Władysław Frasyniuk. He was very jovial and loved to talk about his son. Once he mentioned that his son really wanted to have a harmonica. I asked around and got one from my cousin. I gave it to Mr. Frasyniuk Senior and hope it found its way to his son.

The Committee had broken the seal of silence that so often kept the victims in isolation from the society and allowed the perpetrators to commit crimes without anyone knowing, thus giving them the impression of impunity. I believe this was possible because of the one and a half year of Solidarity movement which created a genuine feeling of solidarity among people. For me personally, the work at St. Marcin's was a lesson on how a civil society comes into being, how people become agents and no longer only objects of actions, how they resume responsibilities as citizens. But it also became a lesson on the importance of plain language.

I remember a middle-aged, well-dressed lady who came to report that her son had been arrested and her apartment searched by police, probably because of her son's involvement in some opposition activities. She seemed embarrassed by the situation, did not know, perhaps, how to behave and who we were. I thought this because she appeared to be using stiff, official discourse when reporting a rather personal experience. In particular, she kept using an official word for a house search (*przeszukanie*), the one that was used by no one but the authorities and the state-controlled media. Everyone else was using a well-established expression, one that has been around for generations, *rewizja*. For my generation, the word *rewizja* is immediately associated with the Nazi occupation and the often-deadly house searches by Gestapo. Some people probably also associate the word with the communist security authorities and their house searches for illegal materials, etc. There is no doubt in my mind that, when using the word *rewizja*, both the speaker and the hearer immediately, even if unconsciously assign the role of the villain to the person doing the house search and the role of an innocent victim, or even a hero to the one whose home is being invaded. The official word *przeszukanie* reassigns the roles, giving the right to perform the action to the nondescript authorities and taking away—or at least attempting to take away—negative connotations. By giving the authorities the right to conduct the search and by legitimizing the activity, the person whose house is being searched becomes an outlaw, a criminal. This may be the reason why the word never became part of non-official public discourse in post-war Poland where communist authorities, in particular police, continued to be assigned the role of the villain, performing illegal house searches and harassing innocent people. *Przeszukanie* corresponds directly to the English 'search', except that in the political context of the communist Poland, a neutral expression for that common act of aggression against people's privacy was out of place.

And yet, the well-dressed lady kept using the word *przeszukanie*. I had the impression that perhaps one of her son's friends told her to report the arrest and that she was almost ashamed that she got herself into trouble with police. When she used that odd expression again, I could not stop myself from interrupting her: "You mean *rewizja*, don't you?" With this word uttered aloud, she visibly relaxed, sighed, and said with immense relief: "Yes, I mean *rewizja*". The use of the word *rewizja* transformed her from someone involved in an illegal (or even criminal, according to communist authorities) activity to an innocent victim. Those who invaded her apartment were put in their proper place as villains violating her rights. And, most importantly, her son was no longer a criminal but perhaps a hero. That one word must have brought an immense relief to the mother.

I saw that same lady several more times in Piwna Street during her son's incarceration, then called *internment*. She made some friends with other parents of arrested students and workers; she learned the lingo of the martial law. I even overheard her instructing another woman, newly introduced to the world of arrests and prisons, about how to send money to her child, the so-called *wypiska*. If nothing else, I think she may have found a common language with her son. I do not remember her name, but I shall not forget the lesson she taught me.

As I was helping in Piwna Street—and I must add that it was a very minimal involvement on my part—I was approached by my former French teacher with a request that changed my academic interests once and, perhaps, forever. He knew that I was a graduate from linguistics and working in the German Department at Warsaw University. He once lent me a German book by Victor Klemperer with a cryptic title *LTI*. He said then that the book, whose full title was *Lingua Tertii Imperii* (Language of the Third Reich) was a must for any German philologist and should be read by everyone. Quite honestly, at that time, I just paged through it as I was too preoccupied with other things. But when my French teacher visited me at home some time in mid-1982, he suggested that I translate that very book into Polish for an underground publishing house. A torrent of thoughts swept through my mind. My half-brother Andrzej, whom I considered a role model, was a literary translator. Literary translation was my dream occupation; I would do almost anything to get my foot in the door and gain experience. It was against martial law to publish books that were political in nature, so there was no point in asking what publishing house would publish the book and how much I would get paid, although, I think, a specific amount of money was named. I agreed without any hesitation. Nothing was signed and no names were exchanged, the teacher departed and I was left with the little East German paperback edition of *LTI* in my hand.

I started to work on my translation almost at once and was immediately struck by the similarity between Klemperer's experiences with the German language of the Third Reich and the situation I was observing daily when watching the news or reading papers. It was truly impossible to escape comparisons and not translate Nazi-branded expressions in German into the Polish communist Newspeak. It was an overwhelming experience. I particularly liked to take the book with me to Piwna and work there. Except for days immediately following demonstrations or important anniversaries (there were lineups then as anniversaries usually triggered demonstrations and demonstrations resulted in waves of arrests), the office was quiet. Before the book, I used to chat with people at other tables or read but now, I had work to do.

In the spring of 1984, the translation was ready. I enlisted the professional assistance of a young historian, also from Warsaw University, who specialized in German and Jewish studies and who helped me with historical footnotes I thought the text required. I offered him money for his help, a portion of the honorarium I was to receive. However, when I finally managed to contact the person who allegedly represented the underground publishing house, I was told that the house went out of operation and that no one would print my translation since a state-owned press, Wydawnictwo Literackie, was about to release an 'official' translation, which, apparently, was kept under lock for a long time by the censorship. This was truly devastating as it was my first attempt at literary translation. It also left me with a debt—I had promised money to my historian colleague (roughly equivalent to a two-month salary of a junior assistant lecturer) and was unable to pay him back. Despite this unresolved financial obligation, we became and remained friends. We both left Poland in the 1980s and ended up in Canada. Piotr Wróbel is now a Professor of Polish History at the University of Toronto. My translation of *LTI* was finally published by the Polish Publishing Fund in Toronto in 1992.

There was one more linguistic influence on my understanding of the Polish reality in the early 1980s: the sermons of Father Jerzy Popiełuszko, a priest from a Warsaw parish in Żoliborz who attended to the striking workers in 1980 and who became a spiritual leader for the delegalized Solidarity trade union after the imposition of martial law in December 1981. His monthly masses "for the Fatherland" (no Nazi connotations in Polish) attracted huge crowds. I never managed to get inside the St. Stanisław Kostka church and stood outside, sometimes in the church yard, sometimes in one of the neighbouring streets. The voice of Father Popiełuszko, magnified by loudspeakers, was clearly audible outside. The atmosphere was remarkable, particularly when strangers were shaking hands with strangers following the words "let us offer each other the sign of peace." Everybody in the crowd was aware that the next person could have been an undercover police agent and so the symbolic handshake always felt a bit like an attempt to convert the potential enemy.

What I remember best was the language of Father Popiełuszko, almost biblical in its simplicity and plainness. He preached tolerance and human goodness. He preached for truth when you were surrounded by lies. And he preached for the love of thy neighbour, even if that neighbour hated you and wanted to kill you.

In the summer of 1984, I left Poland and went to Scotland to do my PhD. In October 1984, Father Popiełuszko was kidnapped and murdered by Polish secret police. His murderers were identified and imprisoned but those who instructed them to carry out that action, i.e., their superiors, were never fully brought to justice. Today, all three convicted killers have left jail and the truth about this murder still remains hidden. In the meantime, Father Popiełuszko has been beatified and even if he doesn't make it to sainthood, for me, he will remain the patron saint of plain language.

In August or September of 1989, I was chatting with a young German couple from Munich. We were in London, Ontario. Wolfgang was doing a post-doc in Canada and we met through a mutual friend, David Stanford, a colleague of my husband from Western University. We were all standing in the kitchen of Wolfgang's rented apartment, talking about politics. I repeated the words of Professor Jan Czochralski, my mentor in the German Department at Warsaw University. He said he was sure that communism would fall but was not optimistic enough to believe that it would happen in his lifetime. I said I had similar sentiments. And yet, the Berlin Wall fell on November 9, 1989, a mere two months or so later. The collapse of the communist system in most of Central and Eastern Europe gave rise to an unprecedented feeling of hope and optimism about the future of Europe and the world. The following unification of Germany and the democratic changes in politics and economy in many of the former communist bloc countries reshaped Europe. Many countries of the communist bloc are now members of NATO and the European Union. However, some of the reforms were rushed and no one had any expertise on how to implement change after decades of totalitarian rule. There had never been a successful transition from centrally planned to market economy before. The sudden change in political climate in Eastern Europe did not necessarily imply that the study of totalitarian frame of mind and its linguistic representations should be put aside as no longer relevant or relevant only for historical analyses. The communist perspective survived the end of the system because people living in Central and Eastern Europe still spoke the same language they used to speak before and it is the language that, covertly and in a clandestine way, sneaks old meanings and attitudes into new expressions. These old meanings are not just harmless antiquated concepts, but continue to serve as means of propaganda and mass deception. And a new hybrid mixture of old propaganda and a new, more Western-style language of politics emerged, different from the traditional 'Newspeak', but equally confusing. We saw this in Russia and in the Balkans, but also in the more democratic and reformed countries of Central and Eastern Europe such as Poland and Hungary. As a linguist, I am particularly disturbed by the spread of such confused language. As a Pole, I am deeply saddened by the return to demagogy of communist-style rhetoric in my home country, by new divisions into 'us' and 'them' and by the simple rudeness of some political leaders and their disrespect for both the 'unquestionable' authorities and for their ordinary countrymen. Unfortunately, it is often the leaders who set the example. If they publicly display disrespect for basic values, it is no wonder many political opportunists will follow.

The most recent years have witnessed a surge in populism across the world. The European Union integration of new member states in Eastern Europe provides an interesting example of how national languages and traditions can be used in order to influence people's attitudes towards the idea of European unity. New member states have a long history of aspirations to "return to Europe" after a period of forced isolation. In this context, it is puzzling that so much anti-European rhetoric is used in public discourse in Eastern Europe. It is a fascinating topic for linguistic research to analyse the corpus of contemporary public political debates in Eastern Europe as it demonstrates how language is used by populist parties, both the extreme left and the extreme right. Such parties are often initially regarded as marginal but are able to rapidly grow in popularity, just as the German Nazi Party NSDAP (National Socialist German Workers' Party) once did. Both extremes use similar linguistic tools, reminiscent of communist and fascist propaganda, but adapted to the new political context of European integration. When I was working on my Polish translation of *LTI*, I was playing with the idea, originally suggested by Klemperer with regard to the emerging language of the German Democratic Republic, of writing about LQI *(Lingua Quarti Imperii)*, Language of the Fourth Reich. In the Polish context, the word 'Reich' would have to be replaced by the word 'Republic'. Interestingly, the populist government of the Kaczyński brothers in Poland (2005–2007) used to refer to the Poland they were trying to build as 'the fourth Republic'. The language they used was often referred to as 'the new Newspeak' because of its similarities to communist propaganda, based on conspiracy theories, enemy figures and conflicts. When this party returned to power in 2015, these similarities only increased and the hate propaganda against various 'others' escalated. The need to analyse this new post-communist Newspeak is a political necessity. This book is in part a reflection of that desire.

And then came the war in Ukraine, confirming my worst childhood fears. When I was telling people that the main reason I 'always', or for as long as I can remember, wanted to leave Poland was because it was too close to the Soviet Union, they likely thought that my fear was irrational and unwarranted. At least from the end of the Cold War, Russia was being seen as weakened, becoming westernized, less of a threat. I did not buy that. My greatest fear has always been the prospect of another war. My Mom used to say that there has not been a generation of Poles who did not go through a war but I was hoping that the martial law of 1981 had been my war. The fear of a Russian, and currently Belarusian, aggression has always been there.

The war against Ukraine will end, sooner or later. Its cost, both in terms of human lives lost and infrastructure (and here I mean not just factories and homes but also ancient monuments of culture) is already enormous. It shattered, for several generations to come, the dream of European peace and safety, already shaken by the Balkan wars and the annexation of Crimea. In this context, the question of language comes up again. Russia and Ukraine have very different narratives of unfolding events. The two sides cannot communicate as they disagree on their descriptions of reality. Russian propaganda dehumanizes Ukrainians, painting them as Nazis (an absurd but very effective invective for the Russian audience). This dehumanization is a necessary prerequisite for Russian soldiers to not feel remorse killing other Slavs. One day, when this war is over, Russia and Ukraine will still be neighbours. How will they be able to live next to each other after such atrocities?

Even before these troubling developments in the former communist countries, the events of September 11, 2001 in the United States gave birth to a new language and a new rhetoric in the West. While this theme goes far beyond the scope of this book, I could not help but constantly make comparisons between my own experience with the language in communist Poland and my research on totalitarian propaganda on the one hand, and the language used to discuss politics in the shadow of terrorist threats on the other hand. The war in Iraq, the situation in Afghanistan, and the fear of a global conflict with Islamic fundamentalists brought a new language to the West. I feel horrified when I see the concept of 'an enemy' (usually in singular, of course) resurrected and the world divided again into those who are 'with' us and those who are 'against' us by virtue of not being 'with' us. I cringe when I hear about 'freedom fries' and when politicians are elected on little more than 'gut feelings'.

This book took more time to write, and even longer to publish than I thought, precisely because of the uncomfortable connection between the growing power of propaganda in different parts of the world. I started writing it in the summer of 2001, just weeks before the attacks of September 11. Like everyone else, I watched with horror as the planes struck the World Trade Centre and hoped against any hope, each time these images appeared on the TV screen, that *this time* the plane would miraculously re-emerge from behind the building without hitting it. But I was wrong time and time again. It seemed that there were no words to describe what had happened. But then words started to emerge. First it was the 'war on terrorism', something understandable in the time of national anguish. And then terrorism became abbreviated to a rather vague and imprecise 'terror' and, day by day, I turned into a modern-day Victor Klemperer, mesmerized by the transformation of English used by the American media.

The war on terror has proven to be a long one and its end is still not in sight. Victor Klemperer once said about the language of the Third Reich:

> … it changes the value of words and the frequency of their occurrence, it makes common property out of what was previously the preserve of an individual or a tiny group, it commandeers for the party that which was previously common property and in the process steeps words and groups of words and sentence structures with its poison. Making

> language the servant of its dreadful system, it procures it as its most powerful, most public and most surreptitious means of advertising.
>
> The task of making people aware of the poisonous nature of the LTI and warning them of its dangers is, I believe, not just schoolmasterish. (Klemperer 2000: 16)

I strongly believe this is true not just of LTI, Language of the Third Reich, but of any propaganda that relies on language manipulation. As long as it continues to take on new spins, the task of making people aware of its poisonous nature remains a meaningful occupation.

CHAPTER 2

The Confusion of Language

There are many ways in which language may be used to distort reality. We rarely ponder what happens when the language used in public domain fails to fit reality. Does this situation happen? Has it happened in the past? Can the misalignment of reality and language be noticed? What is it indicative of? What effects does it produce in the hearer? And, most importantly, how can ordinary people protect themselves from propaganda and language manipulation? Having grown up in a place where language became divorced from reality, I have often asked myself these questions.

Some of these issues concern fundamental problems in linguistics and philosophy of language. Others are more specific to sociology or media studies. The analysis of the role of language in politics is not a new area of research. The 20th century, with its rise and fall of totalitarian powers, provided a particularly rich source of data for the study of propaganda and language distortion. A number of scholars were engaged with the question of propaganda in the last century; here I shall focus primarily on their work published in the 1940s or early 1950s, even though from different theoretical perspectives and based on different experiences. This choice is simply related to the fact that those were the sources that were available to me when I was still in Poland and which affected my own thinking. As many of the observations seem to still apply today, in Eastern Europe and elsewhere, I would argue that we are still dealing with aspects of totalitarian minds and propaganda machines and should therefore remain alert to the dangers of deception through language.

The word that is usually used to refer to a purposeful distortion of reality for broadly understood political purposes is *propaganda*. In the West, the term has mostly negative connotations, which cling more closely to the noun than to the verb—to *propagate*. The word was originally used to designate *Propaganda Fide*, the Vatican Office for the Propagation of the Faith, established in 1622 by Pope Gregory XV in his Bull *Inscrutabili Divinae*. Today, this body, responsible for missionary activity throughout the world, is known as the *Congregation for the Evangelization of Peoples*. This Congregation was renamed in 1982 by the Polish-born Pope John Paul II, and I wonder whether John Paul's experience with the communist use of the term 'propaganda' during his life in Poland had anything to do with that.

The word propaganda was later taken over by non-religious circles to describe a variety of ways in which human conscience, attitudes, and behaviour could be influenced by purposefully used linguistic and other means of persuasion. The clearly negative connotations of the term date back at least to World War I when the ultimate purpose of propaganda became the control of human societies. Horst Dressler-Andress, one of the collaborators of Joseph Goebbels who was responsible for the management of the radio network in the Third Reich, described the purpose of propaganda as ensuring "uniform reaction to events" (quoted after Mazur 2003, 20). In the Soviet Union, the word 'propaganda' was shortened and combined with the truncated noun 'agitation' to produce 'agitprop', a word that described vigorous ideological persuasion, both in political and in literary texts. In the 1950s, a new term came into circulation, coined by the American writer and journalist Edward Hunter: 'brain-washing'. Even though its scientific merits are still debatable, the term is used colloquially for any attempts to manipulate people's thoughts and behaviour.

I started to use the term propaganda for the type of information disseminated by the official media in Poland relatively late, probably only at the end of high school. Before that, the fact that the media (newspapers, radio, television, films, school textbooks, and some—but not all teachers, etc.) lied was for me a kind of shameful family secret, like the fact that some relative drank too much because they could not control their urges. I did not understand why it was so but I knew there was nothing I could do to change it. Later, my thinking of language manipulation was particularly influenced by three writers, all of whom I read while still in Poland. I list them in the order in which I encountered them:

- George Orwell (1903-1950), British essayist and writer. His novels *Animal Farm* (1945) and *Nineteen Eighty-Four* (1949) and later also his 1946 essay "Politics and the English Language" had a profound effect on my thinking of language and reality;
- Czesław Miłosz (1911- 2004), Polish poet and writer, 1980 Nobel Prize Winner for Literature and the author of *The Captive Mind* (1951), where he analyses the mechanisms of attraction that communism, which he calls The New Faith, exerts on intellectuals. This book has been described by *The New York Times Book Review* as "a central text in the modern effort to understand totalitarianism"; and
- Victor Klemperer (1881-1960), a German-Jewish philologist, author of several little-known books on French literature published during his lifetime, and his highly celebrated diaries published posthumously. He is also the author of a unique study on the language of the Third Reich, first published in 1947 under the title *LTI, Lingua Tertii Imperii* and only relatively recently (2000) translated into English.

Even before I left Poland, I became interested in the idea of linguistic relativism, usually associated with two American linguists Edward Sapir and Benjamin Lee Whorf, but applied to the language manipulation in totalitarian regimes. I was introduced to their ideas while taking Theory of Translation class in my third year at the university. After I left Poland, I also read many other authors who dealt with totalitarian propaganda. Of those, the most significant influence on my views was Friedrich August Hayek (1899-1992), an economist and political scientist with a very clear understanding of the communist system of centrally planned economy. I was introduced to Hayek's writings by Philip Booth of the Institute of Economic Affairs in London. I particularly value the insights I gained from Hayek's two books, *The Road to Serfdom* (1944) and the much later book *The Fatal Conceit* (1988).

By naming these authors I by no means wish to minimize the impact that many other scholars and writers had on my understanding of the totalitarian language. Hannah Arendt, Mikhail Heller, Michał Głowiński, Jerzy Bralczyk, Kazimierz Orłoś, Alain Besançon—they all played a critical role in the development of my understanding of the communist system's impact on our thinking, speech, and behaviour.

In writing about totalitarian regimes and their language, it might be prudent to start by attempting a definition of totalitarianism. It is generally understood as a type of authoritarianism, where the group in power exerts complete and total control over every aspect of life and requires obedience and conformity from each and every individual. In order to exert this control, the ruling group needs to control the sources and the means of disseminating information (through censorship and media ownership), the behaviour of the subjects (through secret police and informers), and also the means of production and distribution of food and consumer goods (through centrally planned economy). Totalitarian systems may differ in many ways, and in fact, fascism, Nazism, and communism were very unlike in terms of class support, attitude to private ownership, racial, and national issues, etc. However, they were also similar because they had emerged from "the same seedbed of Romantic Idealism and were based on almost identical pseudo-scientific theories of history" (compare with P.D. Hutcheon's 1996 paper on Hannah Arendt's comparison of the two systems). Where Nazism considered *race* as the driving force of history and the principle of in-group membership, communism used the notion of 'class'. For Kazimierz Orłoś, Polish writer and essayist, what these different types of totalitarian regimes had in common and what distinguished them from other political systems that used manipulation was the fact that, in totalitarian countries, an open dissension from the official line was punishable, sometimes very severely. The two systems—communism and Nazism—had enough in common to allow us to look at totalitarianism as a more general phenomenon and to focus on its attitude to language. It may be worth adding that in our technology-driven and technology-mediated Western world, control of the media may actually become a sufficient condition for the emergence of an almost totalitarian style of political rhetoric. Thus, these observations are not purely historical and oriented towards the past. Unfortunately, political manipulation through language is still very much in use in many parts of the world.

For an historian, it might be interesting to examine why the 20th century was a time of such an unprecedented spread of totalitarian ideology and was witness to equally unprecedented (in terms of scale and brutality) crimes against humanity in the name of a man-made ideology. Millions of people in many parts of the world perished in direct combat and in death camps, purges, and ethnic wars, as well as through forced migration and starvation. Many of those crimes happened because of the rule of terror—in Soviet Russia, in Nazi Germany, in communist China, or in Cambodia. One wonders whether some of these monstrous crimes could have been prevented, if people who committed them were not captivated and blinded by the confused ideologies of their leaders. It seems that one of the reasons why these confused ideologies were able to get their grip on ordinary people was because of the linguistic mastery of their propaganda experts. Thus, the 20th century could also be labelled the century of ideology and mass deception, or, to put it in a more straightforward way, 'a century of lies and liars' (compare with. W. Łysiak 1999). As such, this is a fascinating research area for a linguist.

Language is an indispensable tool for human communication and lying is but one aspect of human linguistic behaviour. Warnings against giving false witness are plentiful in our cultural tradition, but so are lies. The most unscrupulous propagandists, Adolf Hitler and Joseph Goebbels, publicly—and probably rightly—maintained, that the more monstrous the lie, the easier it might be to make people believe it. And making people believe what the leaders wanted them to believe turned out to be probably the most effective strategy of conquest and dominance. It produced obedience with minimal use of force.

This is one of the most startling features of totalitarian regimes: they are not satisfied with the rule of terror. As Joseph Goebbels (in a speech delivered at the 1934 Party Rally in Nuremberg and made famous by Leni Riefenstahl's film *Triumph des Willens*) put it: "It may be good to have power based on weapons. It is better and longer lasting, however, to win and hold the heart of a nation." These words may be easily dismissed as just another example of Nazi rhetoric, but I take them as an expression of a fundamental principle of political propaganda. If you can make people believe what you want them to believe, they will be willing to do what you tell them to do.

In the 1947 foreword to his 1932 utopian (or perhaps rather dystopian) novel *Brave New World*, Aldous Huxley (1946/2007, xlvii) observed that

> [a] really efficient totalitarian state would be one in which the all-powerful executive of political bosses and their army of managers control a population of slaves who do not have to be coerced, because they love their servitude.

No guards will be necessary if the population disciplines themselves. Polish humour of the communist era captured this fact in a famous joke: Why is there no need for guards at the cauldron for Poles in hell? Because, should anyone try to escape, others would pull him back inside.

Thus, both Nazis and communists regularly appealed to emotions and instincts of their people in order to make sure that the official goals would be internalised by ordinary citizens. This was done not because the leaders yearned for genuine love of their people but because, as Hayek observed:

> the most effective way of making everybody serve the single system of ends towards which the social plan is directed is to make everybody believe in those ends. To make a totalitarian system function

> efficiently it is not enough that everybody should be forced to work for the same ends. It is essential that the people should come to regard them as their own ends. Although the beliefs must be chosen for the people and imposed upon them, they must become their beliefs, a generally accepted creed which makes the individuals as far as possible act spontaneously in the way the planner wants. If the feeling of oppression in totalitarian countries is in general much less acute than most people in liberal countries imagine, this is because the totalitarian governments succeed to a high degree in making people think as they want them to. (Hayek 1944, 114)

Authoritarian regimes of earlier epochs must have caused considerable suffering to their subjects but they did not require those subjects to believe that their suffering was for their own good and that the misery should make them happy and proud. If the subjects of the communist system or Nazi rule in Germany did not feel proud and happy, this was their own fault (they were ideologically not mature enough or perhaps they were even class enemies, hostile to the system) and this, of course, was a reason for further persecution. The communist system extended this principle of forced re-education and indoctrination to prisons and labour camps, requiring self-denunciations and confessions of guilt from people who were innocent of any crime. Sadly, often they did confess to crimes they did not commit. It is understandable that someone who faces death may cling to any chance of salvation. Many of those who confessed could have hoped that this would give them a chance to save their lives. Some were certainly tortured into submission. Streatfeild (2007) in his fascinating book *Brainwash: The Secret History of Mind Control*, says that "given enough pressure and fear, [...] everyone will break down eventually" (18).

The mystery of Soviet trial confessions in the 1930 attracted a lot of scientific attention (see also O. John Rogge's 1959 *Why Men Confess*). Streatfeild reports William Sargant's (1956) account of Pavlov's experiments on conditioned reflexes in his book *Battle for the Mind*. By sheer accident, Pavlov, a Russian psychologist and physician who won the 1904 Nobel Prize in Physiology, discovered that extreme trauma (fear of death) could reverse all learned behaviours and cause complete personality change (as a fear of drowning erased learned conditioned behaviours in his dogs when his lab was flooded). Subjected to such critical conditions as torture, people too may develop irrational behaviours and become extremely suggestible. They may actually embrace solutions they would never accept under normal conditions. According to Sargant, who also had experience working with WWII soldiers suffering what we call today post-traumatic stress disorders, this might explain why some people who confessed their non-existent guilt at Soviet trials looked radiant and were smiling in a strangely absent but happy way (Streatfeild 2007, 18).

Orwell masterfully captured this particular desire of the party to mould the human mind in *1984*:

> We are not content with negative obedience, nor even with the most abject submission. When finally you surrender to us, it must be of your own free will. We do not destroy the heretic because he resists us; so long as he resists us we never destroy him. We convert him, we capture his inner mind, we reshape him. We burn all evil and all illusion out of him; we bring him over to our side, not in appearance, but genuinely, heart and soul. We make him one of ourselves before we kill him. It is intolerable to us that an erroneous thought should exist anywhere in the world, however secret and powerless it may be. Even in the instance of death we cannot permit any deviation . . . we make the brain perfect before we blow it out (267).

The very final paragraph of *1984* beautifully portrays the reversed thinking of Winston's tortured mind, the transition from hate and fear to love and willing surrender, to acceptance:

> He gazed up at the enormous face. Forty years it had taken him to learn what kind of smile was hidden beneath the dark moustache. O cruel, needless misunderstanding! O stubborn, self-willed exile from the loving breast! Two gin-scented tears trickled down the sides of his nose. But it was all right, everything was all right, the struggle was finished. He had won the victory over himself. He loved Big Brother (311).

Totalitarianism further introduced a new quality into the area of mass deception by promoting persuasion by means of altering people's perception of reality. This total effect could not have been achieved without mobilising all possible means of (dis)information dissemination, which, in turn, became possible only through advances in technology (radio and film). Totalitarian propaganda was different from propaganda used in other political systems because all its instruments, means and techniques were controlled by one centre and served one goal. Hayek wrote:

> If all the sources of current information are effectively under one single control, it is no longer a question of merely persuading the people of this or that. The skilful propagandist then has the power to mould their minds in any direction he chooses and even the most intelligent and independent people cannot entirely escape that influence if they are long isolated from all other sources of information. (Hayek 1944, 114)

Victor Klemperer, undoubtedly an intelligent and independently thinking man, added a confession based on his own experience of life in the Third Reich:

> I […] know that a part of every intellectual's soul belongs to the people, that all my awareness of being lied to, and my critical attentiveness, are of no

> avail when it comes to it: at some point the printed lie will get the better of me when it attacks from all sides and is queried by fewer and fewer around me and finally by no one at all (Klemperer 2000, 223).

Those were truly prophetic words. Klemperer never gave in to Nazi propaganda. As a Jew, he was an object of persecution by the Nazi system and could not feel any attraction to ideology that denied him and his fellow Jewish Germans humanity. However, after the war ended, he joined the Communist Party and—at least for some time—truly believed the communists would save Germany. The fact that, immediately after the horrors of World War II, many intellectuals felt drawn to communist ideology requires a separate explanation. Maybe it is simply our unconscious defence mechanism that makes us reject the supposition that both sides are equally evil? Maybe it is our human desire to believe in something and to trust someone? Propaganda mercilessly exploits this weakness.

When all media tell the same story and no one dares to challenge the official version because of the fear of punishment, anything can be presented to people as truth. Just one year after coming to power, Goebbels was able to publicly declare:

> There are no parliamentary parties in Germany any longer. How could we have overcome them had we not waged an educational campaign for years that persuaded people of their weaknesses, harms and disadvantages? Their final elimination was only the result of what the people had already realized. Our propaganda weakened these parties. Based on that, they could be eliminated by a legal act. Goebbels (1934)

It is not true that propaganda weakened parliamentary parties in Germany but it probably is true that propaganda weakened the intellectual immunity of the audience and its ability to distinguish between rhetoric and reality. Because it follows an agenda, propaganda, by definition, distorts the relationship between truth and reality; it blurs the notion of truth and tries to get away from it. In effect, the notion of truth is redefined. Here is an example of such redefinition from Goebbels (ibid.):

> Good propaganda does not need to lie, indeed it may not lie. It has no reason to fear the truth. It is a mistake to believe that people cannot take the truth. They can. It is only a matter of presenting the truth to people in a way that they will be able to understand.

These words, written years ago, may be helpful in understanding how it was possible that, in the era of modern and global communication, Slobodan Milošević could successfully persuade many Serbian people that he was *the guarantor of peace* in the Balkans or how, in Serbian media, he could claim victory over NATO forces. The Balkan conflict could serve as a modern example of total propaganda and mass deception with the required attributes of a total media control. Some would claim it was an example of total propaganda on both sides of the conflict.

Perhaps we should not stop here. Perhaps we should ask ourselves: what do we really know about the conflict in the former Yugoslavia or any other of the current conflicts in our global village. We are apparently being better informed about world events than ever before, with various opportunities to find the news in papers, on television, and online. However, are we not getting most or all of our information from one source only, even if it comes via different broadcasters and is written with stylistic variations by various journalists? Are we really justified in our belief that we know the truth or is what we know just the version of the events that someone wanted us to know? I do not intend this to be an attack on politicians: are we even certain that the interpreters are getting the message right? In the spring of 2001, in my conversation with Mr. Christopher Hill, then the U.S. Ambassador to Poland and participant in the Dayton Agreement, he stressed the significance of misunderstandings, resulting from all parties using words and phrases (e.g., 'ethnic equality' or 'multiculturalism') that may have and indeed do have different meanings in Poland or the former Yugoslavia than in the West.

If the regime wants its people to accept and internalise the official doctrine and behave in the expected, (i.e., obedient) way, those people have to be persuaded that the world is indeed as the official propaganda wants them to think it is. This means they have to be taught to see reality through the filter of ideology and not the way it appears to be. Of course, ideally, they should be unaware that this filter exists.

As a child I believed that socialist realist films showed reality. I was sad that my part of Warsaw was not as bright and clean as it looked on the screen, but grey and partly ruined. Although I never had the chance to be in the parts of the city that looked like those in the films, I naively assumed that what I saw on the screen was reality and that I lived in a degraded version. It did not take me long to realise my mistake, but the gap between media images and my everyday life in Poland persisted. By noticing the gap, I learned that the relationship between reality and the pseudo-reality created through language (both verbal and visual) was arbitrary. The pseudo-reality was a utopian goal to some, mostly the idealistic intellectuals, and it was simply a tool of deception to others. In his book *The Soviet Syndrome*, Alain Besançon writes that through all those years of the continuous construction of the paradise on Earth, the scientific utopia of the Soviet system "has not even begun to be born" and the communist ideology remains only "a ghost in search of a body.... The construction of socialism amounted to the construction of fiction" (1976, 93).

In practice, only few people can really be persuaded for any considerable length of time that black is white, but many will learn to say they see things in prescribed colours and they will call them by prescribed names. As long as they play their roles, the regime usually does not mind. It knows well, that playing this game (Orwell's 'doublethink') will soon become second nature for those who engage in it and that simply by using prescribed language their perception of reality will likely be altered. Language provides us with means to label the world and by this, it takes an active part in shaping our perception by imposing those labels as cognitive categories. We use language not only to communicate with others but also to think and form judgements. Ludwig Wittgenstein (1922) said that the limits of his language defined the limits of his world. George Orwell (1946) added the observation that our language "becomes ugly and inaccurate because our thoughts are foolish, but the slovenliness of our language makes it easier for us to have foolish thoughts" (426).

Orwell masterfully developed the idea of controlling people's perception of the world by means of language manipulation in his *1984*, where a new language, *Newspeak*, had been invented specifically for this purpose (for more on reality construction through language see Stroińska 2000).

> The purpose of Newspeak was not only to provide a medium of expression for the world-view and mental habits proper to the devotees of Ingsoc, but to make all other modes of thought impossible. It was intended that when Newspeak had been adopted once and for all and Oldspeak forgotten, a heretical thought—that is a thought diverging from the principles of Ingsoc—should be literally unthinkable, at least so far as thought is dependent on words. Its vocabulary was so constructed as to give exact and often very subtle expression to every meaning that a Party member could properly wish to express, while excluding all other meanings and so also the possibility of arriving at them by indirect methods. This was done partly by the invention of new words and by stripping such words as remained of unorthodox meanings, and so far as possible of all secondary meanings whatever. (Appendix: The principles of Newspeak, 312-313.)

Orwell's idea of 'Newspeak' was based on historical facts and not merely a literary invention. Actually, it was based on elements of two realities, that of the Stalin's Russia and Hitler's Germany. In *The Road to Serfdom*, Friedrich Hayek provides a very thorough analysis of the process of language manipulation through words. It might be interesting to add here that Orwell reviewed Hayek's book at approximately the same time when he was working on his *1984*. Hayek writes:

> The most effective way of making people accept the validity of the values they are to serve is to persuade them that they are really the same as those which they, or at least the best among them, have always held, but which were not properly understood or recognised before. The people are made to transfer their allegiance from the old gods to the new under the pretence that the new gods really are what their sound instinct had always told them but what before they had only dimly seen. And the most efficient technique to this end is to use the old words but change their meaning. Few traits of totalitarian regimes are at the same time so confusing to the superficial observer and yet so characteristic of the whole intellectual climate as the complete perversion of language, the change of meaning of the words by which the ideals of the new regimes are expressed. (Hayek 1944: 117)

Hayek's views could be supported by the living experience of propaganda in the Third Reich as described by Victor Klemperer. He took up a distich by Friedrich Schiller about "a cultivated language which writes and thinks for you" and observed that there is more to Schiller's verses than an aesthetic interpretation. He writes:

> But language does not simply write and think for me, it also increasingly dictates my feelings and governs my entire spiritual being the more unquestioningly and unconsciously I abandon myself to it. (Klemperer 2000: 15)

Klemperer further supports Hayek's observation about the role of single words with twisted and distorted meaning in the process of thought manipulation. He asks "What was then the most powerful Hitlerian propaganda tool?" and then answers:

> ...[T]he most powerful influence was exerted neither by individual speeches nor by articles or flyers,

> posters or flags; it was not achieved by things which one had to absorb by conscious thought or conscious emotions. Instead Nazism permeated the flesh and blood of the people through single words, idioms and sentence structures which were imposed on them in million repetitions and taken on board mechanically and unconsciously. (ibid.)

Michał Głowiński (1990) analyzed more recent language and thought manipulation in Poland. He stressed that by either promoting or excluding certain words, the language can give or deny existence to persons, things, and phenomena. In the Soviet Union, books were rewritten and official pictures were repainted if they happened to refer to a person or event that became an object of disapproval. Among the famous examples of such manipulation of historical facts through their visual representation in art (not in photography, where making changes has been easier) are the alterations of Vladimir Serov's 1947 painting of Lenin proclaiming the establishment of the Soviet power. In the original version, Stalin can be seen standing behind Lenin. He was added to the picture in order to strengthen his claim that he was Lenin's legitimate successor. After Stalin's death, Serov painted a new version of his picture in which the figure of Stalin has been painted over and covered by a picture of another man. The original picture was a historical fabrication but most people would likely accept that Stalin and Lenin must have at least worked together. There is also a picture of Stalin by Mikhail Mikhailovich Bozhi called *Stalin in the Civil War*, painted around 1950. It portrays Stalin at the front line together with some other commander. The picture suggests that Stalin took a more active role in military operations in the civil war than he did in reality.

In Nazi Germany, a famous representation of Hitler in art was the portrait by Hubert Lanzinger, depicting the *Führer* in white medieval armour, on a black horse. Painted in the mid 1930s, it is entitled *The Standard Bearer*. This heroic representation would lose some of its appeal if the viewer were to know that Hitler was allegedly afraid of horses.

In 1995, London's Hayward Gallery had a thought-provoking exhibition entitled *Art and Power: Europe under the Dictators, 1930-45*. It provided an opportunity to compare art from communist Russia, Nazi Germany, Mussolini's Italy, and communist China. All totalitarian countries of that period managed to produce or to legislate art that was in many ways so similar that, as Igor Golomstock notices in the introduction to his 1990 *Totalitarian Art*, "one could only recognize its country of origin by spotting whose portraits adored the walls." What made the art produced by these diverse systems so uniform was the fact that it was realist in form but utopian in content. It depicted reality that did not exist, but it depicted it so well that, just as I believed socialist-realist films and not my eyes, people believed art and not reality. Thus, communist and Nazi art documents the history of fiction.

Through the power of language, verbal or visual, the picture of reality in the minds of those who are subjected to the total propaganda machine can be distorted, and the difference between the given and desired state of affairs blurred (see Głowiński 1990: 8-9, Stroińska 1994, 59 and 2000: 125). Victor Klemperer goes further and keeps asking about the outcome of such continued distortion:

> And what happens if the cultivated language is made up of poisonous elements or has been made the bearer of poison? Words can be like tiny doses of arsenic: they are swallowed unnoticed, appear to have no effect, and then after a little time the toxic reaction sets in after all. If someone replaces the words 'heroic' and 'virtuous' with 'fanatical' for long enough, he will come to believe that a fanatic really is a virtuous hero, and that no one can be a hero without fanaticism. The Third Reich did not invent the words 'fanatical' and 'fanaticism', it just changed their value and used them more in one day than other epochs used them in years. (Klemperer 2000, 15-16)

Today we too use the word 'fanatic' with very high frequency, usually without realizing it. It has been conveniently abbreviated to 'fan' and is being used, mostly by the younger generation and often with intensifying adjectives such as 'great', which indicates that people really do not realize the origin of the word. A 'fanatic' is an exaggerated devotee or an enthusiast going overboard in his or her passion and further intensification of such properties is superfluous. We may think that 'fan' became an innocent word and its overuse does not need to bother the purist. But the way we use language is a reflection of deeper sociological processes. The way the word is being used today signals that our strongest feelings (our fanaticism) is directed towards popular culture and celebrities. This may indicate that they have taken place of what used to stir stronger feelings in the past: religion, politics, etc. It is not my role to judge this development, but it may be worth pointing it out.

There is a famous saying attributed to Confucius, quoted by Hayek, that "when words lose their meaning, people will lose their liberty." In Eastern Europe, this poisoning of language went on practically uninterrupted for decades. Its effects have greatly contributed to the present state of mind of people in post-communist countries. Let us look at some examples to illustrate this phenomenon.

The country where I was born was called not Poland but the People's Republic of Poland. The word 'republic' (from Latin *res publica*) has an old polonized equivalent: *rzeczpospolita.* This is how Poles kept referring to their homeland for centuries: *res publica*, i.e., 'that which is the possession of the people.' However, the adjective *ludowa* (people's), used in many other combinations as well, was one of the Polish weasel words after World War II. The concept of weasel words was introduced into literature by Mario Pei in his 1978 book *Weasel Words: The Art of Saying What You Don't Mean.* There, he actually attributed the coining of the word to President Theodore Roosevelt in 1918, while Friedrich Hayek attributes the origin of the expression to Shakespeare's 'I can suck melancholy out of a song, as a weasel sucks eggs' in *As you like it* (II, 5). In *The Fatal Conceit*, F.A. Hayek (1988) further analyses the phenomenon of weasel words, defining them as words that attach to other words and empty them of their meaning without leaving any visible traces of the operation. Thus, in the new name of Poland, what used to be the property of the people became the new colony of the Soviet Union. In *demokracja ludowa* ('people's democracy'—the official name of the political system of the Eastern European countries) and in *sprawiedliwość ludowa* ('people's justice'), the adjective actually corrupts the meaning of the noun and turns the whole phrase into the negation of the noun. The adjective would be added, almost at random, to nouns in order to make them sound more 'politically correct' in the communist sense: thus, *gospodarka ludowa* would be 'people's economy', signifying something like socialist or centrally planned economy, but more vague and not at all equivalent of the German *Volkswirtschaft* ('economics' or 'national economy'). The word *ludowy* is legitimate when it is used to mean 'folklore-related', as in *sztuka ludowa* ('folk art'). It is a weasel word when it is supposed to relate nouns to the communist system.

A somewhat similar situation happened in German with the word *Volk*. For Hitler, all Germans, wherever they lived, constituted one ethnic group, one *Volk*. The lexeme *Volk*—in this meaning of ethnic togetherness—was added to nouns and adjectives quite freely producing many specifically Nazi words: *volksnah* ('ethnically close,' 'popular'), *völkisch* (a word practically taken over by the Nazis which used to mean 'popular', 'populist' or 'common' but in a positive 'natural' sense), *Volksgemeinschaft* ('a racially unified and idealized community of people'), etc. One German word with *Volk* that survived the Hitler regime and is doing well, skilfully escaping murky associations from the past is *Volkswagen*, Hitler's pet project of the 'people's car'. To fully grasp the effects of adding *Volk* to other nouns and adjectives one needs to understand how the Nazi regime (re)defined the word *Volk* (see the brochure *Faith and Action*. Stellrecht 1943):

> A People *(Volk)*: A people grows from god's will. Woe to him who wishes to destroy the peoples and make people alike. God created the trees, the bushes, the weeds and the grass not so that they could merge into one species, but that each should exist in its own way. Just as a tree, a people grows as a living whole from similar roots, but becoming one, the strongest of its kind. All of the same blood belong to it. A people knows no state boundaries. It is bound by the ties

> of blood that bind all the sons of a single mother. The German people is a nation of a hundred million. Each German belongs to it, no matter where he may live. A people cannot be destroyed as long as its roots draw on the strength of the earth. Summer and winter may come and go. But it always blooms anew in indestructible life and perfects itself in the strength that rises from its roots towards god's will. What does it mean when an individual dies? It is as if the wind blows leaves from a tree. New ones grow eternally every spring. The peoples are the greatest and most noble creation of god on this earth. There is no institution in the world, no party and no church, that has the right to make them the same or to rob them of even the tiniest bit of their individuality. (Stellrecht 1943)

This definition is quite convoluted because of its highly metaphorical form. It is very difficult to discuss the truth—or even determine the meaning—of statements that are expressed as metaphors. This new definition applies to the German people but it does not seem to apply in the same way to other ethnic groups. Thus, it is not clear whether, in the opinion of the authors of the brochure, the Jews too are a *Volk*. If they were, they too would have to be considered "the greatest and most noble creation of god on this earth." Evidently, one should not search for logic in propaganda materials.

In Polish, the noun *brat* ('brother') and the derived adjectives *braterski* and *bratni*, became another contaminated word. In public discourse it no longer signified a kinship relation or shared interests, values and priorities (as is normally the case within families) but was related, just like the concept of *big brother* in Orwell, to someone who is wiser, more experienced, and who can command you. This notion should also imply that the big brother will protect you from the bullies, but exactly the opposite was the case in the communist bloc. The invasion of Czechoslovakia in 1968 by Warsaw Pact troops was officially referred to as "brotherly help", clearly defining the notion as violation of the rights of the people in Czechoslovakia to decide for themselves. They were made into little kids who had to be brought back to order by the caring *big brother* who knew better what was good for them.

For over two centuries, starting with the partitions of Poland at the end of the 18th century, waves of foreign repressions triggered military uprisings, which triggered waves of emigration, first mostly to France, Great Britain, and the U.S., then also to many other countries of the world. There are several million Poles living outside Polish borders today. Among them were Poles who left before World War II, Poles displaced during the war, Poles who left when the communists moved in, Poles who left after each series of 'events', and, of course, Poles who are still trying to find better career opportunities abroad. It would be hard to find many families in Poland who would not have relatives living in other countries. They could be described as "Polish (political and economic) emigration", "Polish diaspora" or "Poles living in exile". These terms imply that those people have left Poland and are not willing to come back. They imply that Poland was or is not a country where they wanted to be or where they could return because of the threat of persecution. However, Polish has also a special term for Poles abroad, it is *Polonia*. This Latin name for the country denotes in contemporary Polish those Poles who live outside Polish borders, but speak Polish and continue to take interest in Polish affairs and culture. It is a 'positive' definition and it makes the members of the Polonia part of the greater community of all Poles. Outside Poland, the term *Polonia* does not have any ties to propaganda. In Canada and the U.S., we have the Congress of Canadian Polonia and the Congress of American Polonia respectively, as the highest level of representation of Polish interests in those countries. However, in communist Poland, the word has been taken over by propaganda. This difference in meaning and connotations is particularly visible for the adjectives *polonijny* (Polonia-related) and *emigracyjny* (emigration-related), especially when applied to 'organizations.' The first ones sent parcels to relatives in Poland, supported the teaching of Polish language and literature, and engaged in folklore dancing; the others supported imperialistic broadcasting such as Voice of America or Radio Free Europe and printed banned books to smuggle them into Poland.

In the 19th century Poland, patriotism was considered one of the top virtues. The Polish fatherland (*patria*) was divided among three foreign powers and working for the survival of the Polish language, culture, education, religion, and traditions were a high priority. The connection between patriotism and religion (with Virgin Mary proclaimed the Queen of Poland by King Jan Kazimierz in 1656) created a very specific brand of Polish nationalism. Nationalism does not have to imply a negative or hostile attitude to other countries, but it usually entails emphasis on ethnic unity of a nation while patriotism was free of any such narrow-mindedness. In communist Poland, the word 'patriotism' became linked with the support for the communist, Soviet imposed rule. 'True' patriots (with 'true', in Polish *prawdziwy*, being another weasel word that corrupts the meaning of the words it attaches to) were those people who 'understood the historical necessities' and 'chose the right side in the struggle for social progress' (or whatever else, I am clearly improvising in Newspeak here). Thus, a *patriot* was no longer someone who loved Poland (their *patria*), but rather someone who loved or at least willingly accepted Soviet domination of their fatherland. So redefined, 'patriotism' was no longer seen by Poles as virtue when applied to communist contexts. Privately, the word would still be used for contexts such as Warsaw Uprising or the struggle of the underground Home Army during World War II, but in other situations, it simply became one of those dull, empty words that were part of the communist ewspeak. In some combinations, as in 'priests' patriots' (*księża patrioci*) it clearly indicated collaboration with the authorities.

More recently, the word *patriotism* seemed to have shaken off the layers of Newspeak and could again be used to talk about the workers strikes in August 1980 or people such as Father Popiełuszko. However, soon after the final collapse of the system in 1989, the word was again appropriated by the chauvinistic faction of the post-communist elite, associated with groups such as the All-Polish Youth *(Młodzież Wszechpolska)*, a militant youth organization sponsored by League of Polish Families (LPR, part of the ruling coalition in Poland between 2005 and 2007). They talked about patriotism, but their definition of patriotism was based on opposition to European Union integration and abhorrence towards

Western (liberal) values, the destructive influence of the English language and Western disrespect for Christian religious traditions. As always, there is an element of truth in that portrayal of post-communist Poland but fighting the spread of pornography or not mixing in English words where Polish terms are available is not equivalent with patriotism. This mix of militaristic nationalism, religious zeal, chauvinistic and xenophobic loathing of anything foreign with an added touch of anti-Semitism is just too much of everything. Even though I never supported communism and I have no problem with putting communist leaders of the past on trial, I would be most definitely opposed to lynching anyone and so the picture of a noose or slogans about hanging communists on trees or street lamps make me immediately reject anyone who would advance such suggestions. Janusz A. Majcherek (2008) observes in an op-ed in *Gazeta Wyborcza* that, as a result of the communist devaluation of the term 'patriotic', the anti-communist movement in Poland preferred to call itself 'democratic opposition.' In the same text, Majcherek also notes another word that became a very popular addition to all kinds of official names in Poland: *national*. A popular communist slogan of the 1970s was "The Party with the Nation, the Nation with the Party" (*Partia z Narodem, Naród z Partią*). The missing predicate allows for any and every interpretation. The official name of the military junta that declared martial law in Poland in December 1981 was Military Council of National Salvation. What exactly was meant here by the word 'nation' is not entirely clear.

Even though I made a choice not to extend my observations past 2010, I feel compelled to say that the 2nd PiS (*Prawo i Sprawiedliwość*, 'Law and Justice') government brought a final devaluation of all these terms. By supporting and encouraging the right wing nationalistic extreme movement and their hate-based discourse, the authorities democratically elected in 2015 and loyally supported by approximately 30 percent of Poles, took Poland back to rather dark times of intolerance for disagreement, choosing party loyalty over competence, fundamentalist interpretation of religion, and disrespect for anyone different than the projected ideal of a Polish patriot: white, Catholic supporter of PiS, against EU, abortion, or admitting immigrants. One fascinating story about the 2nd PiS rule has been the conversion of one of the men negatively associated with the first government of that party. Mr. Roman Giertych, a lawyer, who was the leader of the League of Polish Families, and part of the PiS coalition government (associated with the All-Polish Youth and the Minister of Education who wanted to teach patriotism in schools), made a 180 degree turn and became a very vocal critic of the party. While I was very critical of him in 2005-2007, I must admit that I enjoy reading his witty and intelligent texts now. The conversion of Mr. Giertych shows why PiS supports blind loyalty over intelligence.

The American *war on terror* after 9/11 also brought with it a lot of linguistic twists and turns, best described by George Lakoff, Professor of Linguistics at the University of California at Berkeley, in his March 18, 2003 essay "Metaphor and War, Again," made available on the internet. This date, March 18, 2003, is important. The war in Iraq, the so-called *operation Iraqi Freedom*, began two days later, on March 20. The essay was meant as a continuation (or Part II) of the paper Lakoff wrote in December 1990, during the first Gulf War. That essay was entitled: "Metaphor and War: The Metaphor System Used to Justify War in the Gulf". That first paper began with the words: "Metaphors can kill" (Lakoff 1991).

Lakoff states that the public discourse used by the U.S. government in discussing the decision "whether to go to war in the gulf was a panorama of metaphor." In 2003, he argues that "[m]any of those metaphorical ideas are back, but within a very different and more dangerous context" (Lakoff 2003). Lakoff argues that the war in Iraq has been successfully presented to the American audience as a *just war* because of the way different participants have been portrayed and framed. It starts with personification of nations (e.g. equating Iraq with Saddam Hussein, and Saddam Hussein with Al Qaida, and thus removing civilian Iraqis from the role of the Villain in this picture) and continues with imposing a story on the facts: The war was framed as a self defence of the Victim (average Iraqis who suffered under Saddam Hussein's regime and the neighbouring countries threatened by Hussein's weapons of mass destruction) against the Villain (Hussein himself) by the Hero (the U.S. troops). The weapons of mass destruction have never been found, and there is no evidence of any link between Al Qaida and Iraq, but these are irrelevant details for the story. As Terry Arthur says in his book on political discourse, "for dodgy arguments, attack is the best form of defense." (Arthur 2007, 89).

Lakoff concludes by explaining the importance of understanding the power of metaphors and frames over our thinking:

> One of the fundamental findings of cognitive science is that people think in terms of frames and metaphors—conceptual structures like those we have been describing. The frames are in the synapses of our brains—physically present in the form of neural circuitry. When the facts don't fit the frames, the frames are kept and the facts ignored. It is a common folk theory of progressives that, "The facts will set you free!" If only you can get all the facts out there in the public eye, then every rational person will reach the right conclusion. It is a vain hope. Human brains just don't work that way. Framing matters. Frames once entrenched are hard to dispel (Lakoff 2003).

Lakoff was aware that one linguistic paper may not be able to stop a war but this should not deter linguists from analyzing the power of language and from trying to pass their understanding of what he calls "the cognitive dimensions of politics" to others,

> especially when most of our conceptual framing is unconscious and we may not be aware of our own metaphorical thought. [...] [T]hat analytic act is a political act: Awareness matters. Being able to articulate what is going on can change what is going on—at least in the long run (ibid.)

Language is an indispensable instrument of communication but it can be a dangerous tool. Confused language is particularly dangerous because it poses as a toy gun while it is in fact a loaded weapon. It needs to be handled with care. Learning how to disarm propaganda rhetoric is one such way.

CHAPTER 3

The Ideal Human Being *or* the Roots of Totalitarianism

When I think of my life in Poland and the people I knew there, they seem not unlike those I have met elsewhere. In Poland I met individuals of various kinds, some with nice personalities and good natured, others with violent tempers or seemingly with no backbone—friends and colleagues, relatives and neighbours. I was probably too young to have serious enemies, but there were some people I did not particularly like or for whom I had little respect in my somewhat naive, childish way. Even if I were to put them into only a few broad categories, each one was different. No two people were similar enough to be lumped together into one category. This individuality made them all human. This individuality was also a sure sign that the communist system had failed in my country. Had it succeeded, we would all have been like the proverbial 'cogs in the wheel' that Mikhail Heller described as the ideal of the new Soviet man in his 1987 book *Cogs in the Wheel.* The title of the Russian original was, I believe, an even more accurate description of the idea of human uniformity and worthlessness: *Mashina i vintiki*—'machine and screws'. It seems to me that a cog is a somewhat more important functional part of the wheel than a single screw in a big machine. However, this may just be my personal bias or my own mechanical ignorance. The slight incompatibility of the two metaphors, mixed together, shows in the English translation of a quotation from Stalin, cited in Heller's book: "I drink to the simple people, ordinary and modest, to the 'cogs', who keep our great state machine in motion" (Heller 1987, 1). Screws or cogs, simple people in the Soviet Empire should have had no personality of their own. They were only supposed to have a common and collective function and—what seemed particularly important in times of purges—should have been immediately replaceable.

People I knew were not like that. Again, my experience is only representative for the dusk-stage of the Soviet Empire in Eastern Europe and for one country. Even my limited exposure to people in other communist countries, in particular in East Germany, gave me the impression that the Polish situation was not really typical. This may simply result from the fact that I knew people in Poland in a much more intimate way and the better we know someone or something, the less likely we evoke stereotypical concepts.

I admit that certain features made people in Eastern Europe seem different than those in the West, at least during communist times. The Easterners were—usually—less confident and not as career oriented. Maybe the careers in communist countries were not worth the effort? People in Eastern Europe always had time or at least rarely tried to impress others with how busy they were. And yet one salary was hardly enough to make ends meet and most of my colleagues and friends had more than one place of work or did extra jobs, like translations, language courses or private lessons. I did all of those things myself, in addition to my full-time job as a junior assistant at the university, which was a bit like the graduate teaching assistantship of a PhD student in the West, except that I was teaching a full load of undergraduate courses. As there was no official unemployment in those times, we never worried about losing our jobs and finding ourselves on the street. Our jobs did not pay much but were relatively secure. No one took them too seriously in terms of work ethics. There was nothing morally wrong about going out shopping during office hours if something of interest was 'thrown' into the stores. One never knew when 'they' would 'throw' something and so this activity of shopping during working time was fine with everyone, including many bosses who acted similarly.

While no one really cared about ideology when I was growing up, the generation of my parents (or in particular my parents-in-law, who were significantly younger than my own parents) remembers that most attempts to be different, to deliberately not fit in, to project individuality or to simply resist being *gleichgeschaltet* (made to conform) were discouraged or punished. My father-in-law still remembers a special meeting of the student organization (ZMP—the Polish Youth Association) that was called when a female student at the Higher School of Agriculture dared to wear gloves when picking up potatoes in a field as part of the voluntary social service. The meeting was to consider whether this bourgeois behaviour merited her expulsion from the University. Allowing one student to be different was dangerous. This must have also been the reason why another of my father-in-law's friends from middle school, at the time junior vice champion in tennis, Aldek Kudliński, was almost expelled from school for using both hands in backhand—a move he learned while watching Western tennis players. That too was considered a capitalist aberration. Aldek (Romulad) Kudliński (1931–1994) became a renowned economist and has now a private university named after him.

If we were to look for the origins of the idea that human collective can be shaped according to some philosophical theories or political agenda, we may find multiple examples of such theoretical or practical experiments in the past. We could begin this discussion of totalitarian ideology with a look at the ideals of social development and improvement that go back to Jean-Jacques Rousseau and other writers of the Enlightenment. In fact, we may go even further into the past, to Plato and his concept of an ideal society. This topic is important because it may help to capture the undeniable attraction of totalitarianism in its various disguises.

Rousseau's theory had a significant effect on French political thought over the past two centuries. His political legacy is still debated, especially in relation to the question whether he could be claimed as a supporter of totalitarian rule. According to Neidleman's comprehensive study of French political thought (Neidleman 2001), Rousseau neither supported nor opposed totalitarianism. He was neither a liberal individualist nor a pro-totalitarian collectivist (Neidleman 2001, 28)and anyone who attempts to interpret his writings in such a way is examining Rousseau "through the lens of later historical development, rather than on Rousseau's own terms" (ibid.). Neidleman stresses the importance of "distinguishing clearly between the general will as conceived by Rousseau and the general will as appropriated by later political thought and movements" (ibid.) and emphasises that Rousseau's writings are not a "straightforward prescription for political action" (Neidleman 2001, 58). On the contrary, Rousseau describes an ideal, utopian situation of political unity in order to critique modern society and remind us of what we have sacrificed in joining society. However, this interpretation seems to contradict Neidleman's earlier claim that the introduction to *The Social Contract* refutes such a reading as Rousseau states that the purpose of his book is to examine "whether there can be a legitimate and reliable rule of administration in the civil order, taking men as they are and laws as they can be" (*The Social Contract*, I, introduction, 26; as found in Neidleman 29-30). The claim to be taking men 'as they are', Neidleman argues, shows that Rousseau's theories were based not on a utopian ideal and an equally unrealistic desire to improve human nature, but on real, flawed human character. Another characteristic that sets Rousseau apart from other political philosophers is his emphasis on morality and virtue. For Rousseau, freedom is intelligible only in conjunction with virtue. The paradox is that while freedom is a prerequisite for morality, morality is at the same time a prerequisite for freedom. There is, however, no universal idea of what is 'moral' and this concept will vary from society to society. Again, Rousseau makes no claim that one concept of morality should be imposed over another.

To properly examine these concepts would be beyond the scope of this discussion and also beyond the expertise of a linguist. Instead, I shall try to examine the attraction of the ideals of human improvement and perfection commonly—though in different forms—associated with both communism (social engineering) and with Nazism (racial purity), especially in the case of the intellectual elite. I shall then try to compare Communism to Nazism, in terms of their shallow and populist (i.e., over-simplistic) interpretations of history and evolution and their respective roles in shaping the ideal human being.

One of the astonishing features of the most notorious totalitarian regimes of the 20th century was that many honest and intelligent people had been attracted to them. Even today many still believe that it was only the practice and not the theory that was faulty. While the praise of Nazi Germany and its leaders is less common and perhaps rather unlikely in academic circles, communism, often linguistically disguised and hidden behind some other theoretical or philosophical labels, continues to exert a strong attraction. Many Western academics are openly (neo-)Marxist and see their philosophical affiliation as just that: an intellectual category label. While Eastern Europe was still communist, the popularity of Marxist ideology was mostly characteristic of the West. The following encounter was reported by Friedrich Hayek in 1983:

> I think it was last May, that in my London club I happened to sit on the same table as a Russian scientist, who came to Western Europe for the first time to attend a scientific conference. He spoke quite good English, so I could ask him what surprised him most on visiting Western Europe. His answer was: 'You still have so many Marxists. We haven't any!' (Hayek 1983, quoted after Booth & Stroiński, 2006, 222).

It seems that in some intellectual circles in the West and in some fields, probably mostly in humanities and social sciences, labels synonymous with some brand of Marxist thinking are fashionable, in good taste, or even *de rigueur*.

It is also not uncommon, now even in Eastern Europe, to see people collecting gadgets from communist times or wearing garments with communist symbols. In Russia, these sentiments have taken shape of a new ideology and not even Western democratic leaders seemed prepared to protest when the Moscow celebrations to commemorate the 60th anniversary of the victory over Nazism included strong elements of praise for the former Soviet Union and its leader and commander-in-chief, Joseph Stalin. The discussions about the possibility to return to the name Stalingrad for what is now Volgograd were noted by news agencies, but Stalin is usually referred to as "a controversial figure" rather than a criminal. It is hard to imagine the same newspapers calling Hitler 'controversial.'

In the former East Germany, this sentiment for the communist past has been aptly named *Ostalgie*, nostalgia for things East German, i.e., communist. The popularity of authors such as Jana Hensel indicates that there is a group of people who feel that the change of systems, usually referred to in German as *die Wende*, robbed them of their childhood. In her 2002 book *Die Zonenkinder* (literally 'Children of the Zone'; the English translation of Hensel's book was published in 2004 under the title *After the Wall*), Hensel reminisces about her childhood and how difficult it is to be unable to admit that, despite the communism, it was good. Yet the popularity of her book, described by Susan Wyndham as "a deceptively simple memoir that became an instant and controversial bestseller," shows that there were many people in East Germany who felt the same way. In her lecture at McMaster University in 2004, Hensel said that her experiences are difficult to understand for the generation of her parents but can be easily appreciated by the generation of her grandparents: their childhood and youth happened in the Third Reich, not a period to be remembered fondly. There seems to be a problem of separating private happiness and worry-free time of life from the historical context. Can one have happy memories from the times of mass persecution and murder?

While, again, I do not feel qualified to attempt a historical analysis of the attraction of communist childhood memories, I have the impression, based probably on the language used by those who admit having them, that it was the vision of the *lepsze jutro* (better tomorrow), the possibility of improving mankind, creating an ideal society and the 'new man' that had a particular power over people's imagination. The future society that totalitarian leaders promised to the masses was to be based on scientific principles of philosophy or biology or science in general and had a particularly strong appeal to the idealists who believed that a better and more just organization of the human community was not only desirable but also possible. It also appealed to our childhood sense of fairness and goodness, as was the case of my own childhood admiration for Timur.

The concept of *utopia* was introduced by Thomas More in 1516. His book with the title *Utopia* described an imaginary perfect society. While the word means literally *no place*, people seem to be continuously attracted to the idea of creating a social utopia and are ready to believe that creating such an ideal social structure is not only possible but that, in fact, examples of such an ideal structure already exist. Thus, the word is often erroneously used to mean a 'perfect place.' Some Western scholars, even after having travelled to the Soviet Union under Stalin's rule, kept praising the Soviet system and failed to notice its problems. They saw what they wanted to see (or what their hosts allowed them to see) and failed to observe what they did not want to notice. They were in love with the idea of a social utopia and this love made them willfully blind to the reality of one of the most criminal systems in recent history. Some Western journalists, during the Holodomor, the man-made mass starvation in Ukraine in 1932-33, reported what the Soviet authorities told them to report. They saw this as the price for being allowed to keep working in the country or because they derived some gains from such servitude. We may never know whether they purposefully deceived their readers or were simply unable to comprehend Stalin's criminal policies.

The idea that reality could be better and that people are able to improve their fate and their nature is probably one of the strongest engines of human progress. When dissatisfied with their current situation, some people choose to move to a place where their life could be better, while others work harder to change the reality where they are. This latter approach is indeed commendable as those hard-working idealists may be in position to make life better not just for themselves, as would be the case with those who choose exile, but also for their fellow human beings. As long as they respect the lives and wishes of their fellow humans, they are indeed 'the heroes of progress.' The problems start when these heroes of progress believe they know better and that this knowledge gives them the right or moral duty to change the world at the expense of those they consider inferior.

Some such 'heroes of progress' are using available human resources as slave labour and do not care about anything but the product of their labour or their own profit. This was the case with many 'great' conquerors or ruthless entrepreneurs and industrialists. They may have been be cruel and evil and this evil was often clear and obvious. Some leaders of change, however, do not so much care about the profit or even the product of the labour of enslaved masses, as about the reeducation of those masses and transforming them into willing wheels turning the machine of progress, or, as Mikhail Heller brilliantly describes in his book, 'cogs in the wheel'.

Mark Cooray, in his essay "Communism and Democratic Socialism and the creation of a New Man" (1985), describes the New Soviet Man, liberated from the limitations of the past, as someone who "was to be altruist in spirit, communal in outlook, sacrificial in his labour for the common good, boundless in his fight for world revolution" (Cooray 1985). He further explains the means and methods for the formation of the so-called *Homo Sovieticus*: "The first step was total destruction of the old social order and all of the social and cultural institutions that surrounded and protected the individual." Mikhail Heller refers to this as the process of culturally stripping the individual naked and atomising him so he is defenceless and mouldable by the state in each and every corner of social life.

The next step was the 'nationalisation of time' through central planning. Through the instituting of 'the plan' under Stalin, the State attempted to control and manipulate the very concept of time. All human life existed and continued through the dimensions and durations defined by the plan. The Soviet authorities, Heller explains, tried to set and change the boundaries of 'past', 'present', and 'future' by accelerating, shortening, and modifying the temporal horizons within which all economic and social activity were made to conform.

Finally came 'ideologization', the process through which the Soviet State attempted to fill the content of peoples' minds and influenced the language and thought patterns of 'the people' in whose name the leaders undertook this grand scheme. Under this heading, Heller details the state's control and direction of literature, the arts, education, and the all-pervasive din of propaganda through every mode of communication. Nor does Heller ignore the role of fear, intimidation, and terror as practised by the secret police.

There is no doubt that this process of bringing the 'new and improved' person (as contemporary advertising likes to frame it) into existence would involve a lot of force.

According to Orwell:

> ...the ideal set up by the Party [in *1984*—MS] was something huge, terrible, and glittering—a world of steel and concrete, of monstrous machines and terrifying weapons—a nation of warriors and fanatics, marching forward in perfect unity, all thinking the same thoughts and shouting the same slogans, perpetually working, fighting, triumphing, persecuting—three hundred million people all with the same face.

This is the dream of full control over people.

In Nazi Germany, the ideological concept at the centre of the system was not that of the 'new man' but rather that of the laws of nature and Aryan racial supremacy. According to the American Heritage Dictionary of the English Language, (2003), the term 'Aryan' used to be applied in historical linguistics to the people who spoke Proto-Indo-European, the parent language of the Indo-European languages. The word comes from Sanskrit, the classical language of India, used in liturgical texts of Hinduism, where it denoted 'noble,' in the sense of upper-class membership. The last meaning option refers to the use of the word in the Third Reich where it denoted a non-Jewish Caucasian, especially one of Nordic type, supposed to be part of a master race. It is assumed that the word was a self-designation of some of the ancestral Indo-European tribes. Making the word refer to some ancient blond-haired and blue-eyed Northern race, as the Nazi mythology purported, was a complete fabrication. As a linguist and a Germanist (i.e., German philologist), I feel that a word in defense of German linguistics is necessary here. In the German tradition, Indo-European family of languages used to be and even today often continues to be called Indo-Germanic. One of the possible reasons for this special positioning of the German language may simply be the fact that very many (perhaps most) of the prominent typologists (linguists that research language types and their classifications), as well as historical and comparative linguists were German. The discovery of the common origins of most European and many Asian languages was made by Sir William Jones and announced in his famous "Third Discourse of 1786." The concepts of language families and laws of language change, that would explain how languages so different today could be genetically related, were taken up by other philologists. Friedrich Schlegel, in the 19th century, postulated that the root of the word Aryan is also related to the German word *Ehre* (honour) and so the Indo-European self-description was something along the lines of "we, the noble people." It is possible to also see the link of the Sanskrit word to *Éire*, the Irish name for Ireland. In the 19th century the notion of an 'Aryan race' was postulated outside Germany, first by Arthur Comte de Gobineau (a French aristocrat, author of the 1853-55 book *An Essay on the Inequality of the Human Races*), considered the father of modern racial theory, and later by Houston Stewart Chamberlain, British author, often referred to by the Nazis for his Pan-German ideals. As the original homeland of the Indo-Europeans was at some point associated with Northern Europe, the connection between Aryan and Nordic was an acceptable association. We now know that Indo-European origins are more likely in Anatolia (the region of the Caspian Sea) and that the first Indo-Europeans were not blond. But science and ideology do not need to coincide. Ideology is free from the limitation of scientific evidence.

The so-constructed Aryan race was considered to be superior to all other peoples. As such, this concept was taken over by Hitler, along with some simplistic ideas of evolution, and became the foundation of his racial theory presented in 1926 in *Mein Kampf*, often referred to as "the Bible of National Socialist movement." Many scholars at the time, e.g., the American anthropologist and linguist Franz Boas, repudiated this understanding of human diversity. Nevertheless, this primitive teaching of race became the basis of the Nazi policy of racial extermination.

In the chapter "Nation and Race" of *Mein Kampf*, Hitler introduces the idea of racial diversity among people by comparing human races to various animal species. The logic of his argument is fundamentally faulty but the rhetoric is effective in a very populist sense. Hitler starts by declaring what he is about to say as truth so obvious that it may be difficult to notice and goes on, step by step, repeating at each stage that only weak and racially inferior people could disagree with his argument because his argument is what the personified Nature herself established as law.

> There are some truths which are so obvious that for this very reason they are not seen or at least not recognized by ordinary people. They sometimes pass by such truisms as though blind and are most astonished when someone suddenly discovers what everyone really ought to know.
>
> Thus men without exception wander about in the garden of Nature; they imagine that they know practically everything and yet with few exceptions pass blindly by one of the most patent principles of Nature's rule: the inner segregation of the species of all living beings on this earth.
>
> Even the most superficial observation shows that Nature's restricted form of propagation and increase is an almost rigid basic law of all the innumerable forms of expression of her vital urge. Every animal mates only with a member of the same species. The titmouse seeks the titmouse, the finch the finch, the stork the stork, the field mouse the field mouse, the dormouse the dormouse, the wolf the she-wolf, etc.
>
> Only unusual circumstances can change this, primarily the compulsion of captivity or any other cause that makes it impossible to mate within the same species. But then Nature begins to resist this with all possible means, and her most visible protest consists either in refusing further capacity for propagation to bastards or in limiting the fertility of later offspring; in most cases, however, she takes away the power of resistance to disease or hostile attacks.
>
> This is only too natural.
>
> Any crossing of two beings not at exactly the

> same level produces a medium between the level of the two parents. This means: the offspring will probably stand higher than the racially lower parent, but not as high as the higher one. Consequently, it will later succumb in the struggle against the higher level. Such mating is contrary to the will of Nature for a higher breeding of all life. The precondition for this does not lie in associating superior and inferior, but in the total victory of the former. The stronger must dominate and not blend with the weaker, thus sacrificing his own greatness. Only the born weakling can view this as cruel, but he after all is only a weak and limited man; for if this law did not prevail, any conceivable higher development of organic living beings would be unthinkable. (Hitler 1925/1971, 284-285)

This line of reasoning is presented quite smoothly but any attempt at critical reading shows that there is a fundamental flaw. People who have different skin colour or different ethnicity are obviously still members of one mankind, not examples of different species. Hitler presents himself as siding with Nature, whose laws, he says, are not disputable. He then progresses, smoothly again, though not with any logic to his argument, to the point where he introduces the notion of 'struggle' among individuals, a competition for survival where the best wins, which, in his view, is exactly what the personified Nature desires. This linguistic trick of personification allows him to attribute human-like feelings and actions to Nature, gives the Nature human-like agency.

This struggle, he proclaims, is not the result of any negative feelings but the effect of natural sensations, such as hunger. The racial doctrine of the Nazis is thus conveniently explained as "only too natural" (285).

> In the struggle for daily bread all those who are weak and sickly or less determined succumb, while the struggle of the males for the female grants the right

> or opportunity to propagate only to the healthiest. And struggle is always a means of improving a species' health and power of resistance and, therefore, a cause of its higher development (ibid.)

The above fragment illustrates Hitler's technique of leading the reader to draw conclusions based on confused premises. By the clever use of the phrase 'struggle for daily bread', he further reinforces the idea that the survival of the strongest is presented as the rule for human society not only for the animal kingdom. 'Daily bread' makes it sound almost religious, as if these principles were sanctioned by God or, at least by the anthropomorphic Nature.

While Hitler's logic does not stand to closer scrutiny, it is true that the transformation towards the new man happens almost like a natural stage of evolution that grants the greatest chances of survival to those who follow the new rules of the game. Czesław Miłosz (1951, 76-77) writes:

> Victory in this new struggle seems to belong to a breed different from that which was favored to win in the battle for money in the early days of industrial capitalism. If biting dogs can be divided into two main categories, noisy and brutal, or silent and slyly vicious, then the second variety would seem most privileged in the countries of the New Faith [i.e., communism—MS]. Forty or fifty years of education in these new ethical maxims must create a new and irretrievable species of mankind. The 'new man' is not merely a postulate. He is beginning to become a reality.

Indeed, sixty years later in Eastern Europe or some eighty years later in Russia, it was the "new man" who had survived the collapse of the system but who still speaks the language of the empire. That new man had internalised the ethics and the morale of the system, even if he always saw himself in opposition to its teachings. There is no escape from the social reality (or social fiction) created by totalitarian propaganda, there are only various degrees of immersion or submission. The developments in Poland after 2005, and then again after 2015, the shameless struggle for power and complete lack of respect for others prove that Miłosz was right in his predictions. Until my generation leaves the scene, the children and grandchildren of the Empire will keep the new man's mentality alive. I am growing pessimistic even about the following generation.

From those general considerations about the laws of Nature, Hitler smoothly moves on to the issue of human races:

> No more than Nature desires the mating of weaker with stronger individuals, even less does she desire the blending of a higher with a lower race, since, if she did, her whole work of higher breeding, over perhaps hundreds of thousands of years, might be ruined with one blow.
>
> Historical experience offers countless proofs of this. It shows with terrifying clarity that in every mingling of Aryan blood with that of lower peoples the result was the end of the cultured people. (Hitler 1925/1971, 286)

Aryan blood? This is a rather stretched concept, but not within an ideology where logic is also only for weaklings. It might be instructive to look up the definition of blood in the aforementioned Nazi brochure "Faith and Action" (German *Glauben und Handeln*, Stellrecht 1943). The brochure discusses a set of virtues that were seen as desirable in German youth. The author, Helmut Stellrecht, was in charge of military education for the Hitler Youth. The brochure provides definitions of some Nazi key concepts, such as race, blood, faith, etc., and contains a short exposé for the ideology through the explanation of key words. 'Blood' was, in National Socialism, one of the most important key words.

> *Blood*—You carry in your blood the holy inheritance of your fathers and forefathers. You do not know those who have vanished in endless ranks

> into the darkness of the past. But they all live in you and walk in your blood upon the earth that consumed them in battle and toil and in which their bodies have long decayed. Your blood is therefore something holy. In it your parents gave you not only a body, but your nature. To deny your blood is to deny yourself. No one can change it. But each decides to grow the good that one has inherited and suppress the bad. Each is also given will and courage. You do not have only the right, but also the duty to pass your blood on to your children, for you are a member of the chain of generations that reaches from the past into eternity, and this link of the chain that you represent must do its part so that the chain is never broken. But if your blood has traits that will make your children unhappy and burdens to the state, then you have the heroic duty to be the last. The blood is the carrier of life. You carry in it the secret of creation itself. Your blood is holy, for in it God's will lives (Stellrecht 1943).

When Hitler or other Nazi ideologists talk about *blood*, they do not mean the bodily fluid. They talk about something very different. They use familiar words but change their definitions. There is no possibility of any meaningful dialogue if you do not share word definitions. But, in a totalitarian state, the government or the ruling party are the primary definers of words. They control language and, through language control, they control thoughts.

If someone defiled the blood that was passed on to them by crossing racial boundaries, they would be punished by the omnipotent Nature (again giving nature human-like agency). The effect of such contamination would be the lowering of the level of the higher race by

> physical and intellectual regression and hence the beginning of a slowly but surely progressing

> sickness. To bring about such a development is, then, nothing else but to sin against the will of the eternal creator. And as a sin this act is rewarded. When man attempts to rebel against the iron logic of Nature, he comes into struggle with the principles to which he himself owes his existence as a man. And this attack must lead to his own doom. (Hitler 1925/1971, 286-287)

Here Hitler adds to the pseudoscience of his racial theory an element of pseudo-religion. The concept of 'sin', as presented in Hitler's writing, is interesting. It is understood as a transgression against the laws of personified Nature and also against "the will of the eternal creator." Or are Nature and the eternal creator one and the same? What is their ontological status? If it is the Nature, how can it have a will? And how can one 'sin' against it? The concept of sin leads us to think of the eternal creator as the Christian God since Germany was a Christian country. But Christian God does not divide people into different (superior and inferior) races. On the contrary; Christian God teaches to love the weak. If we look up the definition of faith in our "Faith and Action" brochure, we shall see that this word too had its meaning transformed:

> *Faith*—Knowledge is that which can be measured by reason. Knowledge alone means nothing and is dead. But faith can never fail, for faith is strength. Faith springs from your deepest feelings. It is that knowledge for which there is no explanation through reason. … Because faith is strength, it can do what seems impossible. It is the foundation for every deed. No one can do anything without faith. No one can even jump over a ditch if he does not believe he can do it. The highest and most important in a person is not knowledge and understanding, but rather his faith. Each is worth only as much as the faith he has. … Woe to those who do not believe. They are not on the side of the strength

> of creation, but rather annihilation. They are the destroyers of the Reich. Faith is however stronger than all other powers that can be found in this world (Stellrecht 1943).

One might say that faith may give strength, but it is a different concept altogether when one asserts that faith is strength. It is worth checking at this point what National Socialists understood by 'race':

> *Race* means to be able to think in a certain way. He who has courage, loyalty and honour, the mark of the German, has the race that should rule in Germany, even if he does not have the physical characteristics of the 'Nordic' race. The unity of the noble and a noble body is the goal to which we strive. But we despise those whose noble body carries an ignoble soul. A variety of related European races have merged in Germany. One trunk grew from these roots. Each race gave its best strength. Each contributed to the German soul. We Germans have a fighting spirit, a look to the horizon, the "desire to do a thing for its own sake" of the Nordic race. Another racial soul gave us our cozy old cities and our depth. Yet another racial soul gave us mastery of the magical realm of music. Yet another gave us our ability to organize, and our silent obedience. We can not hold it against anyone if he carries a variety of racial lines, for the German soul does as well, and created out of it the immeasurable riches which it possesses above all other nations. The greatness of our Reich grew out of this soul. But the Nordic race must dominate in Germany and shape the soul of each German. It must win out in the breast of each individual. Today our ideal is not the artist or the citizen, but the hero. Our highest treasure is the soul that we have been given. He who mixes his blood with that of foreign inferior races ruins the

> blood and soul that have been given to him to pass on in purity to his children. He makes his children impure and miserable, and commits the greatest crime that he as a National Socialist can commit. But he who follows the laws of race fulfills the great commandment that only like should be brought together with like, keeping apart those things like fire and water which do not mix. (Stellrecht 1943).

This, in my opinion, is a particularly confused definition. It starts with the provision that the Aryan (Nordic) physical characteristics and looks are not an indispensable part of being of the 'right' race. This is easily explainable if one takes a look at the highest-ranking Nazi officials, particularly at Hitler and Goebbels. They do not in any way resemble the Nordic, blond, muscular ideal male figures that often graced the cover of the magazine *Volk und Rasse*. Their racial purity had to be accounted for on different grounds, thus they were Aryan or Nordic on the basis of their courage, honour, and loyalty and their way of thinking in general, not on the basis of their appearance. This is understandable, but it is also being applied, as I shall argue in a moment, in a very exclusive fashion to established party officials only.

The authors then assert that the current population of Germany had developed like 'one trunk' from very diverse 'roots' that all contributed to its present strength. This would suggest that Germans are not a pure race. Then, however, the authors make another leap: "But the Nordic race must dominate in Germany and shape the soul of each German. It must win out in the breast of each individual." This suggests the possibility of some kind of a racial struggle within individual human beings, with different races competing against each other in us for their internal supremacy. If we let the 'Nordic race' win, we are fine. This would give the individual a certain degree of control over their race. One could decide what they wanted to be. If race was a matter of decision, one could be punished for making a morally or politically wrong choice. Punishment for something that is independent of our volition, on the other hand, invites the accusation of racial discrimination. Here the authors introduce the concept of the soul of the nation but leave it undefined. We only know that it is being somehow shaped by race and it is a valuable treasure. Interracial relationships are vividly described as blood mixing that ruins both the blood and the soul that were to be kept pure for the sake of the future offspring. Thus, mixing blood becomes not just a sin, as Hitler described it, but "the greatest crime that [...] a National Socialist can commit."

The argument presented here is rather incoherent but that is not considered a problem for the Nazi ideology. Hitler explains it best himself in *Mein Kampf* in the chapter on Nation and Race when he says that his theories of race are an example of "those ideas whose content originates, not in an exact scientific truth, but in the world of emotion, or, as it is so beautifully and clearly expressed today, reflects an 'inner experience.' All these ideas ... have nothing to do with cold logic as such, but represent only pure expressions of feeling, ethical conceptions, etc." (Hitler 1925 287)

The definition of race given above is important as the race membership became a matter of life and death for millions of Germans after 1935 when special regulations, so-called Nuremberg Race Laws were introduced. They consisted of a regulation about German citizenship—*Reichsbürgergesetz* and a regulation about the protection of German blood and German honour—*Gesetz zum Schutze des deutschen Blutes und der deutschen Ehre.* The laws defined those who had at least three Jewish grandparents as full Jews (*Volljuden*) and those who had one or two Jewish grandparents, practiced Jewish faith or had a full Jewish spouse as racially mixed (*Mischlinge*). Soon other regulations followed. A Law for the Protection of the Genetic Health of the German People required anyone who wished to marry to undergo a medical examination in order to obtain a certificate stating that he or she was healthy, i.e., "fit to marry." As the Nuremberg Laws were quite complicated, special racial ancestry tables were issued to illustrate the genetic make up of the offspring. Interestingly, the figures representing racially *pure* Germans, full Jews and the mixes were represented with the stereotypical colours: Aryans were white (clean, pure). Full Jews were black (dirty, dangerous, and evil) and the mixes were shaded gray (shady, suspicious, contaminated). It was visually obvious that the white figures must not come in contact with black or shady ones because of the obvious danger of pollution. Thus, marriages of pure Germans with non-Aryans were prohibited and so were the marriages between people of mixed race. The proliferation of regulations continued and, step by step, practically all civil liberties and professional opportunities were taken away from non-Aryans. Finally, having been forced out of their jobs and with degrading living conditions, the Nazi propaganda convinced many Germans that these people were subhuman and should be removed from public view, locked up in segregated parts of towns (ghettos) and shipped to labour or concentration camps where they would be exterminated. The warning that Jews will pay if they cause another world war came in Hitler's speeches before September 1939 and so Germany's invasion of Poland on the first day of that month meant that "the punishment" was coming. The technical aspects of *Judenfrage* (Jewish question) were discussed over the next two years and in 1942 plans were in place for an *Endlösung* (final solution). It only took a few years to progress from a linguistically and logically flawed definition of race in propaganda pamphlets to physical extermination of almost the entire Jewish population in Europe and mass murder of many other ethnic social groups portrayed as a danger to German purity. It happened in a highly civilized, modern country at the heart of Europe. And the general outlines of the plan were already announced in mid 1920s, in Hitler's *Mein Kampf*. It was there that Hitler wrote about Jews using words that would portray them as vermin, taking away their human features. No one can say they did not know what Hitler had in mind. Millions of copies of *Mein Kampf* were published. Free copies were given to every soldier and every married couple. English translations (some with the most anti-Semitic rhetoric removed) were available. Everyone had an opportunity to read it for themselves.

It is difficult and perhaps even pointless to compare two inhumane systems, like the communism in its early implementation and Nazism. Both were deadly and, in both, obedience and participation in institutionalized activities were required. However, in terms of aspirations to mould the new or ideal man, they certainly differed. In order to become a communist, one had to follow a certain, partially prescribed path. This path was not fully accessible to people who were members of the upper class and at different times different social or national groups became class enemies or simply scapegoats and were exterminated through mock trials, labour camps, purges or mass starvation. A false report, triggered by human envy or fear was enough to send someone to prison, and prison often meant death. But communism played the card of resocialization, declaring that it was transforming human beings into something better, educating them, improving them, and with them the society. Communism claimed to be building a paradise on earth where everyone willing to join was welcome if they accepted the rules. All of these were just slogans, not the reality, but these were the slogans that people could find difficult to object to. Who would be against a paradise on earth? Who would not want universal welfare?

In Nazi Germany, the paradise on Earth was also being promised, in the form of *Lebensraum* (living space) and the Third Reich itself; holy, eternal, peaceful, well off. But this paradise was *nur für Deutsche* (for Germans only). Jews, Gypsies, Slavs, homosexuals, disabled, and the elderly were not welcome. In fact, they were portrayed as a threat to the very existence of paradise and as such had to be eliminated for the sake of the superior Aryan race, the race of masters. The membership in the master race was determined by the ancestry; one either was or was not a member of the Aryan race. You could not become one if you were not one. This pseudo genetic determinism was an overruling principle, even though some pragmatic considerations were also acceptable. Thus, as part of the *Lebensborn* program, Slavic children who were seen as fitting the Aryan paradigm (i.e. were blond and blue eyed) were regularly taken away from occupied areas and raised as German.

Once it had been established who the members of the in-group were, the 'new man' had to be educated in the teachings of the system and had to accept the goals of the system as his or her own. In communism, the 'new man' could also be a woman. In the Third Reich, women had special roles assigned to them. They were to be wives and mothers. Their role was mostly reduced to biology as they were defined by their reproductive utility. Interestingly, just as the Nazi leaders did not fit the Aryan ideal in terms of their appearance, their wives and the first ladies of the Third Reich, rarely complied with the Nazi ideal for women (Sigmund 2000).

The new men and women needed to be told what to think. This was the objective of propaganda experts and the task of the propaganda machine. According to Goebbels (in his 1934 speech) propaganda had to:

> find meaningful ways and flexible forms to immunize the people's thinking. The people should know the concerns and successes of their government. Its concerns and successes must therefore be constantly presented so that the people will consider the concerns and successes of their government to be their concerns and successes. Only an authoritarian government, firmly tied to the people, can do this over the long term. Political propaganda, the art of anchoring the things of the state in the broad masses so that the whole nation will feel a part of them, cannot therefore remain merely a means to the goal of winning power. It must become a means of building and keeping power.

In Hitler's Germany, the ministry that controlled the media and all domains of public and private life carried the name "Ministry for Popular Enlightenment and Propaganda." In the Soviet Union, the same role was assigned to the "Department of Agitation and Propaganda of the Central Committee of the Communist Party." The word 'propaganda', as originally used in the Latin name *Congregatio de Propaganda Fide*, referred to the task of spreading Catholicism through missionary work and all other available means. The political associations of the term from World War I onwards include support for political agendas through posters, cartoons and all possible forms of verbal persuasion, leading to the definition of propaganda as the deliberate and systematic attempt to shape perceptions, manipulate cognitions, and direct behaviour in order to achieve a response that fits the desired outcome of the speaker (Jowett and O'Donnell 2006). In George Orwell's *1984*, the Ministry that deals with propaganda is called the Ministry of Truth, or MiniTrue. How fitting!

In Nazi Germany and in communist countries, propaganda has been elevated from what is now generally considered a somewhat dishonest trade of deception and put on a pedestal as an indispensable political art and as a means of educating the masses. It has to be added, though, that it was Nazi Germany and the very person of Joseph Goebbels, 'Our Doctor', the Minister of Propaganda, who really gave the term propaganda its full menacing meaning.

> Throughout the world today, people are beginning to see that a modern state, whether democratic or authoritarian, cannot withstand the subterranean forces of anarchy and chaos without propaganda. It is not only a matter of doing the right thing; the people must understand that the right thing is the right thing. Propaganda includes everything that helps the people to realize this. Political propaganda in principle is active and revolutionary. It is aimed at the broad masses. It speaks the language of the people because it wants to be understood by the people. Its task is the highest creative art of putting sometimes complicated events and facts in a way simple enough to be understood by the man on the street. (Goebbels 1934)

This last sentence was meant to resemble the noble task that Martin Luther put for himself in his translation of the Bible into German so that it could be understood by 'the man in the alley'.

Cooray, in his 1985 essay, admits that seven decades of communism in the Soviet Union have not succeeded at producing the new man and concludes with the somewhat optimistic statement that "human nature and will are ultimately stronger than the State." I am not so sure about that. While he further states that it will take a long time for new, non-totalitarian institutions to grow in post communist Russia, I fear that it will take more than one generation to eliminate the effects of the social experiments of communist ideology and propaganda. *Homo Sovieticus* took on a different meaning than what the communists may have intended. It came to signify a distorted, spineless, degenerate subspecies, the 'silent and slyly vicious' dogs who thrive on biting the weaker ones, and reporting on others. Totalitarian regimes in general abuse people through a wide array of physical and psychological means and create generations of broken human beings. Post communist societies are abused societies that will not heal unless they receive help and counselling. The war in Ukraine is showing the ugliest face of the post-Soviet Russia: immoral, depraved, and cowardly. Another generation of young Russians is infected with toxic propaganda. And another generation of Ukrainians is going through the trauma of war and violence. Will this ever end?

What seems to be a truly positive development over recent years in this ocean of pessimism is that scientists are growing less enthusiastic about the idea of mapping out the exact mechanisms of human behaviour. Huge advances were made in understanding our genetic make-up, genes responsible for various emotions or behaviour patterns have been discovered, however, along with these discoveries came the insight that no one factor can be seen as producing one specific effect. Human beings are far too complex in their thinking and acting to be fully understood and to be considered predictable. In his July 15, 2008 Op-Ed, entitled "The Luxurious Growth" in *The New York Times*, columnist David Brooks writes:

> We all know the story of Dr. Frankenstein, the scientist so caught up in his own research that he arrogantly tried to create new life and a new man. Today, if you look at people who study how genetics shape human behavior, you find a collection of anti-Frankensteins. As the research moves along, the scientists grow more modest about what we are close to knowing and achieving. [...]
>
> The prospect may be gloomy for those who seek to understand human behavior, but the flip side is the reminder that each of us is a Luxurious Growth.

Our lives are not determined by uniform processes. Instead, human behavior is complex, nonlinear and unpredictable. The Brave New World is far away. Novels and history can still produce insights into human behavior that science can't match.

Just as important is the implication for politics. Starting in the late 19th century, eugenicists used primitive ideas about genetics to try to re-engineer the human race. In the 20th century, communists used primitive ideas about "scientific materialism" to try to re-engineer a New Soviet Man.

Today, we have access to our own genetic recipe. But we seem not to be falling into the arrogant temptation — to try to re-engineer society on the basis of what we think we know. Saying farewell to the sort of horrible social engineering projects that dominated the 20th century is a major example of human progress.

We should try to keep it that way.

CHAPTER 4

The Common Good

One Sunday morning, my then-16-year-old son was changing a burnt-out bulb in the brake light of his old Chevrolet Camaro that he was lovingly restoring. When he finally emerged from the garage, he showed me the burnt bulb and pieces of melted and brittle plastic that were stuck to the fixture. He told me that the light was improperly installed and that he had fixed the problem and installed the bulb correctly. He then commented that people at the dealership probably only cared about making the light work but not about proper installation because it was not their own car. He, on the other hand, wanted to do everything right because the car was his and he wanted it to work just right. I had to smile. He had just discovered for himself the reason why communism had to fail. It goes against the basic rules of human nature and psychology to care more about things that are not one's own than about things that are.

The idea that there are some things or provisions that would benefit all or most members of a community and so they should be contributed to and protected by all (or by some group of guardians, e.g., the state) is not a new concept. I am not a historian of ideas or a philosopher but the concept of 'common good' seems to be at least as old as the Golden Rule that we should not do to others as we would not wish them to do to us. Versions of this sentiment can be found in various religions as well as in writings of Aristotle and Plato, and are often referred to as the ethics or reciprocity. In short, they all describe a principle of selflessness and not wishing the other any harm.

But what is this general will? According to Rousseau's interpretation, if one were to take all of the private wills of all citizens, their conflicting elements would cancel each other out and what remained would be the 'general will' (Neidleman 2001, 39). Citizens should meet regularly in order to check whether the existing laws conform to their general will. In larger societies, Rousseau later admitted, the general would have to be expressed by the majority. Here is where it starts to get tricky. If a law is passed with which a citizen does not agree, it means simply that he or she was mistaken as to what they thought was their own general will (43), because the general will cannot contradict itself. This means that, once the general will, and with it the laws are established, each citizen is bound to obey even those laws they did not support: after all, they had a voice when the laws were being passed (55). If a citizen does not obey a law, he should be forced to do so, which, for Rousseau, is only forcing him to be free (34).

Another question arises—how do citizens know what the general will is? According to Rousseau, they do not at first recognize the general will and must therefore be taught to understand it (59). In fact, until they have been inculcated with a "deep emotional attachment to the fatherland," the voice of the people cannot be taken as the general will. This task falls to the Legislator, a man who understands the passions and desires of the people but does not feel them himself (56). However, even Rousseau doubted the possibility of finding such a person. For him, the most important responsibility of politics is to create best men (28). To achieve this goal, Rousseau does not rule out thought control or forms of conditioning (we could call it indoctrination or brainwashing) as possible methods. The end would justify the means. Yet, at the same time, as I described earlier, for Rousseau, "freedom is intelligible only in conjunction with virtue" (52) and so the desired outcome would be a system where the general will would indeed ensure freedom and well-being of all citizens. This idealistic concept of society can be very easily twisted into a more sinister system of total control in the name of some superimposed general will.

Rousseau's is a very different social utopia than the system created by Orwell in *1984*. The IngSoc may have given pretence of caring for the needs of citizens by ensuring food rations and employment for all, however, a more accurate account would be the following cynical description of it by the character O'Brien in Orwell's novel:

> The Party seeks power entirely for its own sake. We are not interested in the good of others; we are interested solely in power. Not wealth or luxury or long life or happiness: only power, pure power. What pure power means you will understand presently. We are different from all the oligarchies of the past, in that we know what we are doing. All the others, even those who resembled ourselves, were cowards and hypocrites. The German Nazis and the Russian Communists came very close to us in their methods, but they never had the courage to recognize their own motives. They pretended, perhaps they even believed, that they had seized power unwillingly and for a limited time, and that just round the corner there lay a paradise where human beings would be free and equal. We are not like that. We know that no one ever seizes power with the intention of relinquishing it. Power is not a means; it is an end. One does not establish a dictatorship in order to safeguard a revolution; one makes the revolution in order to establish the dictatorship. The object of persecution is persecution. The object of torture is torture. The object of power is power." (Orwell *1984*, pages 275-276)

I am not sure whether the ideologists of communism and Nazism believed there was indeed a paradise on Earth awaiting humanity and that they were helping to build an expressway to get there. Unfortunately, I expect they were much more like O'Brien in Orwell's novel. I am quite confident, however, that there were ordinary people and idealistic intellectuals who did believe in social engineering and a better tomorrow. Czesław Miłosz (1951/1990) observed that "men will clutch at illusions when they have nothing else to hold to." This is probably why fear and poverty are often inseparably connected with authoritarian rule. They make it easier to swallow promises of a better future and many other lies of authoritarian propaganda. Tadeusz Borowski, an Auschwitz and Dachau survivor, a writer and a poet, joined the communist party after the war with the intention to work for the common good. Having been through hell, he must have truly wanted to help build something better. Even though, or maybe rather because he had witnessed the arrest of his parents by Soviet authorities in the 1920s when he was growing up in a Polish family in what was Soviet Ukraine and because he had seen unimaginable suffering in Nazi concentration camps, he truly believed that virtue is inseparable from freedom. He wrote, "There can be no beauty if it is paid for by human injustice, nor truth that passes over injustice in silence, nor moral virtue that condones it," (Borowski 1967). He was not a conformist and he was not ready to compromise his values. He truly wanted to believe that a better world was possible and was ready to help build it. Disillusioned by the communist system in Poland in which he put his faith, he died (likely by suicide) at the age of 28. His brutal short stories from Auschwitz are among the strongest voices in literature in defence of human dignity when nothing is left of the traditional social fabric.

Ten years after the *Social Contract*, Rousseau wrote an essay entitled "Considerations on the Government of Poland and on its proposed Reformation," where he tried to apply his political theory to a practical situation. He was asked for his opinion on the subject of reforming Poland by Count Wielhorski, a Polish nobleman and a member of the so-called Bar Confederation (Bar was a fortress in Podolia, then Eastern Poland, now Central Ukraine). Rousseau's comments about Polish politics, completed in the year of Poland's first partition (1772) sound relevant even today:

> While reading the history of the government of Poland, it is hard to understand how a state so strangely constituted has been able to survive so

> long. A large body made up of a large number of dead members, and of a small number of disunited members whose movements, being virtually independent of one another, are so far from being directed to a common end that they cancel each other out; a body which exerts itself greatly to accomplish nothing; which is capable of offering no sort of resistance to anyone who tries to encroach upon it; which falls into dissolution five or six times a century; which falls into paralysis whenever it tries to make any effort or to satisfy any need; and which, in spite of all this, lives and maintains its vigour: that, in my opinion, is one of the most singular spectacles ever to challenge the attention of a rational being. (Rousseau 1772)

It is not a nice picture but it is better to see the reality and react accordingly than to believe in beautiful (patriotic) fiction and do nothing. Rousseau further explains why he (or anyone analyzing the country's situation from outside and without intimate knowledge of the culture) would not be qualified to solve Polish problems. He—modestly—explains:

> I do not know of anyone better suited than [Count Wielhorski] himself to work out such a plan, for along with the requisite general knowledge he possesses all that detailed familiarity with the local situation which cannot possibly be gained from reading, and which nevertheless is indispensable if institutions are to be adapted to the people for whom they are intended. Unless you are thoroughly familiar with the nation for which you are working, the labour done on its behalf, however excellent in theory, is bound to prove faulty in practice; especially when the nation in question is one which is already well-established, and whose tastes, customs, prejudices and vices are too deeply rooted to be readily crowded out by new plantings. Good institutions for

> Poland can only be the work of Poles, or of someone who has made a thorough first-hand study of the Polish nation and its neighbours. A foreigner can hardly do more than offer some general observations for the enlightenment, but not for the guidance, of the law-reformer.

I find this to be excellent advice for politicians today who attempt to decide for other nations what their 'common good' should be and how to achieve it. They try to sell to others whatever ideals worked (or failed) in their own countries, without paying much attention to cultural, religious, and other differences. A little bit of modesty, Rousseau's style, would probably go a great distance.

Was there any 'common good' in a communist society? Were we, the children and adults shaped by life in communism, any better at recognizing the 'general will'? Have we done to others what we wanted them to do to us? Were we charitable, caring citizens of our common homeland? When I look at Polish society today, I have to question the 'positive teachings' of communist education. Pretty much everything was free, universal, and relatively accessible: child care, education, health care, company sponsored holidays. Did it teach us respect or did it teach us to take for granted things, which in other countries people had worked hard to achieve?

One concept from my communist childhood that is very difficult to translate into languages that have not been affected by the 'system' is that of *praca społeczna*. Seemingly translatable into something like 'social work' or 'community service', it completely loses its meaning in translation.

The theory behind the communist 'community service' was that it was a voluntary service offered by people for the good of their community. This is exactly what countless people do in reality in the West. In Canada, retired men and women volunteer in hospitals, greeting incoming patients and visitors and directing them to appropriate departments or wards. Parents, grandparents, and concerned citizens help young school children safely cross the street on the way to and from school. People volunteer to coach children's sports teams, help political parties, youth organizations ,and humane societies. They give countless hours of their time, usually without any remuneration or recognition, out of the goodness of their heart ,or simply because they are lonely and volunteer work is a good way of meeting other like-minded people. I truly admire those people and believe that they deserve more recognition than they get. But what they do does not resemble in any way what we used to call 'voluntary social or community service' in Poland.

I remember my own experience of *praca społeczna* as anything but voluntary. In elementary school we had various community service field trips involving spring clean-ups in the school yard or city parks. This was not much different from my own children's experiences in Canadian schools. The only difference was that our spring clean-ups had the add-on ideology and that, in theory, they were supposed to be spontaneous and voluntary but were instead planned by teachers, compulsory, and we, the students, had absolutely nothing to say about it. We did not mind those field trips, of course. They were fun but only because we were outside and could socialize freely, even when we were 'pretending' to do the work. Perhaps this 'pretending to do the work' was the most negative part of the experience. It was not because the work was always meaningless or impossible to do but the very set up was wrong. We would be given, say, one hour to do something that required several hours of work so there was almost no point to do anything as it would make very little difference. Or we were given the whole day to do something that required an hour of work. There was then no point to work hard as we knew that we would be able to finish it anyway. Very early on, students were being introduced to the fiction of work in socialism: we pretended to do the work and they pretended to pay us for that; if not with money, then at least with marks for voluntary service.

Three voluntary community service experiences stayed in my memory in a particularly vivid way. The first one involved the clean-up effort on the site of the Warsaw Royal Castle destroyed in World War II. In 1971, shortly after the political turmoil of the December 1970 food price hike riots in Gdańsk, the new First Secretary of the Polish Workers' Party, Edward Gierek proclaimed that the Royal Castle in Warsaw would be rebuilt. All that was left of it was one standing wall fragment with the window that belonged to a room once occupied by Polish writer Stefan Żeromski. The Castle used to close off the Castle Square on the river side and was first bombed and partially burned in German air raids on Warsaw in September 1939. At that time, thanks to the efforts of many citizens of Warsaw, most of the treasures (paintings, sculptures, furniture) were evacuated and hidden from the incoming German troops. The curator of the Castle and director of the National Museum at the time, Stanisław Lorenc was instrumental in that effort. In 1944, after the collapse of Warsaw Uprising, Germans blew up what was left of the Castle. The ruins were cleaned up after the war ended, but despite the successful reconstruction of the Old Town and a decision to reconstruct the Royal Castle made as early as 1949, no attempt was made to rebuild it. Perhaps it would go against the new communist ideology to spend money on the reconstruction of the royal past? Or it was simply much too expensive for a poor country? The idea to suddenly reconstruct the Royal Castle and the subsequent launch of the fundraising campaign were great public relations moves and brought an overwhelming and very-positive response from many Poles both in the country and abroad.

In 1971 or so, when we were sent to help with the clean-up in preparation for the reconstruction of the Castle, the space once occupied by the building was empty. I think we were supposed to dig through the remaining rubble, pick up bricks and put them into piles. Or perhaps we were carrying new bricks to be used to reconstruct the foundations of the castle. I just remember carrying rough brick across the empty space. Nevertheless, this was a relatively meaningful occupation as I could imagine the Royal Castle coming into being at the very same spot where I was then digging in the rubble. The reconstruction, financed from citizens' donations, was completed in the late 1980s. In 1984, just before I left Poland, I was able to glimpse inside the splendid, beautifully restored rooms, thanks to a friend who worked there. Each time I visit Warsaw and see the Castle which by now is a familiar part of the Old Town landscape, I recall that clean-up effort called 'voluntary community service' and I think that the only inappropriate part of that name was the adjective *voluntary*. However, I admit that—given a choice—I would have gladly volunteered to do what I was forced to do.

The second community service I remember well involved a different kind of clean-up. When the new Academy of Medicine campus was being built not far from our high school, we were sent there to help with the cleaning of the rooms before they were given over to future users. My class was working in a suite of rooms to be used as prosectorium and my personal task was to clean terrazzo tables that, as I imagined, were to be used for performing autopsies. These tables were splashed with concrete and paint and I had to scrape the paint and concrete off and then scrub the surface to remove the stains.

There was nothing wrong about this activity and I admit that what we were asked to do was useful. It was, simply, somewhat morbid. One needs to see this activity in the context of a regime where people were still being killed by police and secret service. Only a few years had passed since December 1970 when police killed several protesters in Gdańsk and Gdynia. In Poland at that time, as pretty much throughout the entire post-war history, one would likely be as frightened by seeing police at the door as by a burglar. We were in high school, i.e., old enough to understand the brutality of the authorities. In a popular joke, a Russian is asked about his happiest moment in life and he remembers a night when the KGB, i.e., the secret service, knock on his door. He opens in horror and the officer asks: "Ivan Ivanovich?" With a sigh of relief, the man responds: "No. One floor up."

At that time of my life, in the early 1970s, the relatively pro-Western era of Edward Gierek and foreign credits pouring into Poland because of the apparent political thaw, I was actually contemplating a career in medicine, something that made my mother very happy. She kept repeating that my father always wished that at least one of his three children would follow in his footsteps (my half-brothers would have been following the career path of both their parents). Actually, both my half-brothers wanted to study medicine but were told not to even try to apply for admission to the Academy of Medicine because the communist system discouraged creating family professional traditions or 'clans'. When I told my mother that I was contemplating medicine, I did not tell her that I wanted to specialize in forensic medicine. My father, who passed away in 1969, left a large medical library. After his passing, most of his books were stored in different closets in the apartment, but some I kept and read. My favourite one was a comprehensive and very beautifully edited old German book of general medical knowledge for women, bound in red leather. It was written by Dr. Anna Fischer-Dueckelmann, published in 1911 in Stuttgart, printed in Gothic font and lavishly illustrated. This book introduced me not only to the field of human sexuality but also to the German language. I had no idea at that time that this would become part of my professional career. I checked in an old German-Polish dictionary every word in the chapter on sex, on sexually transmitted diseases, etc. When I told my students in German how I became fluent in reading *Fraktur*, the Gothic script, it gives them a chuckle. A second treasured book was a textbook of forensic medicine by professor Leon Wacholz published by Gebethner and Wolff in 1925. This book was in Polish and I read it from cover to cover. My interest in forensic science was related to my genuine interest in chemistry. My interest in medicine as a possible choice for higher education, on the other hand, was purely pragmatic: at that time, in Grades 7 and 8, both my friend Kasia and I very seriously (for our age) discussed the idea of leaving Poland when we grew up and—in a very unrealistic way—I considered medicine a good career choice, unaware of all the difficulties in obtaining credits for foreign training. Later, in high school, my interests shifted to art and art history but I ended up a student of German and later linguistics and I never regretted those second choices. My only connection to the once-attractive field of forensic medicine is through my work as court interpreter in Ontario where I have had more than one opportunity to be involved in murder trials. I am glad I did not pursue a career in forensic medicine, as I doubt I could actually handle the pathology work associated with that profession.

When I passed the university entrance exams to the Department of German, all prospective students had to go through compulsory *praktyki robotnicze* (manual labour practicum). As far as I can remember, the official purpose of this work practicum was for future intelligentsia to gain respect for the working class. I know and respect many working-class people, but certainly not thanks to that labour practicum.

Along with a group of some 20 other girls, I was sent to a company with a heavy-sounding name ŻELBET, a company that designs concrete reinforced with iron rods. The construction site to which we had been assigned was on the other side of the river in the part of Warsaw called Praga. I had to be there for 6 or 7 am and it took me at least an hour bus trip to get there. It was summer and the weather was hot. I do not recall whether we were allowed to wear our own clothes or whether we were issued work clothes, but I seem to remember wearing blue overalls. I was prepared to do some work, however, what I remember is that there really was no work suitable for us at that construction site. We were given orders that made little sense to us—a group of girls about 18-19 years old, all prospective first-years at Warsaw University. One such order was to carry bricks to the second floor of a building under construction. After running up and down a number of shaky ladders, we came up with a primitive pulley and rope fixture, put the bricks into a bucket and pulled the bucket on a rope to the second floor. It worked just fine until our supervisor discovered our invention and told us that we were not allowed to use it. We went back to running up and down the ladder and lost some of our respect for the working class. Clearly, the purpose of the exercise was not to accomplish anything (i.e., really transport the bricks to the second floor) but to keep us artificially busy. We fully expected that as soon as we completed the task of taking the bricks upstairs, we would likely be told to bring them all back down. On another occasion, some intoxicated construction workers drove heavy machinery all around the construction site chasing some girls. I consider it a miracle that there were no accidents.

After one month of the work practicum no work had been done, nothing had been accomplished and no particular respect was gained. Yet I still could not really complain. At the very least, I was happy that I was going to university and not staying at the construction site for good. Also, I had not acquired any phobias. I know of friends who went to work in factories that produced food or cosmetics and having seen the production process could never use those products again. In a country where shelves were becoming emptier every day, this would have been a serious inconvenience.

Perhaps the most absurd community service I have heard of involved the mother of my best friend Kasia, a well-respected obstetrician. Along with her colleagues, all physicians or nurses, she was sent to paint benches in a city park. Could there be a less meaningful employment for a medical doctor? It is, however, somewhat reminiscent of the Canadian concept of encouraging foreign medical professionals to immigrate to Canada only to have them drive taxis because their education and work experience in their respective countries are not recognized here. At least no one here claims that this is done for the common good.

The very idea of working for the common good, that is the good of one's community, class, country or the international community of workers, has a strong attraction for people, especially those who are—often by choice—suffering from alienation: the intellectuals. Some argue that it was this alienation that made some Western intellectuals believe in communist ideals, in this spirit of a commune life and human solidarity which often seem absent from the capitalist world ruled by competition in a free market. In 1980, it was the same need for doing something for the common good that brought together some ten million Poles to join the new and independent Solidarność (Solidarity) trade union. For those of us for whom it was the very first active engagement in politics, there was a wonderful, almost intoxicating feeling that everything was possible and that we could really change things in Poland. We had no fear and plenty of hope. This feeling of people's power started, in my view, with the visit of the Polish pope, John Paul II, to Poland in 1979. It was the first time in my life that I saw so many people gathered willingly and peacefully for an event that had no communist content. Police were everywhere, but they kept their distance and often visibly enjoyed being there for the same reason the crowds did. Even policemen were usually Catholic in Poland. The Solidarity movement that came into being a year later capitalized on this feeling of togetherness that ran across all social and many political divisions. Incidentally, 1980-81 was the only time when I would not have left Poland even if an opportunity had arisen for me to do so because I too was captivated by this chance to do something for the common good. This atmosphere of social solidarity was infectious. In the summer of 1981, at a linguistic conference near Poznań, I met Axel Grunwald, a German linguist living in Paris. He was interested in the developments in Poland and wanted to know more about it. We became friends, exchanged many letters until the martial law imposed in December of the same year cut off correspondence and pretty much any contact with the West. Axel felt devastated by the events in Poland and wanted to show his personal solidarity with the crushed Solidarność by doing something meaningful to help. He singlehandedly collected medical supplies, flew them to Poland and donated them to university policlinics in Warsaw and in Kraków. He made several trips to Poland, with boxes of supplies and usually also with some books cleverly stashed at the bottom of the big boxes. At one time, he was the only person left dealing with customs officers and my husband and I were the only people in the waiting area. We knew that Axel was bringing "illegal" literature, illegal because it was printed outside Poland or by authors whose books were banned in the country. We saw him talking to the officer checking his boxes and finally the officer waved him through. We later asked Axel what he told the officer. Apparently, he suggested that the officer, who said he had some medical problem, could come to Warsaw University polyclinic and see a doctor there.

That was a stressful day for all three of us. Earlier that afternoon, we went to the American Embassy in Warsaw to watch a movie — *Coal Miner's Daughter*, about Loretta Lynn, in its original English version. We were going to the Embassy's library to prepare for TOEFL, GRE and GMAT tests that we had to take to apply for graduate studies abroad. When we were leaving the Embassy building, through the side door on Piękna Street, a police (called in Poland *milicja obywatelska* or 'citizen police') van was waiting and all people coming out were invited into a larger, open-ended police truck, commonly called *buda* (meaning something like a 'shack' or 'shanty. My husband grabbed my hand and we started running across the street. Nobody followed us and we easily got away. We don't know what happened to the others. Most likely they were taken to a police station, IDed, and possibly warned not to go to the Embassy. The main reason we ran was that we were supposed to pick-up Axel from the airport later that evening and if we were not there, he would have no way to contact us—there were no cell phones in the 1980s and we did not have a land line in our apartment in Ursynów.

I suspect another reason Axel got involved in organizing medical supplies was because some of the ideals that were being threatened by the Polish communist junta were too dear to him to idly watch them being destroyed. On one occasion, I took Axel with me to the monthly mass for the Fatherland with Father Popiełuszko. After the mass ended, people quietly went home. It was a warm spring evening. At the nearby Wilson Square (then called Square of the Paris Commune), police water cannons were waiting. Suddenly, they started spouting water at the peaceful crowd of church goers who immediately dispersed. Axel was shocked. He just stood there looking at the scene in disbelief and kept asking: *Aber warum? Why?* He felt part of the crowd. He felt that he belonged to that community.

Axel has been and still is a wonderful friend. During the martial law, he and his wife Noriko travelled to the US where they met our distant cousins and dear friends Kelly and Cheryl Warczyglowa. Warczygłowa was my mother's maiden name. Kelly, born and raised in Pennsylvania, thought the name must have been distorted as he never met anyone else called Warczyglowa. He had a routine of checking telephone directories in every city he visited and he finally found the name in the Warsaw telephone directory in 1976. It was my mother's number—apparently my dad insisted that she kept her unusual maiden name. It means something like 'growling head' and, the family legend says, was a nickname of some great-great-grandfather during the uprising in 1863. Kelly made a phone call, we met and we became really very close friends—all Polish Warczygłowas and all Pennsylvania Warczyglowas. When Kelly and Cheryl and Kelly's parents were in Poland in 1980, after the August strikes, during the short-lived time of Solidarity, we made a pact: if things were to get very bad in Poland, we would write to them and say that we were divorcing. Having received such a signal, they too would divorce and would come to Warsaw, marry us and get us out of Poland. The second code word was 'Kleenex'. We were to use it if we desperately needed money.

When Axel and Noriko visited our cousins, they talked about what they could do and, at some point, Kelly mentioned that we may need some Kleenex. Soon after, we received a lovely care package from Paris with all kinds of nice things and a lot (I mean A LOT) of Kleenex: boxes of tissues, individual pocket packages of tissues, etc. It was a while later, when we all met again, that the story of Kleenex found its explanation…

Just as many people in the West felt solidarity with the Solidarność, many must have felt a similar kind of affinity with the communist movement which offered them a chance to be involved in making history. One could argue that the love affair of intellectual elites with communism bears certain similarity to the modern trend among some Westerners to convert to Islam in search of something to fill the spiritual emptiness of life in the West (as commented by Andrew Hamilton in the January-February 2005 issue of the on-line journal *Eureka Street*). The need to belong, the need to be an active part of a community is a strong motivation for joining movements that label themselves as progressive, working for the general good of the common people, etc.

In his book *The Joke*, originally published in 1967, Czech émigré writer Milan Kundera captures this feeling of attraction in his description of a young communist student talking to his friends:

> We listened to Ludvik with a mixture of admiration and revulsion. We were irritated by his certainty. He had the look all Communists had at the time. As if he'd made a secret pact with the future and had thereby acquired the right to act in its name. Another reason we found him so offensive was that all of a sudden he was completely different from the Ludvik we had known. With us he'd always been one of the boys, full of mockery. Now he was talking pompously, shamelessly using the most grandiose words. And of course, we were also annoyed at the free and easy way he associated the fate of our [folk music—MS] band with the fate of the Communist Party even though not one of us was a Communist.

> Yet his words did have a kind of attraction for us. His ideas corresponded to our innermost dreams. They elevated us to a heroic greatness. (Kundera 1967, 139)

The same phenomenon has been described by Czesław Miłosz in *The Captive Mind*. The book dissects precisely the topic of how communism fogs the mind of intellectuals. It is a question that keeps coming back to me all the time: what defence mechanism could be employed to protect one's own inner freedom? How can you stay free from the fatal attraction of power in a totalitarian system? Is it certain values and beliefs? Is it courage? Is it faith? Is it knowledge? Or is it "the power of taste", as Zbigniew Herbert put it?

I have read books by people who admit that they have felt attracted to the communist idea of human improvement, the paradise on Earth or the utopian community and general will, or who simply think of the past with some soft nostalgia. I cannot say that I feel the same way. I am sorry that my childhood and my youth are long gone though I never feel in any way sorry that the political system that overshadowed them is over. Even my admiration for "Timur" is just like my sentiment for "Lady and the Tramp": I would like my children to help others not because it is what the Soviet pioneers were supposed to be doing but because it is what my parents have taught me to do: help if you can. They called it *Kinderstube*, proper manners acquired in childhood. Those things that we learn to do and learn to like as children usually stay with us for a lifetime. They may even influence our choice of pets: When we were deciding what kind of a dog we wanted, for me, it had to be a schnauzer, one looking just like the Tramp from Disney's movie. One could argue that I liked Tramp, "a mutt of uncertain origin" (as he is described on some websites dedicated to the movie), better than I liked Lady because of my leftist way of thinking. However, I do not think that my preference for schnauzers or schnauzer-like mutts has had anything to do with politics.

Yet, there is no doubt that, deep down, I do believe in the common good, in solidarity among people, in co-operation rather than competition among friends. I am not sure whether my communist upbringing is the cause or whether it goes back to what I was taught, indirectly and directly, at home. I learned to respect others and help if I could. It was to do for others what I would like them to do for me instead of refraining from actions that I would not appreciate others doing to me. I see this as my father's legacy, a legacy of a medical doctor serving everyone in need. I cannot claim that I have learned a lot from my father. He hardly ever talked to me because he seemed to constantly be working. However, I did watch him and witnessed the enormous respect he received from his patients, friends, and even acquaintances. His waiting room (which was the entrance hall in our apartment) was full of patients until late at night, every evening of the week. Some arrived very late with an emergency even though the sign on the apartment door said that Dr. Eugeniusz Piotrowski saw patients between 3 and 5 pm. There were often people sitting there when I had to go to the washroom in the middle of the night. A particular Romani family always came at night, usually with a medical emergency involving a baby. The following day, at dinner, my father would describe the baby's illness, most often caused by inappropriate food, like sausage with mustard. I admit that, when I was little, it scared me a bit when such patients arrived late at night and crowded the small entrance hall. However, they were all truly concerned about the baby and in no way really threatening. All those who knew my father remembered him getting up at night and taking care of emergencies at home or walking to a patient's home, either with his 'domestic help' or later with my mother (this is for instance how Teodor Parnicki, his patient and an accomplished writer, remembers him in his memoirs—Parnicki 2008).

I know few people today who would sacrifice their sleep or their free time (family time) in order to help others. One such special person is Irene, my neighbour in Woodstock, Ontario. Before her retirement, she was a social worker at a hospital, dealing with individuals in crisis. She hardly ever came home before 7 pm and would never leave work if she felt that there was someone who needed her attention. When she returned home, she began an evening of volunteering, coaching this or that team. After the Russian invasion of Ukraine, Irene, herself of Ukrainian background, organized the assistance for Ukrainian refugees in our county, spending many hours organizing the donations, distributing them to those in need, helping families to register children in school, find family doctors, get necessary Canadian documents, or look for a job. Such people are rare. I know that Irene has learned this caring attitude at home, from her parents. This simple legacy of human brotherhood that people are exposed to at home is a much stronger influence than the communist legacy of 'the great fathers of the mankind' that we were taught at school.

Having been brought up and educated in a system that taught us to be socially responsible and to care for the common good, one would think that my generation would freely engage in charitable activities. I see more of such behavior among my friends in the West than in Poland. I am not making accusations. People in Poland often have to work several jobs, struggle to make ends meet, and have very little time to spare. To be perfectly honest, the same is usually true of people in the West. David, a colleague of my husband, a university professor and father of three, spent many years volunteering at a soup kitchen. A school secretary works as a volunteer for The Humane Society, a retired male friend spends half of every day working as the lollipop man helping young children cross the streets to and from school. Surely, they could spend their time doing something for themselves or making more money. Charity (meaning 'love') has to come from the heart. Those who were taught to love, or perhaps rather those who were given the opportunity to learn to love, are more likely to grow up being charitable. Those who were told that they were charitable because they grew up in 'the most advanced political system and in the best country' will have little to no inner desire to show charity. Why would they? Charity was never a genuine feeling they needed to show, so it remains misunderstood.

One notable exception has been the so-called Great Orchestra of Christmas Charity, a non-profit organization established by Jurek Owsiak in 1993. The Orchestra collects money for children's hospitals in Poland, buying medical equipment supplies that the government could not provide. While very many Poles, both in Poland and abroad enthusiastically support the Orchestra, donate money or run local collections, the PiS government cannot find in themselves enough charity to show some gratitude. The equipment bought by the Orchestra and marked with a red heart logo saves lives but the indefatigable Mr. Owsiak has been a target of hate and smear campaigns. Those who read PiS-controlled press and follow government-sponsored television perpetuate the slanders, accusing Owsiak of benefiting financially from his charity work. The good thing is that, every year, the Christmas Charity (the campaign ends shortly after Christmas, thus the name) collects more money, breaking previous year's record. But the hate works. On January 13, 2019, during the final event of the 27th edition of the Great Orchestra, the mayor of the city of Gdańsk was assassinated on stage by a young man claiming to have been persecuted by the liberal government that ruled before the 2015 PiS takeover. Hate brings out the worst in people.

And yet, maybe I was wrong about Polish lack of charitable feelings. The war in Ukraine woke up something in Poles—something I have not seen for a long time. People opened their homes and their hearts to the thousands, and then hundreds of thousands of Ukrainians fleeing the war, mostly women and children, and the elderly. Even without any significant help from the government, or maybe because the government did not meddle with the help effort, people organized places to stay, food, assistance, first with basic needs, then with getting papers needed to register for medical care, schools for children and work permits for adults. It was truly heart-warming, especially since there have been those using not always good experiences from the past history of our two nations, to question the moral imperative to help those who needed help. Let's hope that this lesson in solidarity with Ukraine will help both nations to heal old wounds.

But, maybe, we should not overemphasize the emotional aspect of charity. To work for the common good is not the same as charity. One can work for the common good through creating market mechanisms that encourage people to invest in companies that benefit the community. Services that cater to the common good do not have to be free of charge, but merely affordable for the population. Free health care sounds advantageous but can we expect doctors and nurses to work for free too? I love teaching but I also like to have a salary so I cannot expect any other profession to accept working for charity either. Nothing is really free, but some people think that way or are encouraged to think that way by populist politicians and demagogues. H.L. Mencken defined a demagogue as “one who preaches doctrines he knows to be untrue to men he knows to be idiots.” In terms of the market mechanisms and principles of economy, people who grew up in communism have very little understanding of how these things work and can be easily persuaded. The easiest principle to follow is to remember that the bigger the promise of the common good, the less likely it is to ever become a reality.

CHAPTER 5

The Façade of Newspeak

Officially, contradictions do not exist in the minds of the citizens in the people's democracies. Nobody dares to reveal them publicly. And yet the question of how to deal with them is posed in real life. More than others, the members of the intellectual elite are aware of this problem. They solve it by becoming actors.

—Czesław Miłosz. The Captive Mind, 54

I WAS LUCKY to be born after Stalin's death, when the political system in my native country was but a shadow of what it was immediately after World War II. I was lucky to be born in Poland and not in any other of the countries of the Soviet Bloc because the system in Poland during my childhood was milder than elsewhere. Finally, I was lucky to be born into my particular family, where we were not in open and active opposition to the system but, at least at home, never pretended to support it.

Theories of first-language acquisition, corroborated by evidence, tell us that most children will effortlessly learn the language or languages to which they are exposed. The child constructs the grammar of the language based on the linguistic input he or she receives and not simply by imitating linguistic behaviours of those around. Error analysis provides support for this thesis as children utter sentences they have never heard and create erroneous morphological forms, usually based on the principle of analogy, extending rules they have constructed to forms that adults know are irregular. Thus, forms such as mouses" instead of "mice" and "I go-ed" instead of "I went" are common among children mastering English as their native language. This developmental behaviour is universal and happens to children acquiring various languages. My children used the wrong but morphologically regular Genitive forms like *piesa* or *lewa* instead of the irregular *psa* (dog's) or *lwa* (lion's) in Polish, just like most Polish children do when they are learning the case system, even though they grew up away from Poland and had never heard these erroneous forms used in our family.

The word "Newspeak" was introduced into the general usage by George Orwell in his political dystopia novel *1984*. Newspeak was designed to replace the ordinary language, Oldspeak, in order to prevent people from thinking thoughts the ruling party considered undesirable. As the Party line and the principles of Ingsoc were very narrowly defined, developing Newspeak was really equivalent to removing unnecessary words and making sure that the words in the Newspeak dictionary had only one meaning. There was no scope for the frivolous luxury of synonyms or for any blurring of definitions.

It was intended that when Newspeak had been adopted once and for all and Oldspeak forgotten, an heretical thought—that is, a thought diverging from the principles of Ingsoc—should be literally unthinkable, at least so far as thought is dependent on words. Its vocabulary was constructed to give exact and often subtle expression to every meaning that a Party member could properly wish to express, while excluding all other meanings and also the possibility of arriving at them by indirect methods (Orwell 1949/1990, 312-13).

Unlike any natural language where new words are constantly coined and where meanings change, Newspeak was actually shrinking, with more and more words banned or replaced by simpler morphological forms.

Quite apart from the suppression of definitely heretical words, reduction of vocabulary was regarded as an end in itself, and no word that could be dispensed with was allowed to survive. Newspeak was designed not to extend but to diminish the range of thought, and this purpose was indirectly assisted by cutting the choice of words down to a minimum (313).

The idea that authorities may want to eliminate concepts by removing words from usage is not a literary fantasy. An example of this was that people or historical facts virtually ceased to exist because any mention of them was banned from public discourse. In Poland, one such historical event was the mass killing of over twenty thousand Polish officers and prisoners of war ordered by the Soviet authorities in 1940. The mass graves in Katyń were discovered by the Germans in 1943, but it was clear that the officers were killed in 1940 when those territories were still in Soviet hands. Katyń was a name that was not supposed to be mentioned, not even in the twisted, official version. However, the authorities occasionally mentioned the "Khatyn" massacre and referred to the "Khatyn" memorial, even though any attempt to erect a memorial to Katyń victims was immediately met with resistance by the communist authorities. This was very confusing and made some people believe that Katyń and Khatyn were the same place. But Khatyn was a village in Belarus destroyed by German troops in 1943, another war crime but a different one.

There are many other examples of removing concepts from public discourse or restricting their usage to situations where the concept would apply only to Western countries or to past times. Thus, it seemed that—at least based on official media reports—social problems such as prostitution only occurred in capitalist countries. There, it could have been viewed with empathy. Women were forced into prostitution by poverty and lack of other employment prospects. As poverty and unemployment did not exist in communist countries, according to the government, women had no reason to succumb to that level of destitution. I do not recall any mention of the moral aspect of prostitution but morality, in communist Poland, was replaced by the 'socialist morality', with the adjective 'socialist' emptying the noun of its standard meaning. Thus, that aspect of the problem became irrelevant. And since the problem did not exist in the first place, there was no need to either legalize prostitution or punish it. And yet, in popular opinion, prostitutes were often judged in moral terms; they were considered to be doing their job because they were deeply demoralized and so financial gratification was seen as secondary. This may explain why the vulgar term denoting 'prostitute' was and still is probably the strongest swearword in Polish.

The end of communism brought prostitution to the surface, renaming the upscale version of the activity and changing it into something more acceptable. Advertisements for *agencje towarzyskie* (social agencies) and sexual services can be found in daily newspapers. Poland became a new destination for human trafficking for sexual exploitation purposes. There seemed to be a relatively high level of tolerance for prostitution and many other forms of shady business practices that cross the line of what is legal, making 'honesty' another rather flexible notion. How can this flexible attitude to honesty and morality be compatible with the teachings of the church in this predominantly Catholic country is somewhat puzzling. The long tradition of abuse of both people and words may be a possible explanation.

Unemployment did not exist in communist countries, but this did not mean everyone was really working. Was it truly work when a sales lady spent eight hours in a store that had nothing (sometimes virtually not a thing) for sale? She could have used her time to clean the store, but that was the job of the cleaning staff. Sometimes the sales personnel were present and the store was not empty, but still did not serve customers. A sign with the word REMANENT explained everything. The Polish usage had nothing to do with physics (where it is defined, according to the Oxford Dictionary as "remaining; residua"; used with reference to magnetism to designate what is "remaining after a magnetizing field has been removed"). Polish *remanent* was some kind of inventory check-up (maybe listing what was left?), always done during opening hours and usually taking the whole day. I have never seen stores closed for a 'remanent' in the West but in Poland it was a sacred ceremony that required no justification. I remember several occasions when I would try to open the door to a store only to be shouted at: "Can't you read? It is *remanent*!"

Another special occupation in communist countries was that of the so called *babcie klozetowe*, literally 'toilet grannies', whose role was mostly to collect fees from customers who used the public toilets in cinemas, restaurants, railway stations, etc. As toilet paper was scarce (for no apparent reason), a piece of paper was also distributed to the clients. *Babcie klozetowe* were also responsible for keeping the toilet reasonably clean, but that was another story. The most surreal public toilet I visited in the late 1970s, on the way back from a skiing trip to Szczyrk, was located at the 19th century railway station in Bielsko-Biała. I have heard that the renovated building of that station is now one of the most beautiful ones in Poland. Then, the toilet was as shabby as any public toilet in Poland, but it boasted an oversized board with a price list for the use of the facilities, washing hands (with and without soap and towel), shower, etc. Perhaps there would be nothing special about the board except the toilet did not even have running water at the time, not to mention showers. It was actually so bad that it did not even have a toilet granny to collect a fee.

One of the best (also in terms of artistic talent) depictions of the toilet grannies can be found in the 1981 satirical movie *Miś*, meaning 'Teddy Bear' in English, where they function as a kind of choir in Greek tragedies, providing commentary about the events. Even though there are toilet fee collectors in other countries, Polish toilet grannies were an important part of the communist landscape. Roman Polański's 1959 film *Gdy spadają anioły* (*When Angels Fall*) is about a toilet granny.

Apart from very low-paying jobs that simply kept people employed, unemployment was also offset by a myriad of jobs in the security apparatus: surveillance, censorship, personal information reporting, etc. To keep the appearance that mail was inspected or telephone conversations were controlled, especially after the imposition of martial law, there must have been Poles doing those jobs. After I graduated from Warsaw University, I needed to leave a written guarantee that someone would pay back the cost of my education, should I have decided not to return to Poland after a trip abroad. In some connection to this process of signing the guarantee (the details of which I no longer remember), I had been invited to meet with someone about my job prospects. The meeting took place not far from the university campus. All I remember is a big desk and a relatively young man in a grey suit against a big window frame. He expressed an interest in my knowledge of languages and suggested that I could use it well working for the Office of the Control of Publications, i.e., the censorship office. If I liked to read, he said, this would give me access to a wide range of interesting literature. In retrospect, I must admit that this was, in theory, an interesting employment suggestion. I was, however, not interested and he did not insist.

Having graduated in 1979 and having been offered my first academic position in my home Institute of Applied Linguistics, I was probably in the last class that went through the *kształcenie światopoglądowe* (worldview training) for future academic teachers at Warsaw University. For several weeks, a group of new assistant lecturers and PhD students met weekly in the University's Kazimierzowski Palace with lecturers who were talking to us about all kinds of ideological issues. I did not pay much attention to what was being said. I had several friends in that group and we spent most of the time exchanging messages on pieces of paper or reading books. The only lecture I remember was about using popular figures from Polish history to give legitimacy to the communist regime and to increase its popularity. As an example, the speaker mentioned the fact that Polish banknotes at the time used pictures of Polish kings or famous artists rather than communist activists, as had been the case previously. Indeed, at that time, only the 50 złoty note had the head of Karol Świerczewski, a communist general from World War II. Other notes displayed famous historical figures: Tadeusz Kościuszko (500 złotys), Mikołaj Kopernik (1000 złotys), Mieszko I, Polish prince and the first ruler of Poland (2000 złotys) and Fryderyk Chopin (5000 złotys). Before those new notes were introduced into circulation in the 1970s, the old notes had generic representations of workers and peasants that looked just like the socialist realist monumental sculptures adorning the Palace of Culture (Stalin's gift to Warsaw) or the façades of buildings surrounding the Constitution Square in what was popularly known as MDM in Warsaw.

My first university salary in 1979 was around 1500 złotys. Five year later, in 1984, my final salary before I left was 10,000. This was the amount I was paid a month, in cash, after deductions. At that time, it did not occur to me that I must have been paying taxes and pension premiums. There was no information about any deductions and, of course, no mention about their nature. The six-fold increase in my salary was due mostly to inflation which, e.g. in 1982, was about 100 percent from 1981–1982. This, at the time, was a peak and was likely linked to the martial law of 1981. After I left Poland in 1984, inflation started to steadily climb up, reaching 250 percent in 1989 and the record 585 percent in 1990. Skyrocketing inflation made it necessary to issue banknotes with even larger denominations: in 1987 a 10,000 note with the art nouveau painter and dramatist Stanisław Wyspiański, in 1989 20,000 with Maria Curie-Skłodowska, 50,000 with Stanisław Staszic, one of the leading figures of Polish Enlightenment, and finally 200,000 with the national emblem of the Polish People's Republic.

In 1990, after the official end of the communist system in Poland, the 100,000 złoty note was issued featuring Stanisław Moniuszko, a composer and founder of Polish opera. However, it still had the words Polish People's Republic on it even though the country's name has been officially changed back to Republic of Poland. 500,000 (with Henryk Sienkiewicz, Nobel Prize winning author), 1,000,000 (with Władysław Reymont, a novelist and also Nobel prize laureate) and 2,000,000 (with Ignacy Jan Paderewski, great pianist and Prime Minister of the Republic of Poland in 1919), followed. A 5,000,000 złotys note with Marshall Piłsudski was to be issued but the denomination of Polish currency in 1995 (at the 10,000 to 1 ratio) cancelled that plan.

When the lecturer in our 'worldview training' mentioned the use of historical figures for the legitimization of communist rule, I am sure he thought he was speaking to young communists. I doubt he thought we were true believers. He probably assumed we were as opportunistic as everyone else. I remember raising my hand and asking whether he thought it was morally appropriate to manipulate people that way. I do not recall his answer. It must have been given in Newspeak, which meant that it likely had no content.

The question of money in communism has always been an interesting one. I used to collect stamps as a child and had a few German *Briefmarken* from the period of the great depression and inflation after World War I. Some had the original denomination as part of their design and then the new price stamped on top of it, going from four thousand to ten million German marks. Later, the denomination was only stamped on top of the colourful rectangle when it was ready for sale. It seemed strange and scary to imagine money losing its value. I remember stories about Germans burning banknotes in their ovens because it was cheaper to burn money than to use it to buy firewood. When Canadian and American media reported automobile companies burning billions of dollars per quarter in the more recent global financial crisis of 2008, I pictured in my mind German women throwing banknotes into fire. For me, 'burning money' is still a very productive metaphor. This is what linguists call metaphors that have not lost their ability to produce vivid images in the minds of listeners.

When I was in my twenties, a similar situation was happening in Poland. Tickets for city buses and street cars, cinema or theatre tickets, labels on groceries, etc. had new prices stamped on top of the old ones. I missed the worst of it as I left in 1984 and did not return to Poland until 1991. The strict, unpopular, but thoughtful financial reform (often referred to as 'shock therapy') was led by the first post-communist Minister of Finance, Leszek Balcerowicz and prevented Poland from an economic disaster. As prices went up, most people suffered losses in their income or faced unemployment for the first time in their lives. This made Balcerowicz a target of popular dissatisfaction and of political attacks from populist opposition. He is probably better recognized for his achievements in the West than he was in Poland. The 2005-2007 Kaczyński-led ruling coalition contributed to this unfair perception of the chief mastermind behind Polish economic recovery.

Full employment, lack of obvious poverty, and apparent absence of social problems such as prostitution, drug abuse, domestic violence, AIDS, etc., was intended to produce complete satisfaction of the working class. Communism, after all, is the system where the workers constitute the ruling class and this naturally eliminates conditions that could possibly cause their exploitation, characteristic of the capitalist society. In the capitalist West, we were taught in school, the ruling class represents the interests of the owners of the means of production. Workers are indispensable for the actual production of goods, but they are constantly being exploited by capitalists. However, the fear of unemployment prohibits them from protesting against the harsh working conditions and unfair wages. When the situation becomes unbearable, workers may go on strike. 'Strike' was one of those words that could not possibly refer to anything happening in a communist country. Workers in communist countries could not possibly go on strike. If they did, or actually *when* they did, official propaganda had two ways of dealing with the situation. Either it was not a 'strike' but only a temporary *przerwa w pracy* (work stoppage) or it was not 'workers' who were involved but some 'hooligans', 'brawlers', 'uncertain (or in fact 'certain') elements', etc. In August 1980, propaganda used expressions such as 'street brawls' (*burdy uliczne*) and suggested that the participants were either recruited from 'the margin of society' (the expression *margines społeczny* suggests that even if social pathologies exist, they are a negligible margin in an otherwise healthy society) or were 'irresponsible young people blinded by the enemy' (Głowiński 1996, 83). Workers' protests were usually referred to as non-descript 'events', as e.g., in March 1968 (*wydarzenia marcowe*, 'March events') and were later referred to by time descriptions (October, March, December, June, August—in the chronological order of Polish political unrests). Each wave of 'events' resulted in a following wave of emigration. My wave of emigration is usually referred to as 'post-Solidarity' emigration because the martial law of 1981 was introduced in December and the term December had already been taken by the events of December 1970 in Gdańsk and Gdynia.

Some words disappeared in post-war Poland because they no longer had anything to refer to. One such word in Polish, close to my heart for family reasons, was *aktuariusz*, i.e., 'actuary,' a person using their expertise in mathematics or statistics for the purpose of doing calculations for insurance operations. Poland had an active actuarial association prior to World War II, published an actuarial journal and participated in international actuarial congresses. After the war, the state monopoly in insurance eliminated the need for rigid calculation of premiums or reserves. If the sole state-owned company needed money, the required amount could be taken from 'another pocket', or simply printed. I may be exaggerating here, but not by much. The ideas of profit and corporate capital, along with the profession of an actuary whose job was in the communist interpretation reduced to looking after those profits, were things of the capitalist past. Actuaries were eliminated from the economy and the word *aktuariusz* was eliminated from the encyclopaedia. It stayed in English-Polish dictionaries (translated as *znawca ubezpieczeniowy*, 'insurance expert' in the 1997 edition of the Stanisławski's dictionary) but not in Polish-English ones. The idea that the elimination of the word will make the concept disappear had worked really well and by the end of the 1970s most people in Poland had no understanding that running an insurance company involved complex calculations. After 1989, the profession, all of a sudden required by the insurance reform, had to be recreated from scratch.

Another peculiar lexical phenomenon involved the name of the country that had played an important role in Polish history. After 1922, Russia became the biggest of the republics within the newly established Union of the Socialist Soviet Republics. Many languages—including English, German, French and Polish, adopted the Russian word *soviet* (meaning 'council') as part of the name of the new state. Soviet Union was thus called in Polish *Związek Sowiecki*, a direct equivalent of the English term. The relations between the newly independent Poland and the post-revolutionary Russian state in the East had not been very amicable and the animosities led to an open war that started in 1919 and ended with a truly miraculous Polish victory in the Battle of Warsaw in August 1920. Because the term *Związek Sowiecki*, in particular the adjective in it, acquired definitely negative connotations, the pro-Soviet (or Soviet imposed) government in Poland after World War II coined a new name for the Eastern neighbour. A calc translation (i.e., a translation that copies the structure of the original word) was introduced: *Związek Radziecki*, where the word *rada* is a Polish translation of the Russian word *soviet*. The use of the adjective *sowiecki* in the post-war Poland was considered an expression of a hostile attitude to our 'brother' and was thus banned. The word continued to be used by exile publishers and by the foreign radio stations broadcasting in Polish but was replaced by the Polonized version (*radziecki*) in all official public discourse. The word *sowiecki* was also used by opposition sources in reference to the War of 1920 but that was in fact an erroneous use of the word as Soviet Union really came into being in 1922. Another term in circulation was the "Polish-Bolshevik war" or simply the War of 1920. This was the officially tolerated expression that I remember from my father's obituary in 1969 which described him as a: "soldier in the War of 1920." The official propaganda did not have any problems with how to name that historical fact. It simply eliminated it from history. My father had a life-long problem with the Soviet Union: He was born in Czortków, east of Lwów, in 1900. At that time, those towns were part of the Austrian Empire but his family was Polish, with some Ukrainian connections via marriage. After WWI, Lwów and Czortków became part of Poland but were then taken over by the Soviet Union. In post-war Poland, his personal identification document stated that he was born in 1900 in the Soviet Union. The Soviet Union did not exist in 1900, but this argument was ignored by the government.

Another linguistic phenomenon typical for totalitarian propaganda was the redefining the meaning of words. Victor Klemperer brings many examples for this in *LTI*. If used often enough, new meanings spread like wildfire and take hold of the speakers. One of the examples Klemperer quotes is the noun *fanatic* transformed into a positive description and used by the Nazis to refer to ardent supporters of their ideology. The word, in its adjectival form (fanatical) was often juxtaposed with words such as 'hero' or 'National Socialist' and, as Klemperer argues, quickly became associated with positive personal characteristics to the point that heroism was unthinkable without fanaticism. Today we think that the adjective 'fanatical' returned to its negative meaning (overzealous or obsessed).

Among the words that changed meanings in communist Poland was 'patriotism'. As a result of the partitions of Poland and more than a hundred years of struggle for national independence, patriotism was deeply ingrained into the very way of thinking for several generations of Poles. Except for a short period of time between the two world wars when Poland was independent, there was also an interesting distinction between the nation and the state. The state was usually identified with the occupying power. The twenty years of independence (1918-1939) were followed by the Nazi occupation and then by the Soviet control of Poland. Consequently, for many generations of Poles, patriotism meant fighting for the national independence against the occupant which often was synonymous with the state, government, officials of any rank, etc. This definition of patriotism did not sit well with communist authorities. They were easily identifiable with the Soviet Union, which, in turn, was for many people just another name for Russia, one of the three powers that took part in the partitions of Poland. Thus, 'patriotism' had to be redefined. In his 1996 book *Mowa w stanie oblężenia: 1982-1985* ('Language Under Siege: 1982-1985), Michal Głowiński offers a brief history of this term in communist Poland. He writes that in Stalin's times, the term 'patriotism' was 'a Siamese twin' of another popular propaganda term 'internationalism,' as in, "The love of one's own country had to go hand in hand with the admiration for the first workers' and peasants' state" (Głowiński 1996, 126—my translation). In the following years, the only thing that changed was the slight decrease in the overbearing nature of the propaganda use of this term. Patriotism came to mean as much as being in agreement with the Party. You were either 'with us', the Party or 'against us': thus, patriotism was no longer associated with the love of one's country, *patria* (the fatherland), but rather with the active support for the *partia* (ruling party). I am not sure whether the similarity between these two words was ever part of the process of the semantic shift, but—with time—it could have become an example of the folk etymology. The word 'patriot' became a way of signaling allegiance with the party line, as was the case with the already mentioned *księża patrioci* (patriot priests), i.e. those among the Catholic clergy who, mostly in Stalin's period, collaborated (or were forced into collaboration) with the communist authorities.

In 1982, after the imposition of martial law, a new pro-communist organization was created and given a name that included the by-then empty adjective 'patriotic'. It was Patriotic Movement for National Rebirth (called PRON). It united many pro-government organizations in an attempt to show that the 'entire society' was in support of the government policy against the delegalized Solidarity trade union. As Solidarity had 10 million members, it was difficult to show that the entire nation of 35 million opposed it, but nothing was impossible in communism. As membership in the Movement was organizational and not individual, it was relatively easy to order all official organizations to join it. Głowiński quotes the newspaper headline: "The Movement of All Patriots" (Głowiński 1996, 127) which suggested that all patriots supported PRON, i.e., you could not be a patriot if you did not support PRON. He adds, however, that this title also indicated PRON's possible openness to all those with 'good will'. Here, again, 'good' means what is good for the government, not for the people.

Those people whose patriotism was not based on the support of the Communist Party could not be called patriots. If they were referred to that way, it was usually with the use of the ironic quotation marks, typical for most types of propaganda and very well described by Klemperer (2000 72-73). Thus, the members of KOR, (the Workers' Defence Committee), a civil society group created by intellectuals to help the workers persecuted after the June 1976 workers' strikes in Radom, were referred to as "patriots" in quotation marks and the inspirational teachings of father Popiełuszko were referred to as "patriotic" sermons. In the mouths of the communist regime, the word 'patriot' became synonymous with 'collaborator' (the Polish equivalent of, *kolaborant*, had its meaning reduced to denoting those who collaborated with the Nazi occupants) but it still retained its meaning for most ordinary people. As such, the word *patriota* in Polish was a great example of a user's defined meaning, i.e., different groups in Poland were using this term with different, often mutually exclusive meanings. In the so called 'Fourth Republic' (*Czwarta Rzeczpospolita*), the new Poland the Kaczyński brothers tried to create when they were both holding the two top positions of power in the country between 2005 and 2007, the use of the term 'patriotism' imitated the "best" (I am using the ironic quotation marks here) communist traditions and significantly contributed to the final popular frustration with that word. The Kaczyński brothers talked about patriotism but their definition of patriotism was based on the opposition to European Union integration and abhorrence towards Western influence in general.

In June 2006, the then Minister of Education, Roman Giertych, leader of the League of Polish Families, an ultranationalist party that was part of the minority government of the Kaczyński brothers, proposed to introduce a new subject in schools: 'Patriotic Education'. Some of his colleagues even talked about starting patriotic education in kindergarten. The overwhelmingly negative reaction to this idea was based on several reservations: many people disputed Giertych's interpretation of the word: a right-wing nationalist party, accused of fascist tendencies (the youth faction of the League, the All-Polish Youth, which exhibited many features of a fascist organization), identified patriotism with nationalism or even chauvinism. Some argued that schools were already teaching in the spirit of patriotism and there was no need to introduce special classes to teach that as a subject. Others, e.g., Professor Andrzej Garlicki, argued that patriotism cannot be taught the way one teaches mathematics or physics. Giertych, asked about his understanding of the term 'patriotism' explained it as "teaching history with the emphasis on those things that can constitute national pride" (*Chodzi o uczenie historii Polski pod kątem tych rzeczy, które mogą stanowić dumę narodową*, as reported by Marcin Graczyk in *Gazeta Wyborcza*, June 6, 2006). A change in government in 2007 spared us from the program being realized. After 2007, Roman Giertych left politics, returned to practicing law, and underwent an interesting transformation. He is now considered an outspoken opponent of the former coalition partner Kaczyński who provides great commentary on current political events.

Communist propaganda transformed 'patriotism', one of the key words of the Polish Romantic tradition, into a nonsense word with no mind of its own. It also made many people mistrustful of its intentions. When the USA PATRIOT Act was signed into law by President George W. Bush on October 26, 2001, less than two months after September 11, most people accepted the need to temporarily compromise civil liberties in the face of terrorist threats. The word 'patriot' helped make people believe that allowing government to have access to private information about every citizen was indeed necessary. Few people know that this agreeable sounding name is an acronym for **U**niting and **S**trengthening **A**merica by **P**roviding **A**ppropriate **T**ools **R**equired to **I**ntercept and **O**bstruct **T**errorism Act of 2001. This name is too convoluted to make anyone think that the acronym is just a coincidence. It cannot be a coincidence: it is a *Meisterstück* of propaganda that Goebbels would have commended. In his essays on metaphor and war, George Lakoff (1991 and 2003) suggested that propaganda tends to frame war using metaphors, e.g., disease, business (balancing costs and benefits), or a fairy tale. In the post 9/11 political context, terrorists, Taliban, Al-Qaida, or Saddam Hussein all fit the role of the villain while the USA could be cast as either the victim or the hero or both. In a fairy tale scenario, the hero attempts to rescue the victim from the hands of the villain. In national and international affairs, patriotism is a natural attribute of the hero figure and so hardly anyone questioned the name of the act, even though many questioned its content and its impact on individual freedoms.

In a somewhat similar way, the word 'realism' also came to signify the point of view that agreed with the Party line. Głowiński (1996,132) comments that in Polish history, a reference to realism indicated either a rational and measured approach to the situation at hand or was a sign of opportunism, possibly even treason. After the martial law of 1981, 'realism' meant as much as agreeing that the authorities had no choice but to call in the army. This was the theory of *mniejsze zło* (lesser evil) advanced by the military government. The 'greater evil' was the allegedly unavoidable 'brotherly help' that would have been offered by the Soviet Union and other countries of the Warsaw Pact, i.e., military intervention. With time, 'realism' developed into an empty phrase, used to justify about anything. This means that, as Głowiński argues, it meant nothing (ibid., 133).

Another expression that was used to signify a person who was in agreement with the party line was *człowiek ideowy* ('a man/person of ideas'). The adjective *ideowy* derives from the noun *idea*. While, in theory, this means as much as the English 'idea' or 'thought', in communist Newspeak the meaning was restricted to 'progressive' ideas, and 'progress' was defined according to communist ideology. In similar fashion, 'scientific world-view' meant the Marxist interpretation of the world. Generally, communist Newspeak operated on dichotomies. Everything was presented as black and white, good (progressive) or evil (reactionary). However, I am not sure what the antonym of the communist 'man of ideas' was supposed to be. It needed to be a pejorative concept but *bezideowy*, meaning 'without ideas,' was not common. One that comes to my mind is 'cosmopolitan'. Of course, it does not make much sense on the surface, but a 'cosmopolitan' was someone with liberal and relativist views which makes that concept close to the opposite of someone with well defined progressive views. Yet, 'cosmopolitan' was also most commonly used as the negative version of 'internationalist.' Głowiński notes in 1969 that labelling an artistic movement as 'cosmopolitan' signalled that the authorities were about to hinder its development (Głowiński 1991: 104). He also points out that such labels had no definitive meanings as, for instance, following the March 1968 'events' in Poland, Jews were accused, in turns, of Zionism (i.e., a form of nationalism) and cosmopolitanism.

The newest Polish Newspeak likes the word 'nihilism' and the phrase 'civilization of death' (possibly because of the question of abortion), both applied to liberal, leftist (*lewacki*, as opposed to the less pejorative *lewicowy*) views. These are the fashionable derogatory terms used as opposites to Polish Christian tradition and traditional values. These too shall pass, I hope.

The most bizarre feature of the political discourse of totalitarianism was, in my opinion, what we may call 'the magical character of language.' I find the creative aspect of Newspeak most interesting as it helps to explain that propaganda discourse was able to virtually create a pseudo-reality. By either promoting or excluding words and concepts, language can give or deny existence to persons, things, historical events or scientific discoveries. By doing this, it can blur the difference between the already given and the desired states of affairs, obscuring or distorting the image of reality in the minds of people who were subjected to the total propaganda machine (Stroińska 1994, 59ff).

Language is usually seen as an instrument of communication within a community of speakers. In this instrumental function, language is quite flexible and adapts to its various functions and to demands of its speakers. In this way, it reflects the group that uses it. Edward Sapir (1949) described language as "a guide to social reality." John Austin (1962) described it as "a vehicle for social action." In a totalitarian state, where all information is controlled by a central power, language not only reflects reality but also becomes an instrument for creating a new social reality, as well as a means of imposing that alternative reality on peoples' perceptions of the real world.

In its ability to reflect reality, language has a lot in common with art. This comparison with art is not accidental. The similarities between the official (propaganda) art of various totalitarian states, e.g., Hitler's Germany and Stalin's Russia, are striking. Igor Golomshtok (1990, XIII-XIV) observed that

> [despite] the diverse historical and cultural traditions of the countries in question, there arises a style that one can justifiably term the international style of totalitarian culture: total realism. For it is only by the imprint of racial, ethnic, geographical or other details that we can determine whether a work of art created under totalitarianism belongs to this or that country or people.

While he calls the style of totalitarian art 'total realism,' it is important to note that the realistic depiction is only a stylistic camouflage for what in fact is 'total creationism.' The relationship between the real world and socialist reality created by the language of propaganda (in the news, in literature, or in art) was for the most part arbitrary and socialist reality had very little in common with the real world. This did not particularly disturb its creators. Communism was a scientific utopia that was to be born out of the old world order. But it never was born. It remained "a ghost in search of a body..." (Besançon 1976, 93).

As the postulated reality of communist propaganda was linguistic in nature (i.e., it was constructed through language), it had a somewhat unusual logic. One example was that statements of propaganda could not be easily contested or denied. From the linguistic point of view, the reasons are obvious: many statements used by propaganda cannot be assigned truth value, i.e. it is impossible to determine whether they are true or false. Some are performative speech acts that do not allow for truth value assignment in principle (e.g., promises). Other statements use metaphors that cannot be interpreted literally, contain presuppositions or simply lack predicates.

Most propaganda discourse can be seen as 'perlocutionary' speech acts in Austin's terminology. This means that words are spoken in order to produce certain beliefs in the audience rather than to describe existing states of affairs. I think it is important to keep the perlocutionary character of propaganda discourse in mind when we read sentences that look like statements and seem as if they were being used to describe reality or to report facts. At this point a comparison with visual arts seems justified again. Neither the Socialist Realism of Soviet and Soviet-style art nor the official style of Nazi Germany portrayed reality. In fact, in both countries Naturalism was considered dangerous and politically incorrect because it was often politically and socially engaged. In both countries the official style, almost identical in form, produced optimistic pictures from the everyday work and life of the new society. Golomshtok explains:

> Rather than being derived from the present, this optimism was injected into totalitarian art from the mythical future. As the present day grew more terrible, as the struggle grew harsher and victory drew nearer, as hunger and terror put an end to more and more millions of lives, so the imaginary heaps of food on kolkhoz tables grew vaster and the smiles on the faces of workers more radiant. (Golomshtok 1990, 191)

In the Soviet Union this style was given the name not of surrealism but of *sotsrealism* (short from Socialist Realism—note how the weasel word *socialist* changes the meaning of the word *realism* here). I believe that here lies the explanation of my childhood's belief that the world in sotsrealist movies was real and the world I saw with my own eyes was an inferior version of reality. I preferred to believe the films (art has always been a form of propaganda in totalitarian systems) than my own eyes. Golomshtok explains that in its portrayal of life, *sotsrealist* art reflected not reality, but

> ideology and myth in the guise of reality. And it reflected this ideology only too faithfully. From a method of perceiving the world—like nineteenth-century realism—it has been transformed into a method of instilling into the world

> a particular kind of perception, and as such it was endowed with a dynamic charge. (ibid.; 98)

Propaganda does not want to describe harsh reality. Instead, it tries to create or postulate a better one. One of the most effective ways of imposing cognitive frameworks through language is the use of metaphors and scenarios. The fairy tale or rescue scenario used by both Bushes in both Gulf Wars was also employed, for instance, in the case of the German aggression against Austria, Czechoslovakia, and Poland (to defend the German minority) or in the case of the Soviet aggression against Poland in 1939 (to free Western Ukraine and Western Byelorussia, now Belarus, from the Polish yoke). The usefulness of metaphors manifests itself in the most obvious way through their ability to present complex concepts in a simple way by comparing them to something familiar. Emotions are relatively complex psychological states that are difficult to describe without reaching for comparisons with other, more familiar phenomena. Thus, we say that we are 'boiling' or that we are about to 'explode' when we are angry. The immediate effect is a better understanding, the long-term effect, however, is an oversimplification. Anger does not result from overheating. It may have complex reasons and angry confrontations will not be resolved by lowering the temperature (at least not in its literal sense).

As metaphors cannot be taken literally, it is impossible to engage in any meaningful discussion when they are used. Orwell's example of an incompatible (and dead) metaphor was, "the Fascist octopus has sung its swan song" (Orwell 1946/1972, 432). The metaphors that have been mixed here are 'dead'. We no longer really think of a swan when we hear the expression: 'swan song'. The meaning of this expression is rather a final gesture or performance, often given shortly before death. For the word 'octopus,' on the other hand, a reference to a powerful organization or institution with far-reaching, especially harmful influences is now part of the dictionary definition. The strategy of using such metaphors in political discourse has an added advantage. Whether one believes the fascist octopus has sung its swan song or not, if we use the metaphor in an attempt to engage in a discussion on that topic, we will be uttering complete nonsense.

Communist propaganda used many colourful expressions for enemies of the system. Among many pejorative terms for the USA, one that brings a smile today is 'American pirates'. Until recently, pirates belonged to the past and were used in propaganda discourse simply because of negative connotations of the term. The word also fits the fairy tale or rescue scenario where pirates would naturally be associated with the role of the villain. More recently, popular culture changed the negative connotations of the word by creating the fictional character of Captain Jack Sparrow, the Pirate Lord of the Caribbean Sea, made popular by Johnny Depp. Even more recently, real life ruthless pirates attacking ships along the coast of Somalia became a huge international problem and brought the older connotations back to life. In any case, the expression 'American pirates', attested by Głowiński in 1966, in the context of the Vietnam War (Głowiński 1991, 9) was and remains an oddity of Communist propaganda. It was part of the language that was supposed to make the opposition appear obnoxious and abhorrent.

The worst example of all times in Polish Newspeak was the term used to describe soldiers of the Home Army (*Armia Krajowa*): *zapluty karzeł reakcji* ('the spit stained dwarf of reactionism'). This term was used on a 1945 propaganda poster designed by Włodzimierz Zakrzewski, the author of several propaganda posters and one of the founders of *sotsrealism* in Polish art. That particular poster, with a caption 'Giant and the spit stained dwarf of reactionism,' shows a large figure of a soldier (the Giant) in the uniform of the Polish People's Army, marching forward and to the left (or, maybe, in the direction towards the West) with a gun. The second figure is small and caricature-like. The poster shows a middle-aged man dressed in black, almost like a priest (but not in uniform). The little man (the dwarf) is trying to grab the soldier's one leg, possibly to hinder his progress, while spitting on his other leg. Hanging from his neck is a board with letters AK (the well-known abbreviation for the Home Army in Polish). I am not sure who came up with this metaphor (ugly personification for an organization that most Poles identified with selfless struggle for Polish independence). I came across suggestions that a similar expression was used by Józef Piłsudski to refer to national democrats. As much as the metaphor is unfair, unjust and hurtful when applied to the Home Army, there is little point discussing its meaning. It was not used to describe anyone, only to offend.

Many slogans, not only in communism, are based on sentence fragments without a predicate (i.e., a tensed verb form). Russian *Nashe delo pravoe* ('our cause [is] just) is an example; Russian calls for a special treatment as it does not use the verb *to be* in the present tense. This may have had an influence on the language used in Polish propaganda slogans (e.g., *Młodzież z Partią*—'The youth [is/stands] with the Party'). Similar syntax is used in German *Gott mit uns*—'God [is] with us' or *Um Freiheit und Leben*—[we are fighting] 'for freedom and life.' These slogans are neither true nor false. They lack a predicate and therefore cannot be interpreted. They are intended to be interactive; they make the audience come up with the missing predicates. They may be meant as statements, expectations, wishes, or commands. An additional difficulty is the identification of the speaker. They may be intended as expressions of the sentiments of the 'society,' but this too cannot be fully ascertained. As a result, the slogans cannot be verified but can still impose cognitive schemata on people's perception of reality.

Slogans are often based on presuppositions, i.e., implicit assumptions about some state of affairs based on utterances whose truth can be taken for granted. One of the logical properties of a presupposition is that both a declarative sentence with a presupposition-triggering element and the denial of that sentence share the same presupposition. Thus, whether we agreed or denied that the Party was fighting for 'further amelioration' of the situation of women, we still tacitly acknowledged that the situation of women must have been good to start with. Similarly, the report that President Lech Kaczyński was working on 'perfecting' his English presupposed that the President's English must have already been quite good.

Many features of bad English listed by Orwell in 1946 were common in communist propaganda (e.g., pretentious or foreign words; vaguely defined words or words with shifted definitions, like 'people's democracy' that overlapped in meaning with the 'dictatorship of the proletariat'; multiple negations, as in 'not uncommon,' etc.—for a more detailed analysis cf. Stroińska 1994). Many of them returned in the language of the Fourth Republic of the Kaczyński brothers in 2005 and then again in 2015.

In his analysis of the English language used in politics, Orwell observed that the general tendency of modern prose was away from concreteness. This could be seen particularly well in sotsrealist arts. Golomshtok (1990) noted that individual features of persons and objects have been replaced by 'typical'. "The individual is portrayed only as an embodiment of something more general" (191). The depiction of reality in art had to give way to the creation of a legend.

As a student of languages and linguistics, I was particularly fascinated with the theory of translation and with the concept of linguistic relativism within the philosophy of language. In academic discussions on this subject, relativism, as formulated in Sapir and Whorf's hypothesis, is usually dismissed as an exaggeration. While everyone agrees there is a connection between language and thought, the claim that the way we think is completely shaped by the language we use is considered extreme and untenable. After all, we can communicate across linguistic and cultural borders. And yet, the study of the language of totalitarian propaganda presents an interesting case where the power of totally controlled language truly has the ability to shape people's perception of reality. This happens not only through specially modified vocabulary but also by means of syntax and through the imposition of cognitive models that determine the perception (e.g., through selected metaphors).

Orwell noted in the Appendix to *1984* that the use of Newspeak was not universal:

> In the year 1984 there was not as yet anyone who used Newspeak as his sole means of communication, either in speech or writing. The leading articles in the *Times* were written in it, but this was a *tour de force* which could only be carried out by a specialist. It was expected that Newspeak would have finally superseded Oldspeak (or Standard English, as we should call it) by about the year 2050 (Orwell 1946/1972, 312).

Similarly in Poland, the communist Newspeak was the language of the papers and many of its features were adopted by party activists. It was often the language of school textbooks and propaganda movies. It was all around us. In real life, however, few people truly practiced it in everyday situations.

When I talked about first language acquisition in my Introduction to Linguistics class, I often asked students whether they remembered anyone instructing them on the grammar of their first language. Their earliest memories usually go back to learning in school how to read and write but they do not remember receiving instruction on how to form past tense or plural forms of nouns. It seems that we absorb the linguistic input that is available to us and construct our model of language based on this data. Being exposed to political propaganda and its language would likely produce the same effect. In Poland, the two varieties of Polish co-existed and no one was really exposed to communist Newspeak alone. Particularly important, in this context, was the role of church as a kind of guardian of pre-communist language. The Catholic Church in communist Poland not only used traditional word meanings, it also took up issues that were important to people. When I left Poland, I realized how little I actually knew about Catholic religion. Even though I went to church almost every Sunday throughout my childhood and then—after a long break—again in my twenties, and even though I attended weekly religion classes in our parish all through elementary school and most of the high school, to say that my knowledge of the Bible was minimal would be an overstatement.

I never read the Bible on my own and did not listen with much attention to the readings in church. Sermons, on the other hand, were usually interesting. They may have had some nominal link to the readings but they usually focused on current issues and how those current issues should be interpreted or dealt with according to the teachings of the Church. Religion classes in St. Jakub's church attracted crowds of young people but mostly because of the priest who led them. According to the legend, Father Józef Gniewniak was an engineer or a student of engineering when World War II started. He was deported to Auschwitz concentration camp for his involvement in the activities of Polish underground resistance movement and it was there he made a vow to become a priest if he were to survive. He survived. That was the legend. In reality it was not the Nazi concentration camp that led to his priesthood but rather communist arrest. He was arrested at least twice after the war when he was a student of history in Kraków—which is also where he met the future Pope John Paul II. After the second arrest, he interrupted his university study and entered a seminary. Maybe he supported the legend because it was safer?

He was lively, funny, understanding, somewhat mischievous and, in my opinion, infinitely good. He shared his tiny apartment with dozens of canaries and other pets. My first two canaries were presents from him. He organized summer camps, famous among teenagers in our area. After each religion class, he would let us watch cartoons, from a film projector. Later, he was removed from our parish and placed in charge of a parish church in Międzylesie, a suburb of Warsaw, where he was also responsible for a huge Children's Hospital. I am sure that children loved his visits and the company of his huge Old English Sheepdog. When my good friend Zosia Klimaszewska was getting married and her Belgian husband needed the sacraments, we all went to Międzylesie. I knew that father Gniewniak would not give us any bureaucratic trouble. We exchanged Christmas cards and letters until he passed away in 2000.

The second important factor in keeping undiluted language available to people in communist countries was Western radio broadcasting in Polish. This provided the news without communist Newspeak. Even though foreign broadcasting stations had their own agenda, they played an enormous role by offering people a language to talk about political events. Strikes were called strikes, crimes were called crimes, and patriots were called patriots.

I have been rather careful about my language habits for as long as I remember, yet there are many influences of propaganda that I absorbed without even noticing it. It usually takes an objective assessment by someone with more distance from the Polish context to properly diagnose my errors.

After my Polish translation of Klemperer's *LTI* was published in 1991, a reviewer noted that, in my translator's introduction, I confused terms 'fascism' and 'Nazism'. She was right and I felt ashamed of my mistake. These terms were used interchangeably by Polish propaganda and often simply signified 'something bad'. My erroneous usage was less sweeping, but it was still wrong to identify fascism, a much broader term, with its German variety. I am sure that there are many other aspects of the communist propaganda that became a part of my linguistic habits and that form the basis for my skewed understanding of the world.

CHAPTER 6

Radio Free Europe

"Without Western broadcasting, totalitarian regimes would have survived much longer. (...) The struggle for freedom would have been more arduous and the road to democracy much longer.... From these broadcasting stations, we gleaned our lessons of independent thinking and solidarity action."

—Lech Walesa, from the foreword of War of the Black Heavens, *Michael Nelson*

IN THE EARLY 1960S, it took me some time to understand why, at night, my parents chose to listen to jammed radio stations instead of the 'normal' ones. It annoyed me particularly in the summer when we were on holidays and were all sleeping in one big room. Even though they kept the volume low—probably more to let me sleep than to make sure that people in other rooms did not overhear them—I was hardly able to fall asleep with the constant high-pitched noise. They listened to Radio Free Europe or to the Voice of America and, even though no one explained it to me, I realized that for some reason they took the strange activity very seriously. This listening to the jammed radio every night was somewhat ritualistic, almost like the bedtime prayer, the Sunday mass in church or visits to the cemetery on All Saints' Day (and after my Father's death pretty much every Sunday). I knew that the voice that kept fading in and out was saying things that people suspected but could not find in the papers or on the official radio and television. I just did not know, at first, why it had to have such poor quality of reception.

Radio Free Europe, definitely the one that my parents listened to most often, was established in New York in 1949 and was funded by the United States Congress. Until 1971, this funding was passed to Radio Free Europe through the CIA since the broadcasting activity was viewed as part of a general CIA psychological warfare campaign directed at authoritarian communist regimes of Eastern Europe and the Soviet Union. That the funding for RFE came from the CIA was publicly acknowledged only in 1971. At that time RFE was converted into a non-profit corporation and its supervision was assigned to the International Broadcasting Bureau. In 1974, RFE was merged with Radio Liberty, established in 1951 by the U.S. organization Committee for the Liberation of the Peoples of Russia and the name of the new institution was changed to Radio Free Europe/ Radio Liberty.

RFE's primary objective was to reach audiences in communist Eastern Europe, i.e., in countries that following World War II found themselves behind the Iron Curtain. The broadcast provided the listeners with current and more accurate news than what was available in local media, and offered political commentary about important affairs. The Mission Statement of Radio Free Europe/Radio Liberty (available online) lists the promotion of "democratic values and institutions by disseminating factual information and ideas" as its main objective. RFE/RL considers a well-informed citizenry (ibid.) as the first requirement of any democracy and lists the following activities as its mission:

- to provide objective news, analysis, and discussion of domestic and regional issues crucial to successful democratic and free-market transformations;
- to strengthen civil societies by projecting democratic values;
- to combat ethnic and religious intolerance and to promote mutual understanding among peoples;
- to provide a model for local media, assist in training to enhance media professionalism and independence, and develop partnerships with local media outlets, and
- to foster closer ties between the countries of the region and the world's established democracies.

The first RFE broadcasting station was located at Lampertheim, near Frankfurt in West Germany. It started to broadcast in July 1950 with the first news programme directed to listeners in Czechoslovakia. Programmes were broadcast to Poland, Hungary, Romania, and Bulgaria a bit later the same year.

In those early years, it was not easy to listen to RFE in Poland; the reasons were perhaps more technical than political. Few people had radios and some of those who did only had receivers that transmitted one official station's broadcasts that could not be tuned to anything else. This situation has to be viewed in the context of the post-war Poland: during the war, the possession of radios in private homes was banned by the German occupants. My mother remembered a Telefunken radio that her parents possessed during the war. They kept it concealed in a fake ceiling in their Warsaw apartment. Following the assassination of Franz Kutschera, the SS and Police Commander for the District of Warsaw (February 1, 1944), arrangements for his funeral involved forcing some people who lived along the route of the funeral procession temporarily out of their apartments. At that time, my grandparents had the radio hidden in the box with coal and heating material and were afraid that during their absence someone may enter their apartment and find the radio. Out of concern for the safety of his wife and two daughters (the son was in a POW camp in Germany), my grandfather decided to destroy the radio.

The first post-war Polish radio, called "Pionier" was produced by Diora in 1948. My parents in-law told me they bought their first radio only in 1952. It was a newly designed model called 'Mazur'. The first radio I remember in my own home was a much later model called 'Violetta', produced by ZRK from 1962. There must have been other radios my parents had used before the purchase of Violetta but I do not remember them. I vividly remember a small, portable radio, in a black leather cover, possibly Russian-made, which my parents used on holidays. Later, after my father passed away in 1969, my mother always listened to it at night in bed. She often fell asleep with the radio still on, and when I walked past her bedroom at night, I could hear the low volume, high pitch jamming noise coming from underneath her pillow. I had the impression that she was somewhat addicted to that radio and the RFE news.

Very early on, the U.S. government realized it could use the talents of displaced Eastern European nationals following the end of the war and employ them in broadcasting information to their home countries. Those émigrés represented a huge potential resource as many highly educated and creative people decided to stay in the West rather than return to their now-communist countries. The U.S. recruited them as writers and speakers for the newly established radio programmes and supported the National Committee for a Free Europe (NCFE), later the Free Europe Committee, which was established in 1949. This organization was entrusted with the mission to find work for political émigrés from Eastern Europe. NCFE put their voices on the air in their own languages for audiences in their home countries, and carried émigré articles and statements back to their homelands through the printed word. These objectives were realized through the establishment of a publishing division, Free Europe Press, and a broadcast division, Radio Free Europe (RFE). The Hoover Digest webpage that supports the Hoover Archives where documentation on the history of Radio Free Europe is housed, describes the history of the most popular radio station in Eastern Europe at the time in considerable detail.

A new and larger transmission facility was established in 1951 at Holzkirchen, near Munich. It began transmitting on May 1, 1951. After the war, May Day became an important official communist holiday that was supposed to be a joyful celebration of the working class. C.D. Jackson, the president of the NCFE, is quoted by *The Hoover Digest* saying: "We thought that would be a good day to launch our station and to let some people know out loud, and quite loud, the difference between workers and slaves." On May Day, huge parades marched through the cities of Eastern Bloc countries. They often included a show of arms or were used as an opportunity to display hostility directed at Western leaders, e.g., through a show of puppets and caricatures. Although these parades were presented on television and in other official media as a spontaneous expression of happiness and satisfaction of the working class, they were carefully staged. No unauthorized person could spontaneously lift their child to hand flowers to the smiling and waving first secretaries of the respective Communist Parties of the region. As May Day parades were a celebration of fiction, it was indeed a good day to reveal some of the truths behind the happy mask.

RFE's broadcasts were produced in New York, sent to Europe, and transmitted from Lampertheim and Holzkirchen in West Germany. Establishing a European production site, however, became essential if broadcasts were to be timely. West Germany, sharing a border with Czechoslovakia and East Germany (GDR), had the best location and was still partially occupied by American forces. Munich, the second-largest city within the U.S. occupied zone, attracted numerous East European émigrés. Many émigrés had some experience in writing, editing, or the technical aspects of broadcasting and were happy to be involved. The European branch of Radio Free Europe opened in November 1952 on the edge of Munich's English Garden. It was a modern radio station with 22 studios. In 1952, Jan Nowak-Jeziorański became head of the Polish section of RFE. When talking about him and his WWII service as a courier between the underground movement in Poland and the Polish government in exile in London, many people did and still do use the adjective 'legendary'. For my parents, it was the personality of this 'legendary courier from Warsaw' that made Radio Free Europe particularly attractive and trustworthy. During the war, Nowak-Jeziorański was a special emissary and he had the people's trust. He was a true war hero, in plain Polish, not in Newspeak. There was no doubt of any kind about his patriotism.

Zbigniew Brzezinski, the National Security Adviser to President Carter, a friend of Nowak-Jeziorański and co-recipient of the Presidential Medal of Freedom, the highest civilian award in the USA, said the following about Jan Nowak's service:

> He was a remarkable blend of romanticism and realism politically, of wisdom and emotion intellectually, of passion and loyalty personally.... At some moments, he even almost single-handedly determined the course of Polish history by his realistic convictions.... In 1956, his was the decisive voice from abroad, urging Poles to be cautious and thus to avoid what happened to the Hungarians when

> they revolted and were destroyed by the Soviets. In 1968, his was the decisive voice exposing the chauvinistic Polish communists who tried to use crudely anti-Semitic slogans in an effort to stage an internal coup in Warsaw.

I think it was Nowak-Jeziorański who single-handedly shaped the Polish language service of RFE. I would even go as far as to suggest that some of the success of the Polish opposition movement may be attributed to his broadcasting.

Every night, the speakers of Radio Free Europe or the Voice of America would report events that took place in Eastern Europe, the Soviet Union and Poland in particular—except of course at times when something important was taking place in other countries of the Soviet Bloc. I vividly remember the events of 1968: the March 1968 student unrests in Warsaw and the invasion of Czechoslovakia in the summer of the same year. March 1968 was the first political action by the opposition that I remember.

I was born in 1956, an eventful year in Eastern Europe. It was three years after Stalin's death. In February 1956, during the 20th Party Congress, the new First Secretary Nikita Khrushchev launched an attack on Stalin, accusing him of power abuse, denouncing his purges, and announcing changes in policy. The process of de-Stalinization had begun.

In March 1956, the Stalinist leader of Polish communists, Bolesław Bierut suddenly died, allegedly of a heart attack, while visiting Moscow. He attended the 20th Congress of the Soviet party, the one where Khrushchev delivered his famous, though secret, speech condemning Stalin. Poles had high hopes that the situation in the country would improve following Khrushchev's policy of greater openness in the Soviet Union, but the successor of Bierut, Edward Ochab, was an equally rigid Stalinist. In June, dissatisfied workers at the Cegielski railway car factory in Poznań took to the streets demanding cheaper bread, fair wages, and more freedom. Their peaceful demonstrations were crushed by police gunfire and several people were killed. The estimates vary but it is suggested over fifty people died when tanks fired at the protesting workers. The protest was labeled as CIA inspired and the workers' demands were dismissed. This was the first of the recurring waves of workers' protests in Poland against the government that claimed to be based on and representing the working class. The dissatisfaction did not disappear and the party realized that a new leader should be appointed to avert a crisis. The most popular choice seemed Władysław Gomułka, who was considered a moderate and who was known for his relatively unorthodox ideas. Back in 1951, he was first placed under house arrest for 'nationalist deviation', then imprisoned, and finally was replaced as Party Secretary by Boleslaw Bierut. He was released after June 1956 unrests and in October was the top candidate for the Party leadership. With Soviet tanks ready to attack Poland and Nikita Khrushchev visiting Warsaw, Władysław Gomułka managed to negotiate a compromise with the Russians. It was agreed that as long as the Polish government supported the Soviet Union in foreign affairs and remained part of the Warsaw Pact, they could, to some degree, develop their own domestic policies. Perhaps the Russians did not want to deal with two international problems at the same time since other conflicts in Eastern Europe were beginning to surface.

The agreement with Polish communists was finalized just a couple of days before the people of Budapest took to the streets on October 23, 1956. The protests started with students, and spread to workers and finally Hungarian soldiers. There were marches in the streets of the capital demanding some mild changes, likely inspired by the developments in Poland. The situation became tragic when Hungarian Security Police (AVO) opened fire on the relatively peaceful crowds and killed hundreds of protesters. Soviet troops stationed in Hungary were called to action by the hardliners but refrained from attacking the civilian population.

Political developments moved swiftly. Workers' and national councils were formed and political parties from before communist repressions in 1945 and 1949 were revived. While the majority of Hungarians were in favour of maintaining a socialist form of government, they also supported the demand of the newly formed government of Imre Nagy for a Soviet troop withdrawal from Hungary. The Soviet Union government would not accept Nagy's demands and on

November 4, new Soviet troops entered Budapest. This time, tanks were supported by artillery, air force and infantry. The intense fighting lasted almost a week and ended with a cease-fire on November 10. Thousands of civilians had died and the following repressions added at least several hundred executions, including that of Imre Nagy himself. The year 1956 was not a peaceful one in Eastern Europe. While it remained as a symbol of a rather short-lived hope for reforms and better living conditions (sometimes referred to as 'the thaw'), it has also revealed the ruthless nature of the Soviet system that did not tolerate dissidence. After the Hungarian revolution was suppressed, those who still believed in communist ideals had to actively ignore the brutal reality behind the Iron Curtain.

I obviously do not remember any of these stories myself. I do not even recall the construction of the Berlin Wall that was undertaken on August 13, 1961. March 1968 is my first fully conscious political memory. However, being the only child surrounded by adults and hardly ever excluded from their conversations, I had already been somewhat introduced to politics. I understood, for example, that 'brotherly help' meant 'military intervention' and that the news on the 'normal' radio and on TV were expected to be selective and biased. I also knew that I was not supposed to tell the teachers at school what I knew about the world events from discussions at home and from Radio Free Europe. I did not try to challenge my teachers. My desire to challenge the official façade of the system came later.

In March 1968, my parents and my grandmother seemed glued to the radio reports about student protests in Warsaw that started on March 8, International Women's Day. We were listening, of course, to Western radio stations. My cousin Anna was at that time a student in Warsaw and was living with my grandmother. She was able to bring my parents first-hand accounts and updates about student demonstrations, like the one in front of the Warsaw Polytechnic—which coincidently was also almost in front of the apartment building in Noakowskiego Street, where my grandmother, and Anna, then lived. The official radio, television, and papers reported these unrests and explained the events as hooliganism and irresponsible actions of antisocialist elements, giving me the first practical lesson on how reality that I witnessed myself was being linguistically distorted by the media. I looked at my tall but very feminine cousin Anna. With her gorgeous blond hair neatly arranged in a long pony tail and her high heels, she was far from the epitome of a hooligan.

Michał Głowiński, Polish historian and literary theory specialist, kept private notes on language changes in the period between 1966 and 1971. In 1991, he published these observations in book form. His book, *Marcowe gadanie* (March chatter) reminds me somewhat of Victor Klemperer's *LTI*: Głowiński takes individual words from the public and private discourse of the time and puts them under the microscope, searches for their origins, meaning shifts, and effects on the reader. On September 13, 1968 he noted (my translation):

> Language is a very sensitive instrument. It registers all tremors and shudders in the life of a society, and dramatic events in particular find their reflection in it. The so-called March events immediately—so to speak—entered into language. This became apparent in three ways:
>
> 1. by reactivating formulae from the period of Stalinism proper, that is from the first half of the 1950s;
> 2. by bringing back to life the traditional language of the political right wing, in particular in its shape from the 1930s;
> 3. by referring to the language of the tabloid press, which appeals to the lowest instincts. (Głowiński 1991, 32)

The cancellation by official censorship of poet Adam Mickiewicz's theatre performance of *Dziady* (Forefathers) triggered a student demonstration in Warsaw. These demonstrations came to be known as *wydarzenia marcowe* (March Events) and were recorded in Polish history as such.(Głowiński 1991, 33)

The play was written during the partitions of Poland and, quite naturally, had strong anti-Russian sentiments. The timing was sensitive. The Arab-Israeli conflict of 1967 (the Six Day War) gave pretext for an anti-Semitic campaign in the Soviet Union which spread to other countries in Eastern Europe where nationalistic views often went together with anti-Semitism. Many people of Jewish background became victims of anti-Semitic purges. The Soviet Union, criticized for its actions, was not prepared to tolerate any expressions of hostility. The March unrests were relatively quickly brought down, labelled as hooligan rebellion 'fanned' by Zionist and antisocialist groups who were hostile to 'our Party and our Polish interests'. As the March events involved many students and intellectuals, some of them university professors, institutions of higher education seemed to have been punished most severely. However, in 1994, Andrzej Friszke revealed in his paper "The March 1968 Protest Movement in Light of Ministry of Interior Reports to the Party Leadership", that the arrests during and after the March events were not restricted to students and intelligentsia. He writes:

> 2,180 people throughout the country were arrested between March 8 and March: 21 for their role in the protests. This number includes 525 students of higher institutions, 327 elementary and high school students, 769 blue-collar workers, 288 white-collar workers, and 130 unemployed persons. 831 arrestees were said to have been freed within 48 hours. Over the next few weeks, these figures increased. A subsequent MSW report put the number of related arrests between March 7 and April 6 at 2,725. The largest category here was blue-collar workers (937), next were students (641, including 248 from universities, 194 from polytechnics and engineering schools, and 199 from other institutions). The third largest group was primary and secondary school students ... It is remarkable that the largest category of the arrested and detained in March/April 1968 was workers. After all, the public rallies were composed of students and the intelligentsia, worker participation in them was practically invisible. Would it thus be appropriate to

> amend the conventional wisdom that workers "did nothing" in 1968? In March 1968 workers did not act as a social group, did not organize at their places of work, but took part as individuals or in small groups as fractions of large street demonstrations. In discussions of this article, it was pointed out to me that the number of detained and sentenced workers could have been even larger than that listed in MSW reports. Some of the detained could have been classified as hooligans whose actions were unrelated to the political context. (Friszke 1994)

One of the reasons the March events went down in history as a student revolt and as an example of a popular uprising where the social movement of the Polish intelligentsia found no significant support among the workers may have been the fact that this was how Western broadcasters portrayed that period. Friszke comments not only about the support from the working class, but also on protests at universities and schools outside Warsaw, another little-known aspect of the March events in Poland. It may have been that foreign correspondents could not gather information about developments in other parts of the country and so they concentrated on what was going on at Warsaw University, Warsaw Polytechnic and, to a lesser degree, also the *Szkoła Główna Gospodarstwa Wiejskiego* (SGGW, Main School of Agriculture) where my mother had worked as librarian and my cousin Anna was studying. Information about SGGW may actually have come from those family sources rather than from the foreign radio stations. For obvious reasons, information about more widespread unrests was not convenient for the authorities. This is why it did not find its way into official media.

After March 1968, many people left Poland, allegedly because they were *the enemies of the people* or *antisocialist elements*. In the official media, the events were openly blamed on people with Jewish-sounding names. Many of those who had Jewish backgrounds left Poland and went to Israel. Some took it as an opportunity to escape communism. Professors who left or were forced out were replaced by those who were regime-friendly and servile, even if not always academically qualified. Those with PhDs but without *habilitation* (the next step required in the university career in the Polish university system in order to be promoted to the position of a *docent*) became a new generation of academics, quickly labeled by people as *March docents*. When I started the university six years later in 1974, the term 'March docent' was still in everyday use to refer to academic teachers who moved to the docent position after the events of March 1968.

Political unrest was not yet over. In August 1968 we were on holidays in Rogów, a summer practicum place for students of Forestry from SGGW, where my mother had worked. We were, as usual, all in one room, and I was big enough to actively listen to the Western radio with my parents. This was the first year when I was a part of that family conspiracy because the March events served as my political initiation. On August 21, 1968, in the morning, the Soviet army—aided by troops from four other Warsaw Pact countries, including Poland—invaded Czechoslovakia. Even though at that time I wasn't sure of the exact reasons for the invasion, I knew that it was immoral. I understood that it marked the beginning of the end of the so-called Prague Spring, which symbolized hope that went beyond the borders of that one country. At the age of twelve, there was not much I could do; I could throw stones at trains carrying tanks towards the Czech border and so I did. Together with other kids—either children of faculty and staff from the Main School of Agriculture who were spending their holidays in Rogów, or local youth with whom we were friends—I went to the nearby railway tracks and stood there, in the field, watching slow moving trains going south. They were carrying military equipment, covered with brown or greenish looking fabric. I think there were soldiers there too but I do not remember whether they were Polish or Russian. We whistled and threw stones at the tanks, but they kept rolling past, oblivious to our protest. We did not discuss political issues; we just did what seemed so obviously right to us. We protested in our own childish way. Many years later, during street protests in 1982 and 1983, when I was in my twenties, I did exactly the same: I whistled and watched other adults like me throwing stones at the police. Perhaps the idea was not so childish after all.

The March events in Poland were clearly inspired by Czech ideas of reform. Like in Poland, the dissatisfaction with the communist system was growing in Czechoslovakia. It was fueled by economic problems and, unlike in Poland, by demands from Communist intellectuals for more freedom and pluralism within a socialist system. The Czechs wanted socialism with a human face. In January 1968, the Communist Party's Central Committee replaced the Party's hard-line First Secretary Antonin Novotny with Alexander Dubček, considered a moderate reformer. Dubček responded to the expectations of his fellow countrymen and started the process of reform, gaining support and admiration in his country and giving hope to other countries. In March 1968, Antonin Novotny was replaced as President of the Republic (a function he kept after being removed from the First Secretary's position) by Ludvik Svoboda. "Svoboda" in Czech means "freedom", a coincidence that was exploited in many posters and fliers, particularly during the Soviet invasion, even though Svoboda himself turned against the reform movement.

Both the Soviet authorities and the leaders of the neighbouring Eastern European countries looked with a lot of suspicion and apprehension at the Czech reform movement and worried about the growing popular support for the new version of a nationally-adapted communism. They all knew they would be immediately removed from power if the people in their countries had anything to say about who was to govern them. There was a well justified risk that the revolution-like movement for socialism with human face could be infectious and would spread into other countries of the region.

When, on the morning of August 21, Soviet tanks rolled into the streets of Prague, there was very little fighting, unlike 12 years before in Budapest. However, this does not mean that there was no resistance: for example, some newspapers continued publishing real, uncensored news and some radio stations continued broadcasting, but from secret locations. The magazine *The World in Pictures,* from August 21, 1968 featured a photograph taken in front of the Prague radio station on 21 August 1968, at 10:35 a.m., picturing an explosion. The text underneath the headline, "WHY?", in both Czech and Russian, read: "Our resistance to violence will never cease! We want it to be a resistance of the level-headed calm and spiritual maturity which is native to our nations..." The picture can be seen as part of the virtual exhibition based on Materials from the Labadie Collection of Social Protest Material at the University of Michigan at Ann Arbor. This exhibition was put together to honour Vaclav Havel's honorary degree conferred in 2000.

One of the immediate causes of the Soviet invasion, aside from mounting fears that Dubček could not control popular pressure for change, was the plan to convene a Fourteenth Party Congress in September 1968, whose delegates, it was hoped, would elect a new pro-reform Central Committee. The Soviet invasion changed the planned schedule and the Congress was held, almost secretly, on August 22nd, at a factory in Vysocany, outside Prague. Delegates, disguised as workers, sneaked past Soviet troops to meet and discuss the new developments. This unusual Congress condemned the invasion, proclaimed support for the reform process, and threatened to stage a one-hour general strike. The strike took place, but the situation of the reform movement was getting worse. The reform leaders in the Czech government had been 'interned', a word that always seemed to be popping up on such occasions, and then sent to Moscow for 'negotiations'. Passive resistance continued, with flyers and leaflets published in both Czech and Russian. There were examples of graffiti in Russian, all meant to tell Russian soldiers where they were and what was going on. It was assumed that the soldiers were never told that they were to face civilians of a country that was in 'brotherly friendship' with their own homeland. They likely thought they would be protecting civilians from disguised 'enemies of socialism'. This strategy seems to have been used again very recently, when, in February 2022, Russian soldiers sent to fight Ukrainians were not fully aware where they were going and why.

Interestingly though, both sides in the Czech conflict spoke the same language, calling for *klid a rozvaha* (calm and level-headedness) and striving for 'normalization'. Prague Spring was a movement that originated in the circles of power in response to the general climate of dissatisfaction. Thus, the reformers used the standard clichés of the international workers' movement and were unable to free themselves from the language of the system they were opposing. Perhaps the purges and repressions that followed Prague Spring and the grey and dreary years of normalization and Soviet help in the fight against counter-revolutionary forces were a necessary condition for the liberation of language and the realization that the system cannot be reformed. It took Czechoslovakia twenty-one more years until finally, on December 9, 1989, in another 'calm and level-headed' movement, later labeled 'the velvet revolution,' the country began the process of real change and not just cosmetic surgery. Six years later, in 1995, the headquarters of Radio Free Europe were moved to Prague.

I never questioned the influence that the independent radio stations had on my perception of reality. They were part of my world when I was growing up and suddenly were not when I left Poland in 1984 and was able to enjoy Western sources of information without censorship and jamming. Many years later, Matt Savelli, an Honours History student at McMaster, asked if he could interview me for a project he was working on for one of his courses. He wanted to talk about Radio Free Europe and its impact on people in Eastern Europe prior to 1989. He asked a lot of very good questions and, for the first time, he made me think about these influences.

I believe the Polish language radio stations broadcasting from the West influenced me in at least two significant but, at that time, difficult-to-notice ways. On one hand, they gave me and many of my fellow countrymen, the feeling that the world had its eyes on Poland (or Eastern Europe) and that what was happening in my country was very important. On the other hand, they strengthened even further the already well-established feeling that the United States of America was the strongest ally of Polish people.

The main effect of broadcasts from the West on me and likely on other Poles was probably the feeling of self-importance. The news centered on the events taking place in Eastern Europe (and the news in Polish naturally focused on what was going on in Poland) and how these events were received in the West. The reported reactions of the U.S. government to the developments in Poland and the mere fact that what we saw as Western radio stations (as a child, I did not fully grasp then that these were just the Western stations directed to audiences in Eastern Europe) were devoting so much time to these events gave us, Poles, the impression that everyone's focus was on Poland. But it was not just the feeling of being the centre of attention either. We felt that the West would help us if needed; that we were watched over and protected; that if things got worse, the West, like a real older brother, would tell the Soviet Union, a.k.a. the big bully, off. I should probably speak only for myself, but I suspect this feeling may have been more widespread: I felt like a passive child. The grown-ups were taking care of my needs. I could just sit and watch—or rather listen. Some critics of the Westerns radio stations would say that this is *not* how a civil society develops.

It is, in fact, amazing that, despite my insatiable curiosity about and fascination with totalitarian propaganda, I personally never questioned the role that Radio Free Europe and Voice of America played in my own political education. It was only my conversation with Matt Savelli that made me realize this astonishing blind spot in my past. Matt wrote in his essay that I (identified as "now an academic studying propaganda," Savelli, 22) claimed that I, "never once questioned who was running the station or how credible its message was" (Savelli, 22.). He continued:

> Because she could observe some of the events she heard on the station occurring in front of her eyes, she assumed everything the station said was absolute truth. As a result of this, she later left Poland with what she described as an "extremely pro-American attitude." (ibid)

I blushed reading these words, yet I must admit that they properly reflect my attitude in those years when I listened to Radio Free Europe and Voice of America. Admittedly, I was relatively young and did not know much about politics. The reality seemed black and white. What was said by the official propaganda was a lie and therefore, what was said by the Western radio stations must have been the truth. Both sides could not have been lying! This may seem absurd to me today but the world in the 1960s or even 1970s seemed so much simpler. This attitude to official propaganda—i.e., the assumption that you just negate what they said to get the true picture—proved a bit dangerous to my husband Krzysztof. When travelling for the first time to the United States in 1976 at the age of 21, he was so convinced that what the communist propaganda was telling us about crime in American big cities was another lie that he did not think twice before deciding to walk through a rough neighbourhood in Chicago late at night. He was beaten up by a gang and ended up in a hospital with a black eye and a broken finger—from covering his face while he was being punched. A humorous element in that story was that the young men who robbed him only took his money, he, however, thought they also took his Polish passport. He was more mortified by the vision of problems with the passport office back in Poland than intimidated by his attackers and so he begged them to help him find his passport. The young people who, as he later claimed, were quite nice and helpful—since they only wanted his money and did not really intend to harm him—went back to where they left his bag, brought it back and helped him search for his passport. Their search was in vain and they were, at the end, quite apologetic. They even called the ambulance for him. The passport was actually safe at home and so Krzysztof did not have to face the passport office about the loss of this so important and precious document.

My love for America was deeply ingrained in my upbringing. The official media always spoke of the United States in a most derogatory way and my positive attitude was likely partly the result of typical Polish contrariness. Like many Poles, we had family and friends living in the USA. There were also historical ties such as Polish support in the war for independence. Poles had an idealistic image of the USA as a country of freedom, open space, and opportunity: America, the gentle giant. When I think of this idealism now, I realize that this may be a similar phenomenon to Victor Klemperer's sympathy for the Soviet Russia. When faced with one powerful and evil enemy, one does not want to see the other side as anything but pure. There is a certain limit to the amount of evil that one can accept.

The imposition of martial law in Poland on Sunday, December 13, 1981 was the last time that a radio broadcast played such an important role in my life. Martial law was declared by General

Wojciech Jaruzelski, the first secretary of the Polish communist party, in a speech which was repeatedly shown on TV and played on the radio. I learned about 'the war' in a rather surreal place—in the line-up for tickets for the cable car to the top of Kasprowy Wierch in the Tatra Mountains. Student strikes across Poland had just ended.

My husband had gotten sick and left his university's strike. When he recovered, he decided to go skiing for the weekend before returning to work. I joined him in Zakopane on Saturday, December 12. On December 13, at about 5:30 am, we were waiting in a queue for cable car tickets. There were only a few tickets available for sale and so one had to queue early in order to purchase them. Shortly after six, someone drove up to the closed entrance door, jumped out of the car and shouted, "War! There is a war!" In response, the crowd of sleepy would-be skiers told him to go get some sleep assuming that he was drunk. He insisted on his sobriety and the truth of the news and when the guards finally opened the cable car station, the TV was turned on. There he was, the general in his big glasses (this time regular, not dark glasses), with the Polish flag in the background. The eagle seemed to be hanging sideways on that flag, adding to the surreal atmosphere of that moment. I felt like my grandmother, who was throwing invectives at party leaders giving their speeches on television. "Bastard," I spoke to myself, "what a bastard!"

The general was talking about the Fatherland that found itself at the edge of an abyss and I had to smile remembering an old joke about the definition of progress in Gomułka's era. In one of the official speeches someone was believed to have said: "In 1945 our Fatherland was at the edge of an abyss. Then, we took a big step forward." Jaruzelski then said that in Poland's situation, inaction would have been a crime against the nation. And that one (who, I asked) had to say: enough. *Why? Enough of what? Bastards*, I thought.

War or not, we decided to take advantage of the empty slopes and spent the entire day skiing. The landscape around us was amazingly beautiful. An abundance of fresh snow, blue sky, beautiful mountains, snow-covered pine and spruce trees. The chairlifts in the upper part of the mountain were not operating—Kasprowy Wierch was very close to the Polish state border with Czechoslovakia—and so each time we had to go to the very bottom and buy another cable car ticket to go to the top. There were very few people skiing. Pretty much everyone who heard the news went home. I remember skiing with tears rolling down my cheeks. The world was so wonderful. Why would some evil people want to spoil this beautiful world with their wickedness? I felt trapped in my country like an animal in a cage and I told myself, "I shall escape from this cage as soon as the door is left ajar and will never let anyone trap me there again." This was a memorable day of most wonderful skiing and most depressing thoughts. In the afternoon we returned to our hotel which was next to the lower cable car station (it was out of season and my husband managed to get us a room there—something that was normally impossible to accomplish). Telephone lines were dead. We could not call our parents in Warsaw.

We had return train tickets booked for Monday night so we stayed in Zakopane one more day. However, on Monday the cable car was closed—I think it was left open on Sunday by someone's oversight—so there was no more skiing. We visited some family friends in Zakopane and learned about local arrests and people being held at the local police station. The jail was apparently so full that the doors did not close … or so we were told. The newspapers headlines repeated a phrase from the speech referring to martial law as a 'lesser evil', thus implying that the alternative solution would have been Soviet intervention. Some people believed it, some disputed it. I remember my husband's comment that this discussion distracted people from the real question and led them into disputing the relative size of evil while concealing the simple truth—that the imposition of martial law against one's own nation was nothing short of a crime.

In Warsaw, my husband's parents were waiting for us at the train station with information on the situation in the country. I do not remember whether we were able to listen to any Western news in Zakopane, but we certainly did listen to RFE and Voice of America back in Warsaw in order to find out what was happening, who was arrested, what had happened to hundreds of people taken from their homes and interned, what happened to workers from the coal mine Wujek where police opened fire, killing nine miners. Again, like in 1956, 1968, 1970, 1976, and 1980, the news about events in my country were coming from abroad. However, this time around, the situation was a bit different. The short time when the Solidarność Trade Union was operating legally created a structure of new resistance. There were printing houses, distribution networks, groups of people who knew and trusted each other. Almost immediately after December 13, the underground news bulletins began to circulate. Newspapers were printed by small press operators associated with the Solidarność trade union and sometimes copied on typewriter with carbon paper. There were few photocopiers available at that time. When I wanted to give my students in the Department of German at Warsaw University a test, I had to type it on my typewriter in as many copies as I had students. For a group of 20 students, it would mean typing the questions at least four times as I could not put more than five sheets of thin copy paper and carbon paper into my typewriter. The last copy would be very pale and the typewritten news that we would receive would often appear the same way. They were handed out to those whom we trusted, obtained from those who trusted us. There were elements of comedy in all this, situational humour that reminded me of some WWII movies that I had cherished as a teenager.

I remember a meeting with an older female professor of English in the Warsaw University Faculty Club. The meeting was for the purpose of swapping news bulletins, but we both ordered a cup of coffee and a custard cream pastry. She gave me the *Solidarność Bulletin* folded inside an old issue of a comic book based on the popular television series *Stawka większa niż życie (More Than Life at Stake).* This action-packed TV series told the adventures of a Polish underground soldier posing as Hans Kloss, an officer of the German Intelligence Service for the Armed Forces, the *Abwehr*, run by Admiral Canaris. The movie had a cult status in Poland, despite its significant propaganda content. However, even taking into account the popularity of Hans Kloss, the likelihood that two female academics would meet to swap comic books about his adventures was practically nil and so, if anyone were to observe the two of us, it would have been obvious that we were engaged in some 'illegal activity'. Thankfully, no one did. In fact, even during martial law, the level of trust was high among people. I used to collect membership dues for the Solidarność

(Solidarity) trade union from my colleagues at the university during martial law—definitely an illegal activity—and learned only *post factum* that the partner of one of them was allegedly working for the security apparatus. It did not bother me too much then and it did not result in any problems. Unlike in other Eastern European countries, it could almost be assumed by default that a random person approached in the street would be opposed to the communist rule and to imposition of the martial law. Even if someone did not oppose it, they would be unlikely to report on someone who did.

On April 12, 1982, four months after the imposition of martial law, the underground Solidarność produced its first radio broadcast. It lasted only five minutes to make sure that the radio transmitter would not be discovered by police. At the precise time of the announced broadcast, we (my husband and I, in the company of his parents and at his parents' apartment) were waiting by the radio, prepared to tune in and out of the announced frequency searching for the anticipated announcement. A well-known melody caught our attention and we immediately knew that was it. The tune was *Siekiera, motyka* ("Axe, Hoe"), a spiteful satirical song from World War II. One line of the original lyrics was *Przegra wojnę głupi malarz* (the stupid painter will lose the war), with an easy-to-read reference to Hitler's failed career as an artist. It was this implied reference to losing a war that made this cheerful old tune so appropriate for this very new and different occasion. This was the last time that the radio was the centre of attention, delivering what was unavailable through other channels. This time, however, the message was not coming from abroad. The Polish society was ready to take over, but the authorities were not yet ready to admit defeat.

CHAPTER 7

Lessons from Children's Literature

Most people have favourite routines and rituals. When I was at university, my favourite way to rest and recharge my mind after final exams were over, was to curl up in one of the comfortable armchairs in my mother's apartment and read the adventures of Professor Kleks. *Kleks* is the Polish word for an ink blot and it was a fitting name for the main character in those stories. Not only was he a creation of the fountain pen of the author, but his characteristic silhouette, created by the superb illustrator Jan Marcin Szancer, with unruly hair and a long messy beard looked like a splash of ink. The adventures of Mr. Kleks were written by Jan Brzechwa (1898–1966), one of the most beloved Polish writers of children's literature. Along with Kornel Makuszyński, Ludwik Jerzy Kern, Edmund Niziurski, Zbigniew Nienacki or Alfred Szklarski, Brzechwa made my childhood a happy one.

I was an exceptionally keen reader from an early age on and books were my favourite and most often requested Christmas or birthday and nameday (mine were separated by one day and celebrated at the same time) present. I am not trying to brag about my intellectual inclinations when I was a child. There were no particularly attractive toys available and clothes were even less desirable as a present. Books, on the other hand, were widely available, relatively inexpensive and there were too many of them to ever make me feel that I had enough. Even though my mother was a librarian, she never really made me borrow library books. She always bought books I requested and very early on I had my own bookcase and my own collection of books. I learned to read before I started school which may have been why I started school one year in advance. I felt the need to learn to read since my grandmother, the one who spent evenings swearing at TV news, often fell asleep while reading to me before reaching the end of a story. I loved the children's edition of the *Tales from the Thousand and One Nights*, exquisitely published with illustrations in vibrant colours, ornamented with gold. I knew some tales by heart and I think I learned to read by looking at the text and telling myself the story from memory. I do not remember how it happened, but I was soon able to read the text myself. I am somewhat ashamed to admit that I particularly enjoyed those passages from the *Tales from the Thousand and One Nights* that involved splendid descriptions of jewels and other exotic riches, which filled the book. This must be the reason why I always liked shiny gemstones and bling.

Jan Brzechwa had a very special place among my favourite authors. His poems for little children use simple, but colourful language and his prose creates a parallel world, outside the limitations of time and space. I am not sure when I read the first of my Mr. Kleks stories, *The Triumph of Mr. Kleks*, which was in fact the last one in the series of three. It was published in 1965 and so I must have been given it for my birthday or for Christmas shortly after its publication. I read the first two volumes, *The Academy of Mr. Kleks* and *The Travels of Mr. Kleks*, much later, probably when I was in high school. They were first published in 1946 and 1961 respectively and were not widely available in the late 1960s. *The Academy of Mr. Kleks*, written during World War II and published in 1946, does not make any direct reference to political or social hardship associated with the war. Perhaps the only exception is the story of Mateusz, a prince turned into a talking blackbird, who had witnessed the utter destruction of his kingdom and the death of his parents after an attack by wolves. Although the story is referred to as a fairy tale even by its own characters, it is unclear where and when it takes place. And it does not really matter. Brzechwa's ingenuity in creating a captivating story and setting it in an imaginative world are enough to keep the reader coming back. The stories reveal new layers of meaning with each subsequent reading. There is nothing of the sad and grey reality of the socialism in Brzechwa's stories for children even though, soon after the war, he had apparently also written socialist realist poems glorifying the communist system. Nevertheless, for me, Brzechwa remains a treasury of ideas that inspired my imagination, brightened my childhood, and that gave me many beautiful memories. These stories in my opinion measure up to Harry Potter and are certainly worth translating for a wider audience. I adored Professor Ambrose Kleks so much that I named my second schnauzer Professor Klex. He too looks a lot like an ink blot.

I could have never imagined that my favourite children's writer could possibly attract any serious criticism, especially in modern times. Yet, I came across a 2007 unsigned article in *Wiadomości* (April 26, 2007, page 12), entitled "Red Card for Jan Brzechwa". The illustration for that article is a young man dressed like a soccer referee, with a (presumably, it is a black and white picture) red card in his right hand. His jersey has letters *LPR*, an abbreviation that in April 2007 would be easily deciphered as standing for *Liga Polskich Rodzin* (League of Polish Families), a populist, right wing, nationalist party, at that point part of the governing coalition. Incidentally, the leader of that party was at that time the Minister of Education. The article would be almost funny if it was meant as a satire on the ultra nationalism of the *LPR*. As unlikely and surreal the text is, I am afraid it was meant as serious and it illustrates the political climate of the Poland's Fourth Republic.

The author—whom other Internet sources identify as Mariusz Urbanek, a publicist and writer from Wrocław—mounts accusations, starting with "revealing" Brzechwa's "real" name, Lesman, which is an accusation in itself as it sounds foreign. German? Jewish? Not Polish enough? I used quotation marks around some words in the previous sentence to indicate either the fact of quoting (e.g., the word "real" or the unstated intention of the author, e.g., "revealing"). However, Urbanek himself uses an abundance of so called "ironic quotation marks", whose intention is to indicate his doubts as to the alleged quality of the characteristics described. And so Brzechwa becomes a "God have mercy 'poet'" (I use double quotation marks to indicate a quote and single quotation marks where the author was using the ironic double quote—I know it is confusing). He is "scruple-less in poisoning young Polish minds with the virus of 'inferiority'." There is, in Urbanek's opinion, "no need to say, who, according to the poet by the name Lesman, only hiding behind the pen name Brzechwa the 'superior ones' are." Obviously, the reader is also expected to know who they are. Who are they?

The reason for the article was that the League of Polish Families demanded the removal of Brzechwa's name from the list of eligible patrons of Polish streets, schools, and kindergartens, a demand Urbanek does not seem to dispute. Because Brzechwa wrote some 50 years ago or so, Urbanek hastens to assure us that a poem about a weird duck (*Kaczka Dziwaczka*) could be read as a direct satire with allusions to the Kaczyński twins (popularly referred to as Ducks because their last name derives from the word *kaczka*, 'duck'). Instead, Urbanek explains, it is because of the "seemingly innocent poems through which Lesman-Brzechwa for many decades trickled the venom of inferiority complexes, lack of faith in the might of the nation, and godlessness." Urbanek then proceeds to give the reader some examples of the venom-trickling poems that Brzechwa wrote. We find among them the most popular poems for children where characteristics such as bragging (the poem *Samochwała w kącie stała*), laziness (*Na tapczanie siedzi leń*), lying, etc. were represented in a witty way, easily understandable for young readers. Other poems, e.g., the one where someone makes an economically poor exchange of an ax for a stick allegedly expose Brzechwa's criticism of the Polish economy. The entire text would be truly hilarious if printed in a satirical magazine. In a normal daily newspaper, it was frightening.

There would be little purpose in my extensive quoting from this outrageous article (which by the way triggered a lot of online discussions focusing on the stupidity of the *LPR's* ideas about education—with the leader of *LPR* being the Minister of Education these ideas were not funny) except to demonstrate how, in the year 2007, it made use of many typical linguistic mechanisms of communist propaganda. The text mixes the *LPR's* justification for the demand to remove Brzechwa's name and Urbanek's own opinions. It is possible that linguistic remnants from communist times were the property of the *LPR* document. The effect is nevertheless overwhelming. One feels as if one is stepping back in time.

During the martial law period, I observed that propaganda articles were using a particularly high incidence of negation. Instead of saying "X is our enemy," they would say that "X is not our friend." In 1982, I once bought a copy of a particularly pro-military junta paper called *Rzeczywistość* in order to investigate this impression on some printed data. As the paper was really an example of a pure 'venom trickling' propaganda, I felt I had to somehow distance myself from the very act of buying it and that I had to justify my action in the eyes of the salesperson at the newspaper vending kiosk. I asked how much it was and added that I never buy such material, but I needed it for research, or something along those lines. I don't think the newspaper vendor cared, but my need for self-justification indicates that I assumed everyone was against the junta and the martial law. This was likely only partially true.

When reading articles in that copy of *Rzeczywistość,* I started to underline all uses of negation and in particular the word *nie* (no/not*)*. There were indeed so many that, after a few minutes, my underlining became mechanical and I ended up underlining the word *niedziela* ('Sunday', literally the day of 'no work"). The same overabundance of negation could be found in Mariusz Urbanek's article. I cannot tell whether the negation came from the original *LPR* document (it might) or whether it was the style of the author (I hope it was not). The effect was the familiar confusion of communist negative discourse. One needs to add here that Polish is a language which regularly uses double (or triple or quadruple) negation and where you could amass any number of negative words in one, perfectly grammatical and stylistically correct sentence. We could quote here from Jan Brzechwa, the poet himself, whose early poem is cited in the article as an example of praise for the Soviet style *kolkhoz* economy: *Nikt na nikim nie zarabia* (literally, 'no one is not making profit of no one', i.e., 'no one is making profit of anyone'). This natural tendency to multiple negation is not the same as the negative representation of positive situations typical for communist newspaper discourse. This last sentence could perhaps be seen as an illustration for this phenomenon: I could have said that "this natural tendency to multiple negation is *different than* the negative representation of everything, typical for communist newspaper discourse." Here again I seem to be hypocritical when criticizing others.

When someone says: "and those who do not hesitate to refuse brotherly help are not the true friends of ours," it takes the reader (and especially the listener) considerable effort to calculate the negations and figure out the meaning. In my, admittedly naive view, the main reason for this use of language is to make it more convoluted (Orwell's principle of plain language being visibly violated) and to actually help people to switch off. It is practically impossible to listen to speeches written in that kind of language, especially where the same message is repeated time after time in somewhat different words.

I have my own proof for the content emptiness of communist propaganda texts.

After two years of studying in the German Department, I gave up any hope of ever switching to Art History and decided I liked the study of linguistics better than I liked the study of literature. I loved reading, but I read for pleasure and I preferred to arrive at my own interpretations rather than listen to what other people wanted me to see in literary texts. Therefore, after my second year of studies, I took another special entrance examination and was accepted to the third year of studies in the Institute of Applied Linguistics, just one floor up in the same building. The Institute's director, Professor Franciszek Grucza, looked like a former heavyweight champion in boxing. However, he must have shown a lot of finesse at assuring funding for the Institute because for the next three years I felt as if I were attending an elite institution. The Institute specialized in translation. We had a mini conference room, with equipment to teach simultaneous translation. We also had access to Western teaching materials, really excellent teachers, high-tech language labs, and classes in small groups. The Institute accepted only ten students per language a year. One of my teachers there was Dr. Barbara Jaruzelska, then (late 1970s) wife of the Polish Minister of National Defence. Later, he became the infamous general in dark glasses who introduced martial law. Dr. Jaruzelska was a warm and caring teacher, with good Western tapes for us to listen to. She hardly ever spoke German to us but I benefited from her language classes anyway, in more ways than she could have anticipated.

It was not in her class, but in a consecutive translation class with Dr. Elżbieta Kaźmierczak that I made my little 'discovery' about the empty nature of newspaper discourse. We were translating some texts from the East German party paper *Neues Deutschland* into Polish. It had to do with something or other that the *ruhmreiche Rote Armee* (glorious Red Army) had done during World War II and how it was remembered and celebrated at some party rally in East Germany. My class was quite skillful at putting that kind of stuff into the equivalent Polish political discourse and we could produce texts about *okryta chwałą Armia Czerwona* (i.e., the glorious Red Army) in our sleep—I am talking about our translation skills, not about our political beliefs. After a while our teacher switched to a Polish text from the Polish communist daily *Trybuna Ludu* and here we went, translating similarly general statements about some party rally into German. The difference was that, German being a foreign language for me, I was only able to say the same thing in two or three ways. I was forced to stop at the fourth sentence conveying the same pseudo message but in different words. I did not know more adjectival synonyms in German and, obviously, I could not simply repeat myself or say: "Well, it's just more of the same." I was stuck. Our teacher was not a communist. She did not give us those texts to translate because she believed in the content. If we were to do conference translation or if we were to translate for some foreign delegation, this was the language we needed to master. She was pragmatic. She was also an excellent teacher and the first person to tell me that I was good at consecutive translation. I used to have an incredibly good memory and could memorize almost anything. Remembering several sentences to be translated was not a problem and I was able to regularly surprise people with my ability to repeat long lists of names, countries, languages in a language family, etc. Now, my memory is no longer as good but I still immensely enjoy translation in any form or format. The closest I get to professional consecutive or simultaneous translation is my court interpretation in Ontario and my teaching of translation courses. If I do any of it well, the credit definitely goes to my teachers at the Warsaw Institute of Applied Linguistics.

We did not practice literary translation during my studies, but this was my true interest. When I read the books about Mr. Kleks, I always thought of translating them into other languages. What could Mr. Kleks be called in English? Mr. Inkstain? Mr. Inkblot? In German, could it be Professor *Tintenfleck*? I liked Inkstain best. It had a German sound, like Inkstein. Did I think, like the article by Mariusz Urbanek implied, that Mr. Kleks was German or Jewish? No, such thoughts crossed my mind. I could not care less about people's ethnicities. But Inkstein went well with his title: "Doctor of Secret Sciences," which in turn reminds me of Harry Potter, Professor Snape and the Dark Arts, even though Mr. Kleks' secret sciences had no evil connotations.

I think I liked Mr. Kleks so much because of the contrast it provided to many books we had to read in school. Some time ago, with my cousins who also settled in Canada and are just a few years younger (which means that our school programmes were basically the same), we went through a long list of readings that seemed to be designed to make children feel miserable. We were reminiscing about the poor blind horse *Łysek z pokładu Idy* (by Gustaw Morcinek), working in some coal mine, and another one, remembered only as "our old mare" *Nasza szkapa* (by Maria Konopnicka). We remembered the little orphan girl Marysia and the dwarfs, *O krasnoludkach i sierotce Marysi* (also by Maria Konopnicka), and how everyone was always hungry in that book. I really hated it as a child. Then there was *Janko Muzykant* (by Henryk Sienkiewicz), about a little peasant boy who wanted to play music but who died in his childhood, and a little girl, Rozalka who burned in an oven where some old woman told her mother to put her to heal her from her sickness (in *Antek* by Boleslaw Prus). There were also foreign books selected to fit the same path of individual suffering: there was the little boy Nemecek in the Hungarian book by Ferenc Molnár *The Paul Street Boys* (*Chłopcy z Placu Broni)*, and the little boy from Florence who spent his nights copying something to financially help his poor parents. Actually, this last book, *Heart* by Edmondo De Amicis, originally translated by Maria Konopnicka (the one who wrote about Marysia, the little orphan girl), has been recently retranslated into Polish. I wonder whether this new translation makes it any less tragic. After going through this list of childhood horrors, my cousins and I felt that perhaps we should sue the Polish People's Republic for our pain and suffering as children and for our pessimism and depression in adult life.

All those stories, written well before the communist times and usually by well-meaning and socially engaged writers, were not bad literature. On the contrary, some were brilliant. After all, both Henryk Sienkiewicz and Władysław Reymont won Nobel Prizes for Literature. It was just that our compulsory reading list was jam-packed with those socially engaged books full of death and poverty and social injustice that made them insufferable. This reading list, paired with the less-than-rosy reality surrounding us made some children despair. Part of my negative attitude was that these literary pieces, taken *en masse*, gave such a gloomy picture of Poland (and Europe) before the war that one was forced to believe in the necessity of the communist revolution to right the injustices and to end the suffering of all those children. Did I ever consider that maybe things simply were not good before the war? Yes, but any picture that is black and white is a simplification and a reduction of reality, with all the shades of grey eliminated. What I did not like was the primitive, cartoon-like stereotyping involved in the interpretation imposed by our communist education. Class membership alone determined whether someone was good or bad. There was no difference here between assigning character features based on class membership or based on race, ethnicity, or religion. Stereotyping robs reality of its natural complexity.

My friend Kasia recently told me that once, in elementary school, after reading *Janko Muzykant*, she confronted her parents demanding to know whether her family ever contributed to the suffering of peasants. Janko Muzykant (Janko the Musician) was a peasant boy who wanted to play the violin. Fascinated by the instrument, he entered the house of a wealthy landowner to admire it but was accused of attempted theft and died as a result of severe and unjust flagellation. Kasia was outraged that her grandparents could have been wealthy landowners guilty of death of little children.

In his *Notes on Nationalism*, George Orwell (1945) describes the emotion he labels as 'nationalism' for the lack of a better term.

This emotion, he explains,

> ...does not always attach itself to what is called a nation—that is, a single race or a geographical area. It can attach itself to a church or a class, or it may work in a merely negative sense, *against* something or other and without the need for any positive object of loyalty.
>
> By 'nationalism' I mean first of all the habit of assuming that human beings can be classified like insects and that whole blocks of millions or tens of millions of people can be confidently labelled 'good' or 'bad'. But secondly—and this is much more important—I mean the habit of identifying oneself with a single nation or other unit, placing it beyond good and evil and recognizing no other duty than that of advancing its interests.

If I were to explain, as a child, what I disliked about those compulsory readings, I would have to admit that I only had a very vague idea. However, I knew that I was really bothered by this sense of being told to read a text and to interpret it in a class-based fashion. Maybe I detested people who were always right, people who would never take the blame or admit that they might have been wrong, and people who overused the superlative. Jane Austin has created many outstanding caricatures of this type of personality in her books. It seems times have changed, but people's characters remain the same.

Apart from Mr. Kleks, my other favourite childhood literary hero was *Pan Samochodzik* (literally Mr. Little Automobile), an art historian turned detective, employed by the Ministry of Culture and Art. Pan Samochodzik devoted his time to finding lost art treasures. These books combined historical information with good adventure writing, even though they contained many socialist elements (the author, Zbigniew Nienacki (1929-1994) was a member of The Communist Party) and often portrayed foreign competitors and adversaries in a rather stereotypical way. I would compare the author of that book series to Dan Brown. Mr. Samochodzik tackled some of the most interesting historical secrets, such as that of the lost Amber Room, treasures of the knights Templar, and many others. The combination of mystery, archeology, an intelligent hero, beautiful women, and the secrets of a fantastic old car that gave Mr. Samochodzik his strange nickname was very attractive and much more believable than Indiana Jones movies or Dan Brown's books. Yet, the books also taught the young readers that art treasures rightfully belonged to the state and that money could not buy everything. Mr. Samochodzik often travelled abroad but also always returned to Poland and his low-paying ministry job.

Another writer I liked was Alfred Szklarski (1912-1992). He wrote about a boy, Tomek Wilmowski, whose father had to flee pre-WWI Poland (or rather the Russian-occupied part of the partitioned country) to avoid persecution for conspiring against the Tsarist government. The son joins him and both travel around the world and live through many adventures. While Nienacki wrote about art and history, Szklarski wrote about nature and geography. Both sets of books were a great reading for a teenager, with captivating plots and appealing characters. Unfortunately, they were never translated into English even though they would have a chance to become quite popular in the West. They taught kids about important values without preaching and without direct references to current politics.

One other lovely book for children that I still cherish and which I read to my own children when they were little was *Ferdinand the Magnificent* (*Ferdynand Wspaniały* by Ludwik Jerzy Kern), a story about the adventures of a dog—a great Dane, I think—who starts walking on two legs and everyone assumes that he is human. His adventures are sweet and good humoured and everyone he meets is so kind to him that he spends the entire day not having to pay for anything. I particularly enjoyed the scene when a tailor takes measurements for Ferdinand's suit and asks questions about the details, such as the fabric, lapels, and buttons. To each question of the kind "And what kind of fabric would you like me to use?" Ferdinand replies—"A pretty one." The tailor says at the end that he had never encountered a customer who would know so well what exactly he wanted. The entire adventure turns out to be only a dream, but the book is simply a happy one with no pretence of historical or social significance.

If I were to summarize what I liked in children's literature when I was growing up, I would say: imagination and goodness. I wanted people to be good to each other, friends to be loyal, love to be forever. I liked happy endings. In fact, I still do. I did not like anyone dying or suffering. I also did not like bad people to go unpunished, but I did not like good people to deliver the punishment because it tarnished their purity. Natural disasters were best for taking care of 'the bad guy'. Someone might say that this may be in part the legacy of communism, but I think that is too far of a stretch.

The most lasting influence in terms of values I cherished in people when I was growing up came from war literature. Not from the books we had to read at school, about the Polish pro-communist underground army or about fighting Ukrainian partisans, but the documentary books my parents read. They were about the Home Army and the scouts, about people not much older than I was, dying for what they believed in. I also read Tadeausz Borowski's stories about Auschwitz, I watched films about the Warsaw Uprising. That was the kind of literature where death had its proper place. People were giving their lives for a cause or by a tragic twist of fate, not for an educational purpose or simply to make me cry. I hated people who made me cry to suit a pedagogical purpose. I resented being manipulated. I cried reading those documentary books that no one, not even my parents told me to read. They simply were at home, waiting, and so I read them.

In a very naive way, I thought that there was something beautiful and romantic about Solidarność entering an uneven fight against the Polish military junta in December 1981 and the months that followed. We engaged in some small-scale activity of hiding friends who were wanted by police, distributing news bulletins, collecting money and then working for St. Marcin's (St. Martin's) church. I did it because it was what I felt I should have been doing but I also believed that this was my generation's turn to fight the evil. If I had been offered a chance to be more active in resistance, I would have. At the same time, I was also at times afraid that by getting involved I might have to pay a price I was not prepared to pay. I was conscious of what that price was.

When I started to work for the Committee for Defence of Political Prisoners at St. Marcin's Church in Warsaw, we—the group of new volunteers—had a meeting with an attorney, also a volunteer, to prepare us for the possibility of an arrest and to teach us about our rights and also about common sense behaviour if such a situation were to arise. He took us outside, to a spot on the Old Town city walls (the rooms at the church could have been bugged) and gave us a lot of useful information. What I remember best was his request to define for ourselves what was truly important in our lives. What was my most valuable 'possession'—a person or a thing? He said that we needed to be aware that this was likely what the interrogator would threaten us about: if it was so important to us, someone could have reported it to the security authorities. I am sure that 'family' would have been high on anyone's agenda and so it was for me although my mother was retired, my father passed away years before, and I really had no siblings who could lose their jobs. My husband was just starting to work and my father-in-law was enough of an expert in his field to think that he would not be endangered by anything I could do. I had two very weak spots that I was aware of. I really wanted to complete my PhD and continue with my academic career; I could quite well imagine that an arrest could prevent that. Also, I was twenty something and I really wanted to have children. If faced with the alternative of spending time in jail, which could perhaps make it impossible for me to continue my education or bear children, or of doing something I thought was unethical, what would I choose? When I read about heroes who died for what they believed, I always wanted to believe that I too would have made the right choice. But would I? I could not live with myself if I betrayed my ideals. I truly wanted to be able to always look at myself in the mirror without contempt. Quite honestly, I did not want to face the dilemma. I felt that no one should have the right to make me choose. I wanted out of the country where I would have to potentially make such decisions. This, truly, was the reason I left Poland and this is the reason why, so far, I do not feel like returning.

When I lived in Scotland, I was amazed by the horror content in stories for children and in folk tales. Later, I was puzzled by the attraction exerted by places such as London Dungeons or the Chamber of Horrors at Madame Tussaud's. The evil in human nature is interesting to study, but it is not a source of entertainment for me. The history of my part of Europe was much too violent to ever think that way. This is also why the tradition of Halloween has been so difficult to accept for many Poles, both those in Poland and those living in countries like Canada. Death is not something to take lightly. In Poland, the Grimm Brothers' fairy tales were edited for children, resembling more their Disney versions than the often very-bloody original stories. I read the original versions in a prewar Polish edition as a university student but I read their censored versions as a child and admit I liked them better that way.

I was once given a fairy tale called *Bluebeard*. I may have been six or seven years old at that time. I am not sure whose gift idea it was, but it was not my parents'. I read the book, with all its suspense, up to the moment when the young queen enters the forbidden chamber and sees the dead bodies of Bluebeard's other wives and I could not read any further. I put the book under my bed. Then, still scared by its physical presence, as if it were cursed, I hid it under the wardrobe. I could not fall asleep until my mother assured me that she had removed the book from the house. I hated the feeling of fear instilled in me by the author. This was the only book that has ever made me so frightened that I could not distinguish between the medium and the message.

When our children were young, they shared a bedroom and in the evening my husband and I would take turns reading to them. First, we only used Polish at home and so the stories we read to them were in Polish. When they started school, we would also read English books, but Polish children's literature always had its proper place to make sure the children learned the language. They became familiar with many Polish children's classics we ourselves enjoyed as children. My husband is a great fan of Sienkiewicz, particularly of his *Trilogy* and, within it, particularly of *Potop* (The Deluge). Once, when it was his turn to read, he chose *Potop* as the next reading. The children were at that point already familiar with another book by Sienkiewicz, *W pustyni i w puszczy (In Desert and Wilderness)* and so we did not consider this a bad choice. I read *Trilogy* with burning cheeks over the summer holidays one year in Grade 6 or 7 and loved its fast-flowing action and plot full of unexpected turns. Yet, after a page or two my husband stopped reading. First of all, there were too many archaic Polish words that required explanation, thus putting the children to sleep almost immediately. Also, the imagery was so brutal and ethnic references so politically incorrect that we decided to switch to another book instead. The world has changed or maybe we just moved to a part of it where this kind of writing would not appeal to children. Thankfully, a language barrier concealed the brutality of the opening scene and instead put them to sleep.

Were Western books for children available in Poland? Yes, and between Kasia's home library and mine, we had a good selection of children's classics, from *Alice in Wonderland*, *Winnie the Pooh*, *The Secret Garden*, Karl May's books about the American Old West, *Anne of Green Gables*, adventures of Sherlock Holmes and novels by Agatha Christie. We read *Dr. Doolittle* and *Mary Poppins*. Of course, we read them in Polish. My favourite in that group was *A Little Princess* by Frances Hodgson Burnett, also the author of the *Secret Garden*, and Edith Nesbit's books *Five Children and It* and others. I also enjoyed several of the books about Anne by Lucy Maud Montgomery. I think that by reading those imaginative and lively books in my free time I learned to enjoy reading, something that all those pain and suffering books at school would not have taught me. Interestingly, I do not recall any Russian books for children that I read. Later, I discovered Dostoevski, Bulgakov and Venedikt Jerofejev (who wrote what I once thought to be a hilarious account of a drunken train journey from Moscow to Petushki) but I was already past my childhood.

Sometime in the late 1960s or early 1970s, my mother received a carbon copy of a typed translation of George Orwell's *Animal Farm* in the mail. The Polish translation of *Animal Farm*, first published in 1956 in Munich by Radio Free Europe, is normally attributed to Teresa Jeleńska. The name of the translator was not listed on the copy that came in the mail. It was typed on tissue thin copy paper. My mother thought that the translation could have been done by one of the ladies who worked with her at the library, but I don't think she ever asked her about it. I don't know what happened to that manuscript and so I cannot check whether someone retranslated the book or whether he or she 'only' retyped the foreign-published (and unavailable in Poland) translation by Jeleńska. The translated title for *Animal Farm* certainly contained the word *Folwark*, but I do not remember whether it was *Folwark zwierzęcy* (Jeleńska's translation), *Zwierzęcy folwark* (the title of the first published edition), or, as I am inclined to believe, *Folwark zwierząt*. I immediately read the text, prepared for a fairy tale as the title suggested. I loved the book and never forgot its impact on me. Its moral message was put in such a simple way that a child could understand it, even if this understanding was not fully and properly based on the knowledge of its historical and political references.

I read *1984* much later, probably in 1978 or 1979, this time in English. Polish translations of Orwell, as well as all kinds of books previously impossible to obtain or forbidden (which was basically the same thing) became widely available after 1980 when many independent publishing houses came into operation. After the imposition of martial law in December 1981, the possession of such books became illegal again. In early May 1982, our apartment was searched by police. They found and confiscated the English copy of *1984* and some other books published by independent publishers, among them the *Psalms*, translated by Czesław Miłosz. Joking with my husband, we laughed that at least they did not take away our typewriter (but they took a sample imprint of its letters) or pencils. The fact that we had so many books kept them busy longer than they were planning. I almost felt like offering them tea, but thought it inappropriate. They were not guests. We had a quotation from Lenin on one of the bookcases: "A police state is a state where a policeman earns more than a teacher." They did not tell us to take it down. It was, after all, Lenin.

My love for books has always driven me to buy more books than I have time to read. I also used to buy a lot of books for my children, just like my mother used to buy books for me. Nothing made me happier than when they asked for a book. I am always running out of shelf space and always despair that there are more books out there than I can possibly read. I am a compulsive reader. I always have a book with me just in case I have the pleasure of having to wait for someone or something.

If I don't have a book, I read all that there is to read around me which effectively drives me insane when I am using any mode of transportation anywhere in Poland. Polish highways are inundated by hundreds and hundreds of signs of various sizes, advertising everything that can be bought or consumed in nearby villages and towns. There are so many of them that it is truly impossible to read them all when in a moving car or bus. My desire to do just that verges on an almost insatiable need. This information overload makes the landscape invisible behind the wall of signs and, along with the persistent chaos of building permits and general mess of urban planning makes Poland look like a third world country. I used to keep begging my husband to slow down not only because driving in Poland was dangerous, but also because I simply could not read fast enough.

When my children started to read for their English classes in elementary school and later in high school in Canada, I always tried to get hold of the books they read. I considered it important to be able to discuss the books with them and I felt that it was also part of my transition to becoming a Canadian myself. However, my children, two grades apart, often read different books. Apparently, there is not one centrally planned list of Canadian compulsory school readings. Or, if there is one (in fact, I am sure there is one), it is long enough to allow some variety and some teacher's choice. For me, the advantage was a larger selection of books for me to enjoy.

What we read and watch as children stays with us not only through our childhood but often through our entire life. Some memories are distorted but even these distortions play a role. Sometimes it is not what we remember but how we were made to remember something that is potentially significant. When I left Poland and started my PhD studies at the University of Edinburgh, I spent the first several months in the university library trying to read everything I thought had anything to do with linguistics or any other of my interests. That I was able to walk among bookcases, look at the books, pull them out, page through them and touch them was entirely new to me in academic sense. In fact, it was not really new, but familiar in a very special way. As a child, I used to run between very tall and old bookcases at the library where my mother worked, at the Main School of Agriculture (SGGW). When I visited her at the library, I was allowed to venture everywhere. I visited various ladies working there, had my special friends among them who would show me interesting things or simply allow me to play with their typewriters, rubber stamps, etc. During my student years, on the other hand, I spent many hours in the (old) Warsaw University library, but was never allowed to the secret and sacred part of the collection where the books were housed. Only the reference collection was directly accessible to the public. After going through the card index, writing down what I thought I wanted on a special order slip called *dezyderata*, and giving the order to the librarian on duty, I would wait an hour or so to get the books that had to be located and brought to the front desk by another librarian. Many times, I found myself frustrated when I eventually obtained the book because it had nothing to do with my research problem. The fact that, in Edinburgh, I was finally able to endlessly walk around that sacred inner temple of the university library and see for myself what the books were about was a revelation. I thought I would never have enough of it. Even today, when I go to the library to get a specific book, I usually end up leaving with five or six other books I spotted on my way. When I worked for a year and a half as a researcher at Kingston University in London, I did the same, only to be told that my borrowing limit was ten books and I would be over my limit if I took out all the books I wanted to borrow. The soft-spoken librarian added: "You cannot be reading all of these books at the same time anyway." Well, maybe I can. Or maybe books have a fetish status for me, I need them around, they form my safety zone, a familiar environment.

The second book-related revelation I experienced after I left Poland was of a different nature. I discovered during my PhD studies that I considered the printed word, especially by a respectable writer, as something authoritative. If it had been published, it must have been a valid opinion. In fact, it pretty much must have been the truth, I thought. Of course, there were some books not to be taken seriously as they were ideology rather than science, but everything else was as solid knowledge as if it were literally carved in stone. I was prepared to learn from it, interpret it, but I was not ready to challenge it. Who was I to challenge a book? In Edinburgh, I saw postgraduate students and professors in the Department of Linguistics take apart various theories, critically analyze them, and challenge what they thought was not correct. I was not just astonished; in some ways the very foundation of my worldview was shaken. It meant that scientists did not know everything—that science (including linguistics, the science of language) was not a finished product that I could simply master. I understood that my task as a PhD student was to add to that already collected body of knowledge, but, in my view, that did not include showing that parts of that structure needed to be demolished and rebuilt. To witness theories being worked out and published, only to be reworked and republished in a new form or version was an unbelievable experience. To see that some of my examples from Polish syntax or morphology could make some of the theories under construction collapse, only to be reformulated in such a way that my counterexamples would be accounted for, was like a breath of fresh air. There was still work to be done. Linguistics was not a finished product. In fact, it is one of the most unfinished products in the manufacture of science as we still know very little about many aspects of language acquisition, loss, or representation in the human brain. I fully realize how silly and naive my beliefs were, but there is no point in denying them. I was a product of my upbringing and my education. I had to take a good look at myself and adapt to the new situation.

I wonder where my belief that whatever has been published must have a high degree of authority has come from. I can see two sources for it. One was the fact that my father had an extensive medical library, with many books in German, printed before WWI. Some may have been his textbooks from the time he studied medicine at the University in Lwów. Lwów, now Lviv in Ukraine, was in the part of Poland occupied by Austria and so the language of education was German, until 1918. Had my father lived longer, I would have learned that he had to keep on top of medical developments—he was reading medical journals and receiving pamphlets from pharmaceutical companies in Germany and Switzerland. But as a child, I did not understand it. I assumed those old German textbooks represented the ultimate, unchangeable wisdom. The other reason could have something to do with the fact that throughout school and university, we all had to read the same selected books.

Even if we did not like them, we did not challenge the way they were selected and so we probably ended up believing that there are some books that are unquestionably valuable readings for children or students. Also, the books that were selected allowed for some range of interpretations, but not for challenge. Some people liked the little orphan girl Marysia, some did not like her. There was nothing to agree or disagree about. No one even tried to persuade us that we should like those readings. Michał Głowiński, Polish expert on communist Newspeak, observed that totalitarian propaganda does not try to persuade the audience of anything. It gives orders on how to behave and what to think. Persuasion assumes a potentially active role of the audience. Propaganda forces its audience into passive reception of commands (Głowiński 1996, 241-42). The mock essay topic for Polish literature classes was "What do we love this or that great poet for?" It was not whether we do but why we do. No controversy. No need to look critically. I have to add that this mock essay title comes from a pre-war novel *Ferdydurke* by Witold Gombrowicz (1937). In it, Gombrowicz pokes fun at many Polish national traditions, including the religious reverence for patriotic writing of some of our literary masters. Even though the book made fun of Polish pre-war society, it was blacklisted in communist Poland, maybe because it was funny. We read it in our Grade 12 Polish class with Miss Rożalska who introduced our class to several unorthodox readings. There was little humour in our other compulsory readings. That too made it easier to keep students within the limits and lines of a prescribed interpretation.

If we were taught anything about rhetoric and argumentation, it was at most how to argue a point, not how to argue against someone else's point. In fact, the arguments of the other side were hardly ever given. They were condemned *en bloc*, but not analyzed or discussed. It is a bit like the opening scene in the film adaptation of Orwell's *1984*. It shows the Two-Minutes Hate. On a large screen, we see the face of Emmanuel Goldstein, the Enemy of the People. We see his lips move, but the fanatical screams of the audience, their hisses and shouts drown the words of Goldstein. In the book, it is only towards the end of the two minutes that the hate rises first to a frenzy, with the voice no longer audible and then to its climax, with the face on the screen dissolving and transforming into the figure of a Eurasian soldier who seemed to be advancing, huge and terrible, his sub-machine gun roaring, and seeming to spring out of the surface of the screen. In the book, the arguments are spelled out but described as just plausible enough to fill one with an alarmed feeling that other people, less level-headed than oneself, might be taken in by them. This is, I guess, why it is safer not to provide the 'enemy' with the opportunity to present their point of view. We do not need to know what they are saying; it is much easier to simply know they are wrong. I strongly believe some Polish problems today, many years after the collapse of the communist system, still result from our inability to discuss things properly, to argue both for but also (in a civilized way) against ideas. I do not mean quarrel but to present a line of argument: a set of assumptions, premises, and consequences. We don't know how to agree to disagree, to accept that we may still leave some problems unresolved, that we may end up with an unfinished problem. It is much easier to use *ad hominem* argumentation and attack the very person of our opponent, either because we don't like them or because we do not like what they stand for, just as I did not like the little orphan girl Marysia in Maria Konopnicka's book.

CHAPTER 8

Pouring Water

I DO NOT RECALL anyone telling me how to speak when asked questions about Polish history in school or, for the most part, what to say and what not to say. Yet, I was always aware there were things I should not say in school and there were things I was expected to say and write. Some of the effects of propaganda can only be analyzed through honest introspection. I believe that there is an important lesson to be learned from understanding how language distortion seeps into people throughout their lives, starting at a very young age. If this chapter seems too personal or too anecdotal, this is because my own thoughts on language distortion are the best and most reliable material that is available to me.

I think the only instance when I had ever been specifically instructed not to talk about something the way it was talked about at home was the infamous murder of several thousand Polish officers, prisoners of war, by the Soviets in Katyń. The official version attributed this murder to the Germans, claiming it happened in 1941 or 1942 while 'every child knew' (as we say in Polish) that it had happened in 1940 when the area was still in Soviet hands. Even though the truth about Katyń was an established fact during the Nuremberg trials, it was only recently that Russia accepted some of the blame for the crime. Until 2009, the Katyń tragedy remained a symbolic point of contention between Poland and Russia. In 2008, a Russian court declared that Katyń murder could not be prosecuted as a political murder as there had been no specific order of the Soviet authorities to that effect. Indeed, the orders may not have been issued at any public or official forum but there is historical evidence that the proposal to eliminate Polish officers had been discussed and approved. To add even more insult to injury, the 2008 court verdict also stated that only the victims themselves, i.e., the murdered officers, had the right to appeal this decision. I can almost picture the upheaval this decision must have caused in heaven. I think I was instructed not to talk about Katyń because my parents did not want me to repeat the official version and knew that talking about the true course of events could bring some form of school-related punishment. As I mentioned earlier, my father was very lucky not to have ended in Katyń himself after he was taken prisoner of war by the Soviets in September 1939.

Despite the lack of overt instruction, I quickly became a very skillful practitioner of the juvenile version of Polish Newspeak, at least at the level of elementary and high school education. We called this particular skill *lać wodę* (the ability to pour water). When I think about this metaphor today, I see its meaning as related to the fact that water increases volume, for example when added to soup. It also seems to lack substance, exactly like what we had to write in essays or say when called upon in class. I was quite good at writing essays about pretty much anything, using big words and convoluted syntactic structures. I could vary my register, from dramatic to reflexive. Communist ideology in the elementary or high school version, in subjects such as Polish literature or history, seemed to me to lack any real substance, just like water, and I had little respect for the few 'facts' that may have been presented. Unfortunately, I overgeneralized this approach to the history of modern working-class movements, simply by analogy. My high school history teacher, nicknamed Brzuch (Belly) due to his protruding stomach, did not seem to care much about historical facts pertaining to ancient Egypt or the French Revolution. He usually read directly from the textbook in class and the student at the front of the classroom, whose desk was touching the teacher's desk, was often entrusted with the task of flipping pages when Brzuch wasn't looking. Brzuch would then start reading from a completely different chapter and everyone in class would have a chuckle. His lack of attention to his surroundings was also likely responsible for the amusing heading of a wall display in his classroom, referring to the length of the 1939 military campaign in Poland that lasted from September 1, when the Germans attacked Poland to October 5, when Hitler received German military parade in Warsaw. The heading read, "35 days of September." It stayed on the wall for many weeks. Clearly, it did not occur to Brzuch to ever look at it more closely. More than once, when asked about names of the political figures from a specific historical period, I would invent them on the spot, making sure that they sounded French when talking about French history or English when talking about British or American history, and, I regret to admit, I was never caught by Brzuch. I tried to do the same when asked about the names of those who were part of the first communist government of Poland, formed in Lublin in 1944. While I was standing there, inventing the names the same way I did for previous epochs and assuming that there must have been some *Kowalskis* (Polish equivalent of Smith) there, I got an immediate and angry reaction from Brzuch: "What kind of nonsense are you telling me, Piotrowska? Sit down." Clearly, for Brzuch, communist history did not allow for pouring water.

The other class that seemed to lack any substance other than empty ideology was Military Preparation. The building of Elementary School Number 93 which I attended in Grades 7 and 8 was physically attached to my future high school. Since a teacher was available and keen to further extend his ability to enlighten the young minds, we were 'privileged' to start Military Preparation in Grade 8, unlike most students who started it in high school. What I remember from that class better than anything else were the boards that the teacher would eagerly bring into the classroom to illustrate his lessons. They depicted the mushroom shaped nuclear cloud, or (naked!) men taking a shower to wash down radioactive contamination. We would learn about nuclear explosions and where to go if that happened. We would be told not to pick up colourful or shiny objects from the ground because they could be mines or some other explosive devices dropped by the Americans who wanted to kill us. Not that long ago, I was reminded of that teacher's words when listening to a television programme about children in Afghanistan maimed by Soviet-made explosives, shiny objects that they were curious about and picked up. It felt like a full circle.

My neighbour in Woodstock grew up near Windsor, Ontario, across the river from Detroit. She recalls many nuclear attack alerts she had to go through as a child and she found them frightening. Nuclear shelters and the threat of Russians dropping a bomb were very real for her, perhaps because her parents emigrated from Ukraine and understood the dangerous side of the Soviet foreign politics. I was growing up with the threat of an American attack, something I never really took too seriously. More recently, I talked with my Japanese friend Yasuko about those Military Preparation classes and the threat of a nuclear attack. I was surprised that she found it very funny. Having grown up in the country that has experienced the effect of a nuclear explosion, she saw the Polish fear as pretentious and unwarranted.

Our Military Preparation teacher seemed very devoted to his subject, but also rather distracted. We had exercise books that we had to fill out weekly and leave in a big pile on his desk. We would get them back the following week, either with no comments or with check marks. It did not look like he ever read our answers, but only checked whether we had done the work. I could have simply copied answers from the textbook—I am quite sure we had textbooks for that course but I do not even remember them—they too must have been full of 'water'. However, I had a better idea. Instead of copying meaningless text from the textbook, I copied novels or poems (written down in a continuous format rather than in verses), making sure that they did not contain question marks or exclamation marks that could make my answers look suspicious. I did that for as long as we had Military Preparation and was never caught.

It was only in the last grade of high school that I realized that I could actually use my writing skills in a meaningful way. In Grade 12 (or Grade 4 of high school), we had a new Polish Language and Literature teacher, Miss Bożena Rożalska who had just graduated from the University of Warsaw and who taught us that literature could be fascinating. I cannot remember the first topic we had to write about but obviously this was not something about which we were expected to pour water. And so I did not. I shall never forget that mine was the only A in a class of over thirty students. I'd often had As and high Bs in Polish before, but so did others and the situation where I was the only recipient of a good mark was a bit unusual. There were several other students who, in my opinion, had justified reasons to believe that they knew more than I did and were better writers. They were probably both surprised and disappointed. That first essay was followed by many others and I kept receiving very good marks. In that class, we read the best of Polish literature and not just the compulsory readings. I stopped pouring water and worked very hard to stay on top. I felt a great respect for our Polish teacher and really wanted her to think highly of me. I never had courage to ask her why she treated me so well, but I owe her much gratitude and, thinking of her from today's perspective have an even greater respect for her. Very few teachers throughout my 12 years of school were ever really bothered to teach us to reach farther and to aspire higher than what the curriculum specified. Miss Rożalska was an inspirational teacher who taught us to be critical readers and to have our own opinions. If you are reading this, Miss Rożalska, I want to thank you, for there were very few teachers as open-minded as you and who had such an impact on our young minds.

Despite growing up in a country that was 'on its way to communism', I never had to read anything by any of the so-called great philosophers and so I never did. I never had to memorize their biographies. I have never seen any communist books at home though at some point there must have been some as my two half-brothers attended university in the early 1950s and were certainly forced to read more rigidly prescribed types of books. They must have taken those books with them (or, more likely, must have thrown them away) when they moved out.

I had to learn some poems by heart but there were no religious poems about Lenin (Stalin was long passé by the time I went to school but Lenin was still revered) or current Polish leaders among them. Those were usually the standard patriotic poems by Mickiewicz, Słowacki, or Norwid that even our parents had to learn by heart when they went to school. I liked learning poetry by heart. There were all kinds of assemblies at school for anniversaries of all kinds but no one made us listen to any of the speeches with attention and I have never been asked to give a speech myself.

I was never forced to join any organization. However, in Grade 7 or 8, together with my friend Kasia, I decided to join Scouts. We made a *blitzschnell* (lightning fast) career and after only a few months made it to the rank of group leaders (*zastępowe*). Together, we were responsible for a group of younger girls, perhaps Grade 3s or 4s. As the first task, we had to find a fitting name for our team and the girls had two competing ideas: *Samanthas,* because of the American television series *Bewitched*, immensely popular at the time, or *Archeopteryxes*, because of the age-typical fascination with dinosaurs and other ancient creatures. I think we selected the latter. Any ideologically proper names did not even cross our collective mind. We joined the Scouts for the fun of the outdoors and we enjoyed it for one year. The following year we were both expelled. Apparently, we missed some team meetings and our team reported us to those higher up. I actually did not think that was the case as we had a good relationship with the girls and attended all meetings. There must have been another reason and maybe indeed we were not diligent enough about the political profile of the organization: for example, we managed to magically disappear when told to attend the May 1st parade with our team.

This is where my voluntary organizational membership ended until I joined the Solidarność (Solidarity) trade union in September 1980. I think I was part of the teachers' trade union during my first year of work at Warsaw University (1979–1980) but that would have likely been an automatic membership.

When I moved on from high school to the university, pouring water was no longer such a valuable tool but writing well was very useful. The difference was that, in the Department of German, most of the writing had to be done in German, which posed quite a challenge. Reading in German also posed a challenge, but of a different kind. There were some one hundred-plus registered programme students in my year in the German Department. We had a number of compulsory classes. In fact, most of our timetable, if not all of it, was set with very little freedom of choice for electives. This meant that all hundred-plus students would be doing the same thing in their parallel literature classes. We were supposed to read quite a lot and some of the tasks were truly insurmountable. It was not just the fact that reading several books in German would take longer than the amount of time we were given to complete the task but that the library only had so many copies. It was impossible for a hundred students to read, say, *The Magic Mountain* by Thomas Mann in German in a few weeks when there were, say, only three to five copies of it in the library. Even if other Warsaw libraries had a couple of copies and if some students read it in Polish (as I did since we had a copy of it at home), which was discouraged for good pedagogical reasons, it was still pretty impossible. Faced with an impossible task, the students all engaged in some fiction. In our seminar groups of about 15 to 20 students, we would divide the reading list, read specific books each and then meet to share what we read. Most of our exams in literature were oral and I remember talking about books I never read and discussing them with my professors. I feel ashamed of it now but back then we felt it was the only solution.

In one subject, we had to read at least one article from a specific academic journal and be prepared to discuss it in the exam. In this particular case I made a rational decision to simply invent an article. The teacher could not have read them all, I thought. I certainly spent longer inventing the article than it would have taken me to read one so saving time was definitely not the purpose. I invented an entire theory, based on some existing linguistic concepts, specifically those of two German grammarians Weisgerber and Trier. I still remember my theory, all these years later even though, I am pretty sure, I would have long forgotten any actual article that I would have read. I gave the author of my invented theory a good German name—Apfelbaum. I got an A+. Have I learned anything from doing that? I definitely have. If someone is telling me about something I have never heard about, I do not pretend that I know what they are talking about. I always think: what if it is just another Apfelbaum theory? I admit my ignorance and investigate.

One of the last experiences of the abyss that separated reality from Polish Newspeak and that required some use of my water pouring skills were my repeatedly rejected passport applications. Except for a few holiday trips to the countries of the Soviet bloc for which we only needed the *wkładka paszportowa* (passport insert'), I had only been to Italy in Grade 11—on a group excursion organized by a travel agency, with my mother and with my cousin Leszek, and to Sweden, with my friend Kasia, after the first year of our university studies. It was my trip to Sweden that had caused me a great number of problems.

Poles were only allowed to take the equivalent of something like ten or twenty American dollars in official exchange (i.e., officially purchased at the official rate, several times lower that the black-market rate) when going abroad. This was another fiction, of course, because no one could get by on that amount of money for more than a day or two. We probably had a bit more from our parents and we had a contact address in Stockholm where we could stay for a few days. We also had the intention to find jobs, work for a few weeks and then do a bit of sightseeing and shopping. We were aware that it was illegal for us to work abroad as we had no work permit. We also knew that working abroad was not allowed by Polish authorities. I do not recall whether it was prohibited by any specific law or whether it was common knowledge that one would be punished by repressions of some kind upon return. This knowledge, however, had no impact on our decisions. Part of growing up in a communist country was that you knew that laws and regulations were there to be circumvented. Unfortunately, this became an inborn tendency that is difficult to shed and I still find myself thinking the same way many years later while living in a democratic country. Even in Canada, there are regulations that simply invite this type of reasoning.

Finding a job in Sweden in 1975 was easier than we had anticipated. We simply went to an employment agency in Stockholm and were hired almost immediately by a tourist hotel in Visby on the Island of Gotland. We had to register there with the local police and fill out tax forms, which we dutifully did. The visit to the police meant a stamp in our passports, but at the age of 19 one does not really worry about the future implications of something as ordinary as a stamp. After two months in Sweden, we returned to Poland. The return trip was an adventure. We took a train from Stockholm to Malmö where we wanted to spend a couple of days before taking the ferry back to Poland. The train stopped in Malmö at four or so in the morning, but we were deep asleep and woke up only after the train crossed the border with Denmark. We were petrified. We had no Danish visa! We were not worried about Danish authorities; no one checked our passports on the way in. We were afraid of the Polish passport office, as we were sure we had done something terribly illegal from their point of view. We got off in Copenhagen and our only concern was how to get out of Denmark without getting a Danish border control stamp in our passports. After a few days there, we ended up taking a small tourist boat from Copenhagen to Malmö and so our visit to Copenhagen remained a secret.

On my way back to Poland, I bought a few German magazines—*Stern, Spiegel*, perhaps something else. I was after all a student of the German language and treated this as an obvious way of practicing the language. We used texts from these magazines in our classes and I saw nothing wrong with the practice. The magazines I bought would give me extra reading material for several months. Unfortunately, and stupidly, I also bought a copy of *Playboy* as a funny gift—or so I thought—for my half brother Andrzej. I was attracted by its cover which that month featured a girl in a white and red striped suit that looked a bit as if it was made out of Polish national flag.

I paged through the German magazines on the ferry to Szczecin, in our cabin, and I could swear there was not a single mention of Poland. The summer of 1975 was rather peaceful and uneventful and Poland was not in the news. When we landed, I put the German magazines in my backpack and concealed the copy of the *Playboy* magazine in my jacket. I was stopped at customs, my backpack was checked with the copies of the German magazines taken out and I was asked to a little room where I was ordered to undress—completely undress. The copy of *Playboy* was easily found in my jacket and added to the German papers. I was told that bringing these magazines into Poland was not permitted and that I would be called to a lesser court called 'collegium' (*kolegium*).

I was never called to any court. Some time later, however, a letter came telling me that the *kolegium* looking at my case had met (I was never notified about that) and had decided I was guilty of bringing into Poland "materials that were slandering the good name of the

Polish People's Republic" (*materiały szkalujące dobre imię Polskiej Rzeczpospolitej Ludowej*). I do not recall any punishment specified or imposed for that crime in the text of that letter. Maybe being found guilty was a punishment in itself. However, when I applied for passport in 1976 (passports had to be surrendered to the Passport Office upon return from abroad and applied for when one wanted to travel again), my application was rejected. It was justified with paragraph 6, which, as I managed to find out, said that the rejection was motivated by "the interests of a person staying in the country and being dependent on the applicant or other important social reasons" (*inne ważne względy społeczne*).

Of course, I appealed that decision, using my skillful rhetoric of pouring water but to no avail. My friend Kasia had to travel on her own and—looking at that from today's perspective, it probably affected, at least for some time, our very close friendship. After many years together in elementary and high school, we both went our separate ways at university. She studied psychology and I studied German philology and later linguistics. Holidays were our time to reunite and after that was taken away, we simply stopped seeing each other regularly. However, we are still in touch, both living in North America now—Kasia in the USA and me in Canada. We have revived our friendship, have done some academic joint work, and returned to travelling together.

In 1977 the same thing happened: my passport application was refused for the same unspecified "important social reasons." I appealed it again and the same authorities confirmed that they were right the first time around and supported their own decision. It was in that year, I think, that I requested a meeting with someone higher up. I went to a gloomy building at the corner of Aleja Róż and Koszykowa Street and after a long wait was seen by a nondescript officer. He had my file in front of him. The name was right: Maria Piotrowska. However, it was not my file. Maria Piotrowska in Polish is a bit like Mary Peters or Jane Doe in English. In the telephone directory of any Polish city there are many Piotrowskis and Maria is a common first name. Even my parents, who after all gave it to me, never called me that and always used my middle name Magdalena. Maria Piotrowska, whose file was on the desk, was a different person, with a different day of birth, different parents, different address and, obviously, different life history. We managed to establish that quite quickly. I never found out what she had done to deserve a rejection and I never found out whether my bringing those German magazines and the *Playboy* into Poland was indeed the reason for my rejection. Having no evidence on the table, the officer told me that "we all know why young Polish girls want to go abroad and what they want to do there." I said that I did not know and asked him to tell me. He said that if I did not know then, he would not tell me. This is how our conversation ended. I still did not get my passport.

In 1978, I applied again, this time under my new name as I got married in January and changed my name to Stroińska. Again, I received a rejection. Maybe my marriage was now added to the other Maria Piotrowska's file. That summer I was hoping to go to the US with my husband and was really looking forward to that. After receiving the rejection, I asked my father-in-law to help me with my next appeal letter and discovered that I found a true master. He was not cynical but simply pragmatic and he believed in doing things professionally. If he were to write a letter of appeal, he would write it in such a way that it would have to be successful, taking into account which arguments would work and which arguments would not work with that particular addressee. He understood that instead of telling the authorities that they were doing something wrong or illegal, we should rather simply ask them to do what the regulations said. As communist laws were part of the communist façade, they were really a kind of legal and legislative fiction and no one believed that the authorities ever intended to obey them. It was like that with elections being a legal fiction, and with many other regulations. The idea that one could simply pretend the laws were there to be obeyed by the authorities was a clever one. They could not disagree. They simply had to pretend that they indeed obeyed the fictional laws they wanted us to pretend we believed in. They were doing themselves in with their own fiction. It was a pleasure to watch that happen.

My father-in-law's letter was a masterpiece of pouring water. He pulled all the right strings and used the argumentation that could not be refuted: that I was an exceptionally good student (well, maybe I was not exceptionally good but I was definitely good) and deserved to be rewarded with the summer holidays with my new husband; that I studied languages and should be allowed to practice them over the summer (as if I could really practice German in America) as this would prepare me better for my future role as a language teacher; that I still had one year of studies ahead of me and would have all the right reasons to return to Poland after the summer abroad. It must have been seen as a masterpiece by the Passport Office as I was given my passport that summer.

However, the following summer, 1979, the situation repeated itself. I was given a rejection when I first applied and then received the passport later, after my father-in-law's appeal letter. Maybe they liked reading my father's-in-law letters there and only gave me rejections to get them. That year I had graduated from Warsaw University but was offered a job there as a junior assistant lecturer and so we used that argument instead to show that I had all the reasons to return to Poland. This actually was a valid reason as I was in fact motivated to return and when my husband suggested that we could stay in the USA, I did not want to consider it. That I did not get my passport when I wanted and was delayed for almost two months had one advantage: In June 1979 I witnessed the first visit to Poland by the newly elected Polish Pope, John Paul II and this experience was very educational.

In 1980, for the first time in five years, I got my passport without appeals and returned to Warsaw from Holland on August 31, the day when the Gdańsk agreement between the striking shipyard workers and the government was signed. When the plane was approaching Warsaw, the sky was dark grey as if there was a thunderstorm gathering over Poland. During the month of August, I had followed the news from Poland as much as possible in the Dutch media and it was on Dutch television that I first saw Lech Wałęsa. I was excited but somewhat apprehensive. I had just changed jobs. My job in the Institute of Applied Linguistics turned out to be a one-year contract which I did not know when I signed it. Still, I was very lucky to get an offer from the Department of German at Warsaw University and was looking forward to working there. It was another reason to return to Poland. My husband graduated that year and had just started a new academic job. So, indeed, we both had good reasons to go back and we had high hopes for Poland. When I was watching the signing ceremony of the Gdańsk Agreement on TV later that day, I was not emotional. Unlike people who witnessed developments of that month day after day, I just wasn't sure what to make of it. Who was Lech Wałęsa? My understanding of Dutch was limited (I had taken Dutch as one of my language electives) and so was my access to papers, radio or television in Holland. Was he honest? I was sorely missing the access to the Radio Free Europe and their commentaries that summer.

One more encounter with fiction is worth mentioning here. When my husband and I were finishing our university studies, instead of being happy to graduate and start working in our chosen fields, I remember us being anxious and apprehensive about the perspective of my husband Kris having to spend one year in the army. University graduates had their army duty reduced to one year, instead of the two-year service that had to be done by those who did not pursue higher education. How to avoid army service was one of the main topics in any discussion among friends at that time. People would fake accidents or a serious illness; they would pretend to have mental problems or would even marry and have children to become sole supporters of families. It would be interesting to collect people's stories of how they avoided military service in communist Poland into a book. With a friend, Jerzy Wilde, we contemplate doing that one day.

With some medical doctors in the family, we first tried for stomach ulcers. My aunt, a radiologist, took X-rays of Kris, literally punching him in the stomach when the picture was being taken (I hope that she did it with the necessary precautions to protect herself). Interestingly enough, I personally do not know any child of a medical doctor in Poland who would have served the year in the army. Clearly Polish doctors had very sickly sons. One of Kris' best friends had undergone lumbar punctures, an unpleasant and potentially dangerous spine examinations to avoid the service. One of my upper-level students of German did something that gave me a better idea. He wrote to the army command that, as a student of German, he would highly appreciate the opportunity to do his army service in the Federal Republic of Germany so that he could practice and improve his German. I am not sure whether he received any response to his letter but he was never called for his army duty either. Definitely, he was considered an 'uncertain element'.

We decided to try to beat the system with its own weapons. I reported on Kris as having a medical condition that he did not want to disclose. I wrote to the army command asking whether they could make sure he could continue the treatment while in the army. I asked them not to notify Kris that I told them. I said he would kill me if he found out that I reported him. An answer to my letter reporting on my husband never came, but neither did an army call for Kris. Reporting on people truly was a weapon of choice in communism.

'Pouring water' was not just simply what students did in school in order to get by or to get good marks from some teachers who did not care too much about our education; there probably were teachers like that but they constituted a minority when I went to school. We were virtually surrounded by the proverbial verbal *water* in the papers, in TV news, and in the so called 'publicist programmes' (*programy publicystyczne*) which usually consisted of commentaries to current events or staged discussions with most parties to the debate representing the same opinion. From a linguistic point of view, it is actually quite an interesting question: How do you keep talking without saying anything or without committing yourself to anything tangible that someone, at some later stage, could possibly hold you accountable for?

There are many ways to do so. The simplest one is to say things that cannot be possibly contradicted. If the politician said that he or she advocated safe school environment for all children, would anyone want anything else? No one wants their children to spend any time in schools that are dangerous. So, there is no message there. If Ministry of Health in Poland or Canada (both with national medical care that covers all citizens) informs that it is working on ensuring timely quality health care for anyone in need of treatment, well, what else would you expect that Ministry to do? Some years ago, a colleague from McMaster University, Dave Parnas, wrote an editorial in the local paper (*The Hamilton Spectator*) on how to listen to a politician and see what the real message is. He suggested a useful technique to get to the essence of political (and other) speeches. His advice was "to look at each sentence and consider its negation. If nobody would utter the negation, the sentence wasn't really saying anything. For example, if a Canadian politician says, 'We will listen to Canadians', they have told you nothing about their policies." (McMaster Faculty Association's public e-mail exchange on mufagab on July 12, 2008; for the original editorial cf. Parnas 1993). In many political speeches we hear today, most of the content would likely disappear after such a test.

Here is yet another test for the fit between Newspeak and reality. In 1985, Polish writer Kazimierz Orłoś published in London and in an underground publishing house in Poland a novel called *Przechowalnia* (which could be translated as 'Depot' or 'Storage'). After 1973, he was banned from publication in Poland upon release of a book in Paris. Clearly, he published it in Paris because he was not able to have it published in Poland. *Przechowalnia* is a very curious and truly unique text. It tells a story of a 'drunk tank' (endearingly referred to by its clients as 'przechowalnia') in a thoroughly corrupt small town. The local alcoholics who all spend regular time in the drunk tank feel that they are being taken advantage of by the staff (who steal money from them while they are there) and decide to go on strike and stop drinking. The plot may seem surreal, but it is not the plot that makes the book special. With the story line about heavy drinking and various, rather unpleasant, physiological consequences thereof, the book is written in a language used by communist newspapers of the time. As alcoholism, dirt, poverty, or any other forms of social pathology did not exist in official propaganda, Orłoś was describing the reality Poles knew from everyday observation using language they knew from the description of fiction. These two did not go together. Describing binge drinking with the official word 'consumption' or drunk and stinking workers as 'malodorous representatives of the proletariat under the influence' had an illuminating effect. The language of the papers was unable to cope with reality. There really was a reason why Kazimierz Orłoś was not allowed to publish in communist Poland.

For me, the use of empty language or any attempt at manipulation through linguistic distortion is indicative of social or psychological problems. The use of Newspeak is usually a symptom of an intention to deceive. My reaction to it has developed into some form of anxiety or panic that I have problems controlling. In March 2003, just before the invasion of Iraq, the intensity of the US Newspeak (I am truly sorry to use this term but it seems to me justified in that context) was such that, for the first time in my life, I was afraid to speak my mind in the classroom. I only teach linguistics, not political science or history, but in a class on discourse analysis, intercultural communication, or even morphology, there are always opportunities to talk about social practices and the language that goes with them. In Poland, in the 1970s and early 1980s, I knew no one was a going to report on me as no one really believed in communist propaganda any longer. But in 2003, some people in North America were serious about weapons of mass destruction and terrorism and I felt that things were becoming black and white. I was scared because I felt language was closing up on me, suffocating, hateful and ominous.

At approximately the same time, something wrong was also happening in my department at the university. People were being dismissed from their posts without clear justification. We were told we were 'dysfunctional' as an administrative unit, but there was no explanation what it meant (and most of us did not think we were dysfunctional). We were even told at some point that we were not supposed to exchange e-mail correspondence within our department and no one said a word in protest. To be honest, no one, as far as I can tell, obeyed that order either. Finally, there was a very unpleasant meeting where the person in charge of the Department at the time (and the one who seemed to be the source of all these strange developments) wanted us to admit our wrongdoing and as we could not (I don't think anyone really knew what we did wrong), she said, in a slow and calm voice, that we would stay in that meeting or meet over and over again until we understood our wrong ways. She had time, she said. I had a regular panic attack then. I had to get up and leave. I later felt embarrassed by my hysterical reaction and apologized. Her language reminded me of the Polish police and I simply could not take it. Indeed, she reminded me of that officer in the passport office who told me that if I did not know what I did wrong, he would not tell me.

Panic attacks are not the best reaction to propaganda, but they may be useful as warning signs. It would be convenient to have a bodily reaction to lies, something like a mild allergy, an itch or rash. In the absence of it, we just need to listen carefully and critically.

The skills of 'pouring water' that I acquired in school and the skills of writing appeal letters I learned from my father-in-law are still very useful. I occasionally help friends in writing all kinds of appeals and I enjoy doing that. I also enjoy writing letters of recommendation for my students. It makes me feel that, at last, I am putting skills acquired by necessity and for all kinds of wrong reasons to a good use.

CHAPTER 9

People and Things

I STARTED THIS BOOK with my memories of post-war Warsaw and how I wished my city and environment were more beautiful and colourful. Even though the city has changed over the past three decades more than I ever imagined possible, I still wish that it were prettier in many ways. The Warsaw I knew as a child and as a teenager, actually up into my late twenties, was not a beautiful city. I read many accounts of how magnificent it once was and I can see it changing from year to year. It is becoming more and more beautiful, even though mostly in a modern, rather than traditional sense. I am not disappointed by this and am happy to see the Palace of Culture and Science surrounded by new highrises. However, I am always more attracted to old buildings, even historical ruins, old houses, churches, and palaces.

The wartime destruction left Warsaw in ruins. There are cities all over the world that are sites of huge trauma. Sometimes the trauma resulted from natural disasters, earthquakes or volcanic eruptions, as was the case in Skopje or Pompei. Sometimes trauma was caused by people's actions, especially wars. I imagine the Japanese cities of Hiroshima and Nagasaki will forever be associated with the atomic bomb. I visited Dresden in 1970 and was very moved by the field of ruins in the city centre, around the *Frauenkirche*. At that time, that area was left in ruin to commemorate the destruction of the city by allied air attack on Valentine's Day 1945. The firestorm that resulted from the air raids killed thousands of civilians (there were no military targets in Dresden) and obliterated a lot of the city's infrastructure. Kurt Vonnegut Jr. brilliantly described it *Slaughterhouse-Five or The Children's Crusade* (1969).

Warsaw was the city of several traumas during WWII. First bombed in September 1939 and forced to surrender to the invading German army, then divided into a Jewish quarter, a non-Jewish part and a German district. Warsaw before the war had approximately 1.2 million inhabitants, one third of them Jewish. When Ghetto was cut off from the rest of the city, this one third of Warsaw was crammed into less than 3% of the area of the city. Then more than one hundred thousand Jewish people from other towns were deported to Warsaw Ghetto.

My maternal grandparents used to live at number 9 Bonifraterska Street, close to the Old Town, vis-à-vis the old psychiatric hospital and church of John of God (a Portuguese saint, *João de Deus*). For a long time, it was the only psychiatric institution in the Russian-occupied part of the partitioned Poland. When Ghetto was being established in 1940, my grandparents had to leave their apartment and move to 6 Nowiniarska Street, apartment 12. This address is listed in the *Kennkarte* (ID) of my mother's sister Wanda. They lived there during the Ghetto Uprising in April 1943, witnessing the burning of the Ghetto and destruction of its remaining inhabitants—most, by that time had been transported to their death in Treblinka. After the uprising was crushed, Germans leveled the ruins with the plan to establish a big garden there, of course for Germans only. Visitors to Warsaw may wonder why huge areas in the centre of Warsaw do not have a single old building standing. Well, that is where Ghetto used to be, and the sheer size of that space empty of anything pre-WWII is really eerie.

The Warsaw Ghetto Uprising was followed, just over one year later, on August 1, 1944 by the Warsaw Uprising. My mother told me about seeing people jumping out of the windows of the burning psychiatric hospital, located at the Jan Boży Convent across the street from their old apartment in Bonifraterska Street, a strong centre of resistance during the Warsaw Uprising, turned into rubble by the end of fighting. After 63 days of fighting and over 200,000 deaths, this uprising too was crushed and the remaining population of Warsaw was forcibly removed from the ruins of the city. When people left, Germans began a well-organized destruction of what was still standing, until they in turn were driven out by the Soviet army. By the way, the Soviet army watched the uprising and the death of the city from across the river but did not offer any assistance. One could say it was understandable as the motivation for the uprising was to liberate the city before the Soviet Army could take it over.

I was born 11 years after the war but I still grew up in the city of trauma, in a city that was a huge cemetery. In addition, I virtually grew up visiting actual cemeteries. It is part of Polish tradition to visit the graves of the family and friends and I had more dead family members than live ones.

I was also surrounded by many memorials of the trauma of German occupation: almost every street, many houses or wall fragments had plaques listing how many people were shot there during the war or during the Uprising. For many years, the memory of the Uprising was somewhat secret but even as a child I knew by the dates what happened when. The unimaginable horrors of the war in in general and the particular traumas of Warsaw were mixed in my mind with the accounts of heroism of those who fought against the occupants and the suffering of the victims. The number of people killed in single events was beyond comprehension, e.g., *Rzeź Woli* (the Slaughter of Wola), a premeditated massacre of the civilian population of the Wola district in Warsaw, resulted in between 25,000 and 60,000 deaths. As corpses were almost immediately burned and disposed of, the numbers are not precise. As someone (it is usually attributed to Stalin) said, a single death is a tragedy, a million deaths is a statistic.

Warsaw was rebuilt on ruins, sometimes, especially where Ghetto once was, on the graves of the war victims. What was built after the war was either the monumental socialist realism style of the Palace of Culture and the Constitution Square, or cheap apartment blocks. While some monumental buildings of the Stalin era look better now than they did when they were constructed, with some patina of the past 60 or 70 years, the apartment buildings are more haunting and dilapidated. Some are being refurbished and covered with new façades but for some there is no saving grace. The parts of Warsaw that I like best are the 19th century residential buildings in Aleje Jerozolimskie, Lwowska Street, etc. There are many other streets that also have the 19th or early 20th century architecture, but the buildings seem ugly in a similar manner as the post-war, faceless apartment blocks. This, taken without any deeper consideration or thought, made me often question the assertion that Warsaw used to be a beautiful city before the war and to see it more as a patriotic boasting than reality.

When visiting Warsaw in the 1990s and early 2000s, I was usually hurrying through its streets, busy with my children's problems, my parents' issues, tasks assigned to me by my busy husband, or other personal or work-related worries. If I paid any closer attention to architecture, it was either the modern buildings or office towers that started to emerge in Warsaw in the mid 1990s or the splendid façades and interiors of old churches, always open to the public and always a wonderful shelter from the commotion and bustle outside. The ugly old buildings were usually an eyesore not worth a second look—at least not until the summer of 2008, when, for the first time, I had the luxury of taking an unhurried, lonely streetcar ride through Warsaw on my way to the Bródno Cemetery, one of the largest in Europe, to visit the graves of my mother, her siblings, and my maternal grandparents. The streetcar was passing through parts of town largely unfamiliar to me. We were far enough from the city centre for the streets and neighbourhoods to remain unaffected by the recent development of office and retail space. It was late morning, the streetcar was almost empty and I had a seat so I was able to pay closer attention to the buildings we were passing.

There is a special category of buildings in Poland that could also be seen in many East German (maybe also Soviet) cities for many years after the war: multi-storey brick houses whose façades were stripped of wall plaster and stucco ornaments by the war—bombs, shells, bullets, and grenades. Red brick façades have a look of flesh wounds, not fresh and bleeding but old, with blood all dried up and flaky. These buildings are typically missing balconies, with only steel rails (often looking actually just like two cut off pieces of railway tracks) sticking out of the wall and the balcony floor and balustrade gone. Balcony doors were opening into a street abyss, threatening anyone who would open them with a free fall several storeys high. To prevent accidents, the lower part was often secured with boards or bricks, allowing only the upper part to open and protecting people from accidentally stepping out into the air. The long rectangle of the balcony door, usually surrounded on both sides by shorter rectangles or squares of windows, looked like a face of a gagged person, mouth covered by stripes of tape or filled with plaster, like the skulls of soldiers or civilians found in some mass graves from wars long past. When I was growing up, there were hundreds of houses like that, probably thousands. It would have been too expensive to restore them on the outside, but the interiors were still suitable for habitation. Sometimes the front façade would be covered with plaster but the back yard wall would be left bare. No one cared about the back side. Only the public view was important.

In the early 1980s, my husband and I went to Zamość, a beautiful small town in south-eastern Poland. It is famous for its Renaissance city hall, splendid town centre, and magnificent city walls with ramparts. We went to visit the parents of our friends whom we had helped hide from authorities after the imposition of the martial law on December 13, 1981. Zamość was selected to be the site for a nation-wide Harvest Festival (*Dożynki*) celebration in 1980, a celebration that, amid workers' strikes in August 1980, had been cancelled and replaced with a smaller scale local event. However, the effects of the preparations that had taken place for the big Harvest Festival could still be seen in 1982 or 1983. The Old Town had been renovated, painted in cheerful bright colours that would look good on TV. Even the old city walls have been partially repaired—one could easily recognize which bricks were new. Renovating cities to look good on camera is a bit like building film sets: they do not have to be done well or last long and they do not need to be solid. They just need to look good on the screen. The paint was already peeling off the newly brushed up walls and it was enough to turn into any side street or, God forbid, look into any backyard, and the pre Harvest Festival poverty and filth were in plain view, particularly around the part of the old Zamoyski Palace that has been used for offices since the 19th century and was partially converted into council flats. A similarly shabby paint job was done in the Nowy Świat Street in Warsaw for some state visit—possibly the first visit of Pope John Paul II in 1979. Only the ground floor level of the houses received a fresh coat of paint as that was how high the cameras would go showing the crowds welcoming Karol Wojtyła to Warsaw.

The idea that putting up an appearance is more important than making any real change is not specific to communism. One could find equally absurd (in my view, of course) behaviours elsewhere. In 1987, we visited an old friend Larry who was a school teacher in a rough South Bronx neighbourhood of New York City. In the evening, he took us on a car tour of the part of town where he worked and it was an unforgettable experience. I was prepared to see a very poor and rundown neighbourhood, but not ready for the urban desert we encountered. Many blocks of houses had been completely demolished because it was seen as the only way to eradicate local criminal activity. In this desert or moon-like landscape, the remaining buildings—an old police station, an old post office, etc, boarded up and empty, surrounded, some distance away, by burned out, but still standing multi-storey buildings, looked like a ghost town, or actually like the levelled areas of the Warsaw Ghetto.... On the following morning, when we were on the way to Manhattan, Larry pointed to the houses of South Bronx visible in the distance. From where we were, they looked just like any apartment blocks. Larry explained they were all empty, but the city spent a considerable amount of money to cover the missing windows with boards with painted curtains so that, from the highway or from the trains bringing people from the suburbs to work, the houses would not look abandoned.

In the recent years, with more money and more attention to the aesthetic value of the city, I see more and more old buildings in Warsaw being properly restored to their former beauty. All of a sudden (suddenly for me because I usually come once a year and see the changes in an incremental fashion), an old, partially ruined or badly damaged building is transformed into a beautifully ornamented 19th century residence. Nothing of the former, post-war bare or plain plaster façade had even indicated the pre-war architectural richness that makes other Polish cities, such as Kraków or Łódź, so remarkable. Recently, one such remarkable transformation was completed in the Wolf Krongold building at 83 Złota Street. A large drab 5 or 6 story building now looks like something you could see in Paris or Vienna. I can see now why people used to say that Warsaw was a beautiful city.

In the 1990s, my husband organized an Actuarial Summer School in Warsaw. Many Western actuaries volunteered as teachers—it was an interesting moment of a communist-style economy developing market mechanisms. I bought them maps to help them navigate the city. A newly published map of Warsaw had a border running around it with pictures of historical buildings. Many of these buildings were labelled as palaces of certain families. I was surprised as I never thought that Warsaw had so many palaces until I realized that I was familiar with the buildings as seats of various ministries or government offices or as public buildings of different types. Thus, the Czapski Palace was one of the buildings of the Warsaw Academy of Fine Arts and the Tyszkiewicz Palace was part of Warsaw University. The Branicki Palace now houses Warsaw City Hall. Some palaces were referred to by their function: the Potocki Palace was known as the Ministry of Culture and Fine Arts. The 17th century building known as the Staszic Palace was purchased at the beginning of the 19th century by Stanisław Staszic, one of the leading figures of Polish Enlightenment. It was redesigned as a home for the Society of Friends of Science, and now is the seat of the Polish Academy of Sciences. It is still referred to as *Pałac Staszica*. The Krasiński Palace houses some of the collections of the National Library and is also referred to as *Pałac Krasińskich*. A special place among Warsaw palaces has the Mostowski Palace, almost always referred to with its aristocratic name. It has been, for as long as I can remember, the seat of the Warsaw's police headquarters and, as such, is not a popular tourist destination. Even during the 19th century, the palace housed the offices of the Commission of Internal Affairs and Police and was later used by the Russian Army. I wonder whether the name *Pałac Mostowskich* was a euphemism promoted by the authorities as an innocent sounding equivalent for police prison.

As I was travelling through Warsaw on the streetcar that morning in May 2008, I realized that many of those ugly pre-war buildings, with plain façades, no balconies and the unimaginative rectangles of windows, probably used to look quite different. They were renovated at the lowest cost possible in the post-war times of apartment hunger and poverty, adapted to the post-war communist style, *gleichgeschaltet* to the Stalinist way of building. They probably made people from out of town think that Warsaw's residential architecture before the war was as ugly as the one being constructed after the war so that they would not feel cheated of the beauty of their living surroundings. It was not difficult to do when one was surrounded by a sea of ruins and when many people only came to work in Warsaw after the war and did not know it before its destruction.

Those apartment buildings that survived the war were very precious, not necessarily in architectural terms, but as living space for people who were returning to Warsaw in the early spring of 1945. There was nothing left of the apartments where my mother's family used to live, in Bonifraterska or Nowiniarska Street. This part of Warsaw was badly destroyed, first in the Ghetto Uprising in 1943 and then in the Warsaw Uprising one year later. Very few items were salvaged from its ruins after the family returned to Warsaw in January 1945. They first found shelter on the other side of the river, in Praga. My maternal grandfather was a highly trained artisan carpenter, making beautiful pieces of furniture, with intarsias, wood inlays with different coloured pieces of wood. I have heard that there was a beautifully ornamented table in their apartment, hand-made by my grandfather. Apparently when the apartment was being searched by Gestapo, the German officer asked whether it was okay to put his hat on this magnificent piece of furniture. Unfortunately, the table burned together with most other family treasures at the end of the Uprising. After returning to Warsaw, my grandfather immediately found a job installing wooden window frames in Hotel Polonia, one of very few buildings in the centre of Warsaw that were still standing. He walked to work several kilometres every day, through snow and ruins. He developed pneumonia and died on April 2, 1945. There were no antibiotics to cure my grandfather. It was while caring for her dying father that my aunt, my mother's sister, Wanda decided to become a doctor.

With no apartment to go back to, only a pile of rubble to be sifted through in search of whatever scraps of their former existence they could find, my grandmother, mother, and my aunt Wanda settled in one room in a still-standing pre-war apartment building. It was on the fourth floor, at number 12 Noakowskiego Street, with a window and balcony overlooking the street and facing the Warsaw Polytechnic. The apartment used to belong to the family of Professor Makowiecki, a pre-war ethnographer. His wife still lived there, in one of the rooms. When I visited my grandmother, the room I had to cross in order to get to the communal kitchen (dark, as it was looking into the well-like courtyard) had walls completely covered with shelves full of folk art ceramic objects—plates, jugs, figures of birds and, what both I and my cousin Leszek remember most vividly, witches and devils. It was a scary place for a child. One room in the same apartment was occupied by Mrs. Michalska, a high school teacher of Polish. I went to her for some extra lessons when I was preparing for my high school entrance exams. Her room was filled with all kinds of antiques crammed into a small space and, like my grandmother's room, had a beautifully ornamented, very high ceiling. Modern apartments were much lower, especially those in post-war apartment blocks. There was also a communal bathroom in the apartment, with floor tiles and a huge steel bathtub that used to be white, but was worn by several years of usage by multiple families. It must have once been a beautiful apartment. Divided among at least three or four families, it was surreal. When I read Bulgakov's *Master and Margarita*, I always pictured my grandmother's apartment as the setting for Voland's residence in 302B Sadovaya Street in Moscow.

My father, with his first wife and two children moved to Warsaw from Lwów in 1935. They first lived at 42 Częstochowska Street but during the war, when his wife and children were trapped in the Soviet Union, my father moved. I don't know why and there is no one left to ask. In his book, my brother Andrzej suggested that the building in Częstochowska had been damaged during the war, probably in the bombing in September 1939. He chose a three-room apartment (with the so called 'little room' (*pokoik*) for a nanny or other domestic help) in a large apartment building at number 62 in Filtrowa Street, just a few streets away from Częstochowska. The building belonged to the Polish Social Security Institution (*ZUS* or *Zakład Ubezpieczeń Społecznych*) where my father worked before (and after) the war. It was finished in mid-1930s and represented the modernist style—simple shapes, spacious rooms, but not as high as some of the older apartments. The building suffered considerable damage during the war. Part of the front façade collapsed in the Warsaw Uprising and the outside walls were covered with bullet and grenade holes, with bullets still buried in dark, never repainted plaster. This is where I was born and where I spent most of my life in Poland, except for 18 months when we had our own apartment in Ursynów, one of the new subdivisions at the outskirts of Warsaw. When I was born, the three-room apartment was pretty full. There was my father and his new wife—my mother. There were his two grown up sons Renek and Andrzej, and, I believe, for a short period of time, also their new wives; there was also a live-in domestic help, the *pomoc domowa* or *gosposia*; the word *służąca*, 'female servant' was considered offensive and we never used it. It was also considered offensive by the official propaganda as servants existed only in capitalism; we had 'helpers.' I don't remember my parents ever using the word służąca in their conversations; they always used the word *gosposia* instead, but I do not think they did this for the same ideological reasons. Amongst all this, there was also me, the baby.

I never found out where my bed was when I was little. One room was my father's office where he saw patients. One room was occupied by my two half-brothers and their wives; the third room was the living room by day and my parents' bedroom at night. The 'little room' next to the kitchen belonged to our *gosposia*. My guess is that maybe I did not have a bed and my pram was pushed under the grand piano that took up almost a quarter of the living room.

As I said, one of the three rooms was taken up by my father's office (*gabinet*) where he saw patients every day after his office hours at the *ZUS* Social Security Institution where he worked as a medical doctor. The apartment was crowded, but I do not recall anyone complaining since there were no other options. Few people were in a better position. In an old joke, a poor man from an overcrowded house asks a wise elder for advice about his housing situation. The elder urges him to buy a goat and bring it into the house. The poor man complains that this is impossible, but finally follows the recommendation. A few weeks later the man returns, even more unhappy, and begs the elder for a different solution because, with the addition of the goat, the situation became insufferable. The elder calmly tells him to get rid of the goat. A few days later the poor man comes beaming with happiness. The problem was solved: with the goat gone, everyone was happy.

I am sure my arrival at 62 Filtrowa Street made the housing situation intolerable, especially to my two half brothers. They soon moved out to their own tiny apartments; my father moved his office to a smaller room (where my brothers used to sleep) and I had a crib of my own in the room that used to be my father's office. One has to understand that, in Poland, such notions as a bedroom, living room, or sitting room meant, and still mean very little. If you have only one room, it has to be your living room and dining room and sitting room and possibly also your office during the day and, of course, your bedroom at night. The dining table has to double as a desk and the couch or sofa that is used to sit on opens into a bed at night. And so my parents used to sleep on the couch in the living room, which we called 'the big room', and I slept in 'the other room.' My dad saw his patients in his *gabinet* and they waited for their turn in our hallway or entrance hall that was full of chairs. The situation in the apartments of virtually all my friends and relatives was the same or worse. This experience gives certain flexibility about almost everything to those of us who grew up with this multifunctional nature of space and objects. We are adaptable.

The shortage of apartments contributed to the creation of the concept of 'surplus space' or 'excessive space' (*nadmetraż*). After my brothers left, my father was using one room for his office, and my mother, as a librarian, got extra space permit as she belonged to the category 'teacher.' Then there was our *gosposia*. I am not sure I counted but four people were allowed to occupy a 70 something m^2 (approx. 800 square feet). When my father passed away, my grandmother moved in from her room in Noakowskiego Street. When she passed away and the *gosposia* was gone, it was just the two of us—my mother and me, and we certainly had 'surplus space' for communist standards. Fortunately, the authorities were becoming more and more distracted and we were never forced to take an extra tenant into our apartment. Nevertheless, *nadmetraż* was a serious problem and a great inconvenience for many people. It was also a problem created out of nothing, a fiction. As it was a fiction, the best way to fight it was also through fiction. This is why people would register fictitious relatives as living with them in order to avoid paying for their surplus space.

To be fair, post war socialist architecture has also created some interesting buildings. Several such places come to mind. There was a very interesting station building of the suburban light rail network in Ochota, not far from where I lived. It was built in the mid 1960s and it had a lightness of design and imagination missing in most other, heavy and grim socialist structures. Its roof looked like a sheet of paper gently folded, with the opposite corners turned up. There was something in its shape that made the viewer think of a bird or a butterfly taking off. The glass structure supporting the wings—the middle was much lower—contained ticket wickets or a waiting room. When new, it was light, bright and shiny; truly innovative, pretty, and simply different. After 1989, one could hardly see it from behind ugly kiosks and booths selling fast food or newspapers and cigarettes. It looked neglected and dirty. Fortunately, the station was renovated around 2009 and given heritage building status in 2012 which gives hope that it will not be demolished when a rich company decides to buy land in this potentially profitable location. If it were demolished, one of very few valuable examples of creativity in the communist architecture would vanish.

One other such example was the first Warsaw supermarket, the so called *Supersam* (the suffix *–sam* means 'self'). It was built in the early 1960s, designed by a group of architects who won an award at an Architectural Biennale in Sao Paulo for their project. It was a large glass hall with an interesting roof construction, turned up at one end. Inside, it had a very original ceiling, made of wooden panels that were formed into irregular wave-like shapes. For over 40 years, Supersam was a popular grocery store, functional and relatively well supplied even in the worst years of socialism. It served a large community in a highly populated and central neighbourhood.

My in-laws lived next to it and it was my mother-in-law's go-to store. In the late 1990s, a toy store, a McDonald's restaurant, and some other stores moved into one part of the building. Architects agreed that it was a valuable building, representative of best architectural traditions in Poland. Perhaps it needed some maintenance and restoration, especially if the roof was unsafe, but there was no obvious reason to demolish it. Yet it was demolished in 2007 and, for a while, there was no sign of anything being built on the site. Then, a modern shopping mall with office space was erected in its place, with a big grocery story in the basement. Now, even that reduced grocery store has closed, perhaps to make room for a more profitable venture, leaving a big neighbourhood without a general store.

My guess is that the architectural design of the original Supersam was great but the building was poorly maintained. Its demolition did not make front page news, like the award in Sao Paulo. It was an old story, and people were not interested. This really is a sad pattern: we build something, but then let it crumble due to neglect. We praise people's achievements, we encourage them to strive for more, but we let them die lonely and in poverty when they get old and can no longer produce. In some way it sums up the socialist idea of humanism and art. Or maybe it is just the modern view that only values utility. In the little town of Woodstock, Ontario two old and beautiful churches have been demolished over the past two decades. One could not find a buyer; the other had some structural problems. There also used to be an old movie theatre, originally built as one of the first opera houses in the province. It too fell into disrepair and was demolished. Canada is not a country with a surplus of historic buildings. To demolish the few old buildings we have is a sign of disrespect for the past and a sign of cultural short-sightedness. How will children brought up in the age of utility take care of our generation when we become no longer useful?

The way people treat lifeless objects, other people, nature, or animals speaks volumes about their character. Similarly, the way a political system treats architecture, stray dogs, or the sick and the elderly is a good indication of the system's true nature. Am

I making a dangerously large leap from one to the other? Heinrich Heine, German poet (1797–1856) of Jewish descent, wrote in 1823 in his tragedy *Almansor* the prophetic words: *Dort, wo man Bücher verbrennt, verbrennt man am Ende auch Menschen* ("Where they burn books, they will also, in the end, burn people"). While in his text Heine was actually talking about copies of the Quran burnt during the Spanish Inquisition, in the 1930s this statement sadly applied to his own books that were burnt in public by the Nazis. The destruction of books was indeed followed by the destruction of the people whose thoughts or race were wrong from the point of view of those in power. Books are more easily destroyed than buildings, but the latter too may appear threatening as they provide something people tend to identify with: history, tradition, or simply something familiar or aesthetically pleasing. After the downfall of the Warsaw Uprising, in the late fall of 1944, the already-retreating German army put a lot of effort, and used a lot of dynamite trying to erase Warsaw from the map. House after house was destroyed. Documentary films show multi-storey buildings falling down. Walls come down in a slow, almost soft motion, somewhat like a curtain after a theatrical performance or people falling down to their knees. There is something utterly humiliating about buildings falling down, similar to large, proud animals falling after they were hit by a poacher's bullet. It seems that if aggressors cannot bring the conquered people to their knees, they do it to the buildings instead.

In 1997, after two years of working at a university in the UK, my husband decided that his actuarial consulting company in Poland required his full-time attention and moved back to Poland and I returned to Canada, with the children. We continued to spend summers in Warsaw. In 2000, my husband bought an apartment in Aleja Szucha, close to his parents' place. Every morning when I put the kettle on to make myself my morning cup of coffee, I would see another building out of the kitchen window that made me think of the twists and turns of Warsaw's history. Located next door was a 19th century urban *petit palais*, built for Maria Agapiyeva, wife of a Russian general. The building used to be hidden behind a brick and iron fence and among tall trees. From the street, it was almost invisible. There were two house numbers on the gate post. A contemporary one that said that the street name was Aleja Szucha. The old one, on a lamp with broken glass, gave a different street name: *Aleja I Armii WP* (The First Army Street). The number has stayed the same: 17/19. Through the large but locked entrance gate, a passerby could see several empty aluminum tins that some compassionate souls used to feed many stray cats that had their home in Madame Agapiyeva's house. The house was a ruin. A two-level neo-baroque building, with walls of yellow brick, with many beige ornaments, must have been a beauty, at some point. I do not know what happened to it during the war but the entire street was a *Nur für Deutsche* (Germans only) area, separated from other parts of town. The infamous Gestapo headquarters were just a few houses away, in the building of the pre-war Ministry of Education. After the war, the Ministry returned but the basement was designated as a museum in memory of hundreds of people who lost their lives at the hands of Gestapo during brutal interrogations in the rooms of this buildings. When the war was over, the *petit palais* found itself under the administration of the Soviet Embassy in Warsaw. Eventually it was turned into a kindergarten for Russian children. There were rusty pieces of playground equipment still scattered around the building in the 1990s and 2000s. Next to it, closing the area off and facing Litewska Street, a high-rise apartment building was constructed to house families of the Soviet personnel. The location was excellent: next door to the Polish Ministry of Foreign Affairs and across the street from some other government buildings. Some people maintain that the buildings had some intelligence applications but we shall not find out about that any time soon, I guess.

For years, when I looked out of the kitchen window, the picture I saw had an eerie resemblance to photographs taken in Chernobyl, many years after the 1986 disaster. The *petit palais* had broken window panes and crumbling walls. Inside, one could see pieces of furniture or wooden boards piled in the patio. More than a decade-old trees were growing in the middle of the driveway. In the apartment block behind, some windows were open and moved in the wind. There was furniture left and curtains in the windows. It looked as if something terrible had happened and the people who lived there had left suddenly, unable to collect their possessions and close the windows before their departure.

When I think about the actual Chernobyl catastrophe in April 1986, what I remember best is the complete disregard shown by the Soviet authorities for people's health and safety—not just in Chernobyl, in Ukraine, or in the Soviet Union but in the neighbouring countries, in Europe, and in the world. The nuclear accident happened on Saturday, April 26, 1986, very early in the morning. Evidence of increased radioactivity was discovered in Sweden on Sunday, but the source of contamination could not be found in the country. On Monday, Swedish authorities confronted Moscow and information about the accident was made public in the West. However, it was only on Monday evening, April 28 that any information about the accident was announced in the Soviet Union. In many ways it was 'façade thinking' all over again: let's keep up the appearance. Maybe if we say nothing, the problem will disappear or no one will notice. On Monday morning, in Edinburgh, Scotland, on my way to the university, I bumped into my British-Ukrainian friend Peter Szalapaj in front of the Edinburgh's Old College. I had never seen Peter so distressed before. He had heard the news and, being both passionately Ukrainian and intelligent, understood its importance and was devastated by its perceived and anticipated effects. I immediately went home to call my mother and my husband's parents (we did not have cell phones yet).

The weather in Poland on that particular April weekend was beautiful. My in-laws and my mother spent the weekend at my in-laws' little cottage outside Warsaw. They did some maintenance on their little wooden house, took the carpets out, let them air in the sunshine, and later beat the dust out of them (which was probably by then radioactive). They spent the whole day outside, enjoying the sun. They were relatively far away from Chernobyl and did not suffer any immediate health consequences. We were in Edinburgh, much further away, where the weather was bad and where we spent the weekend mostly inside. How many people, who were much closer to the accident site, enjoyed the spring sunshine on that weekend? The authorities in the Soviet Union never disclosed the full impact of the accident. How many people died in the rescue operation and immediately after? How many people died or are still dying of thyroid cancer or other health problems caused by radioactive fallout?

Why did the accident happen? Was it an accident or the effect of a test gone wrong?

A few days after the accident, we had a meeting of our East-West student society (which Peter and I established) at the University of Edinburgh, with Andrzej Mierzejewski, a Polish physicist and a postdoctoral fellow in the Department of Chemistry, talking about the science behind the disaster. Andrzej spoke about his knowledge of and experience with health and safety standards in Soviet nuclear research facilities, recollecting a scene reported by another colleague: an elderly cleaning lady, with no protective gear, dusting and mopping (probably on her knees, with a wet rag in her hand) the insides of a chamber where the reactor was housed. Quite likely no one ordered her to do that but also no one warned her against it. Almost exactly ten years later, Andrzej died of cancer at the age of 47. His wife told me that several colleagues from his institute in Poland had suffered from or died of various cancers and that some people believed there may have been some health and safety issue there too.

I wonder what defines this basic respect for the lives and welfare of others that is so often missing in totalitarian systems. Where does this indifference and lack of empathy come from? How can we protect ourselves from it? It seems sometimes that even in non-totalitarian countries our societal networks of friendship, compassion, and mutual trust or respect are breaking down. The media are creating a moral panic about youth violence. Walking at night through major European cities is often not a pleasant experience, with lots of intoxicated people. It feels unsafe partly because of the violence we read about in papers and see on TV. Respect for the individual human being, especially those who cannot effectively claim it themselves—children, the elderly, the disabled—seems so old fashioned, but it is, in my opinion, the best safeguard of a healthy human environment—I am trying to avoid the weasel word 'society'.

In 2006, I did a small survey on motivation to achieve good grades among first-year university students at McMaster. I expected that students would be motivated by the prospect of better jobs or admission to graduate programmes, but the number one motivator was respect. Students said that they were willing to put more effort into classes where they felt respected by the instructor (Stroinska 2006).

The issue of respect is in my opinion related to another characteristic feature of our times: the disposable nature of things. Even two or three decades ago, things were still made to last. Not just in Poland, but everywhere. Even stockings and pantyhose were repaired. We did not throw away letters after we read them. Sometimes they were kept for decades, passed from one generation to the next. I never threw out any toys. Even when broken, they still had a role to play.

Once I washed a plastic doll and all her pretty hair came off. It turned out that, underneath the glued-on hair, the doll had short hair moulded into the surface of its head: instead of going into the rubbish, the doll could now be a little boy or a cancer survivor. I loved to play with building blocks—the ones at home were likely from before the war, wooden, some dyed in different colours and some covered in greenish-brown paper, quite ugly. It did not bother me too much when I was building castles out of them. I also had a number of tin knights on horses, actually quite pretty. They could be used to play the battle at Grunwald, between the Teutonic Knights and the Polish and Lithuanian forces. I had Ulrich von Jungingen and Prince Witold and some other horsemen in historic uniforms. The knights could be taken off their horses but they had very badly curved legs (to fit their horses). Thus, my biggest problem was to imagine these crooked legs away and see them as beautiful. With Kasia, when we played at my place, we used to put all of my dolls together—they came in different kinds and sizes—and played two households—that of JFK and that of Martin Luther King Jr. We did not have any adult male dolls (like Ken, Barbie's boyfriend), and thus we chose two famous widows. That must have been after 1968 when Martin Luther King Jr. was assassinated. All the other dolls were the children. Another pastime was related to our walking home from school, after Grade 7, when we moved to School No. 93 and took a streetcar home. We would say goodbye at the big iron gate of Kasia's apartment building complex between Asnyka and Niemcewicza Streets. She would be on the other side of the massive bars and we would have whole pretend dialogues, one of us being imprisoned Lenin and the other Nadezhda Krupska, his wife. This was our way to de-compress from the political propaganda and ideology at school. But, in the end, it showed how much we have been shaped by that environment.

In the world where things were scarce, with a bit of imagination, a role could be found for almost anything and defects could be imagined away. This ability to do without or to do with imperfect things comes with poverty but some of this tolerance for imperfection is quite healthy. I believe it is healthier than a situation where, in order to play Snow White and the seven dwarfs, children need a specific Snow White doll and seven smaller dwarf dolls. Six dwarfs or seven larger dolls would not do.

In the past, if something broke down, it was repaired, not replaced. There were toy repair shops too. There was one two streets away from my house, on the corner of Grójecka and Niemcewicza Streets. It had naked and broken dolls in a tiny display window, with eyes or hair missing. Some were missing the tops of their heads. The dolls looked old and dead. The store looked scary to me when I was a child. Later, its memory brought to mind the display cases with broken objects collected in the museum at Auschwitz. Here is my inherited, intergenerational childhood trauma speaking again.

The need for repairs in communism resulted from the simple fact that it was at times difficult to buy almost anything in order to replace a broken item. I am not nostalgic about the long queues and the situation where only single mothers of disabled children had a chance to buy a refrigerator or a washing machine. There is nothing I miss about my life under communism except for my own youth and the relatives and friends that are long gone. However, I do miss the fact that in the past we had more respect for things in general. The need to repair broken appliances created a huge demand for people who could fix things. In Poland, they were commonly referred to as the 'golden hand' (*złota rączka*) and could repair broken radios, fix sawing machines, paint windows, and make book shelves. Now, with 'planned obsolescence', it is cheaper to buy a new TV or cellphone than to look for someone to fix the old one.

Some things simply cannot be fixed. They have to be disposed of and replaced. Even people who run repair shops advise you to just buy a new thing and not bother fixing the old. To fix would be more expensive than to buy. You have to pay the repairman a first world salary while the TV was produced somewhere where people were paid a fraction of its cost. We do not respect things the way previous generations used to because most things today are only valuable through their usefulness. A broken modern desk lamp or a broken clock are not objects of beauty worth saving for their looks. If they stop working, they usually have to go.

This urge to replace instead of fixing makes me fear the time when I am old and when my body will stop working properly. Will anyone bother to repair what is not working or will I become human waste, to be disposed of, tossed to rubbish, maybe not literally but simply by being removed to a nursing home? A broken lamp to be placed in the attic, out of sight?

While a mere identification with possessions, including houses and national treasures, is not a good way to find your own sense of self, we do owe some respect to what other generations have created, whether in literature, art, or architecture. Destroying their creations is like erasing the people themselves. I extend this to special achievements of every era and system, including totalitarian regimes. I do not mean by this that monuments of Stalin, Hitler, Dzierżyński, or Saddam Hussein should be kept in public spaces and I perfectly understand people's urge to destroy them. If this is really a spontaneous desire, it has to happen and maybe it has a function in the process of societal healing after the abuse. However, the organized destruction of the remnants of another regime, be it books or paintings or monuments or buildings, can be seen as a prelude to more atrocities.

Also, without keeping the art of totalitarian regimes available to younger generations—with an appropriate historical commentary—it becomes difficult to explain why those systems were fundamentally wrong. If you look at Soviet propaganda pictures from the 1930s, they portray happy peasants gathering rich harvest. They radiate optimism about the achievements of agriculture under communist rule and are making the viewer feel good about the fate of those who lived in such prosperous times. The problem is, of course, that such pictures were painted at the time of the horrible man-made

Holodomor Great Famine in Ukraine, when several million people starved. Whether the famine resulted from a pseudo-scientific experiment and a wrong central decision what to plant or whether it was meant as a punishment for Ukraine's reluctance to implement forced collectivization, the tragedy of the Ukrainian peasants remains in sharp contrast with the sunny depictions of a plentiful harvest. Many years later, Ukrainians are still in the process of changing street names that were associated with the organizers of the *Holodomor*. Very few painters at the time dared to depict the reality of Ukrainian suffering. Among those who did was Kasimir Malevich (1878–1935), whose ascetic images may be not realistic in form, but capture the suffering of the people. Modern Ukrainian art is filling this void today, trying to find language—both verbal and visual—that would be appropriate to the enormity of the Ukrainian *Holodomor* (literally, 'death through hunger'). It is difficult to comprehend the vicious nature of communist propaganda without examples such as Soviet harvest art from the 1930s. An additional aspect of that kind of art is that, through its purported realism, it is a double lie. It tells a false story, but it makes the viewer believe that the setting is real. Obviously, the logic behind this thinking is faulty. There was no harvest, thus there were no happy peasants. Not even the landscape is real in this propaganda art.

The monumental nature of Nazi architecture also merits some form of commemoration, not for its artistic level of accomplishment but at least for didactic purposes. The Colosseum like Nazi Congress Hall and the imposing party rally grounds in Nuremberg or the Olympic Stadium in Berlin, all of them a fitting backdrop for Leni Riefenstahl's 'artistic documentary film propaganda' (or 'propaganda films') are overwhelming and help contextualize the atmosphere of the period. The Nazi love for fire, especially for its primeval effect in the darkness of the night, exemplified by marches with torches, survived the regime in the form of the familiar Olympic torch, first introduced into modern games at the 1936 Berlin Olympics. In association with the Olympic ideals, it seems benign, but in association with the burning of books it shows its inherently violent nature. One should remember the ugly origins of some seemingly innocent symbols.

Similarly, people may look at the Warsaw Palace of Culture or the Lomonosov Moscow State University and see their similarity to familiar American architecture in New York City or Chicago from the first half of the 20th century. The monstrosity of Nazi or communist architecture is only partially dependent on their visual shape. They truly become inhuman in their hypocrisy when one thinks of Nazi concentration camps or Soviet labour camps erected at the same time and by the same political leaders. Time works against us, giving the ruins of the empires past a shimmer of romantic nostalgia. Tourists looking at the remains of the arena in the ruins of the Roman Colosseum may no longer think of countless slaves or animals who died there. They are more likely to admire the power of the Roman Empire and the skill of its architects. How can we learn to see the true nature of political systems when they are so skillful at disguising atrocities with euphemisms and hiding them behind either the well-meaning and humanist looking art or behind intimidating, pompous architecture. What sixth sense can we use to see through the façade?

Zbigniew Herbert (1924-1998), in his poem "The Power of Taste" (translated into English by John and Bogdana Carpenter), suggests that the sense of taste, aesthetic taste, may perhaps be the key. He wrote:

So aesthetics can be helpful in life
one should not neglect the study of beauty

Before we declare our consent we must carefully examine
the shape of the architecture the rhythm of the drums and pipes
official colours the despicable ritual of funerals

Our eyes and ears refused obedience
the princes of our senses proudly chose exile

It did not require great character at all
we had a shred of necessary courage
but fundamentally it was a matter of taste

Yes taste
that commands us to get out to make a wry face draw out a sneer
even if for this the precious capital of the body the head
must fall

During my life in Poland in the 1960s, 1970s, and until 1984, heads no longer fell all that often. Courage became a bit cheaper than it had been for my parents' generation. But even for my generation, the fundamental sense of taste was something that could be trusted, at least most of the time. The examination of 'the shape of architecture', the aesthetics of communism, Nazism, or any other -ism, exemplified by the illustrations of textbooks, party posters, the officially sponsored popular music, should allow a careful and meticulous viewer to see beyond the shallow water of appearance. This principle is still relevant today. Whether it is the ugly monuments of Lech Kaczyński, the Kaczyński twin who died in the plane catastrophe at Smoleńsk in 2010, the tasteless opulence of palaces built by Putin and his oligarchs, the disco-polo style of popular music in Poland, our sense of style gives us a warning. Herbert urges us to retain this basic sense of what is beautiful and what is not, and keep our language plain so that we cannot be seduced by the mask—the façade.

CHAPTER 10

Post-Communism
The Blurring of Definitions

THE FALL OF THE BERLIN WALL in 1989 and the collapse of the communist system in most of Central and Eastern Europe created a new hope that political and ideological conflicts of the past had found a peaceful resolution. However, even if that initial hope had not been dashed by new conflicts, the study of totalitarian ways of thinking and the language of totalitarian propaganda should not be put aside. They remain relevant for a number of reasons. New threats have emerged over the past four decades and new varieties of sophisticated propaganda, more effective and dangerous than ever before have been developed. Most importantly, however, the communist frame of mind, shaped by the prescribed perspective on reality, has survived the end of the communist system. It is easier to transform economy than to change patterns of thought and alter linguistic habits. Many people in Eastern Europe still speak the same language they used to speak before and, usually unconsciously, refer to the old meanings of words. You cannot use some words without bringing back to life and giving new powers to the old way of thinking and black and white value judgements. A new propaganda, a hybrid of communist Newspeak and populism has emerged. It is aggressive, high-tech, often vulgar, and always confusing. It often follows Western models, putting a 'spin' on things rather than telling primitive lies, as it did in the past. But a spin is also a distortion and propaganda in glossy magazines and on colour TV is no more truthful than those same lies printed on cheap yellowish newsprint or shown on TV in black and white.

There are some conceptual traps today, more than three decades after the fall of the Berlin Wall, that still hinder communication between people from the West and people from the East. Thus, some of my observations on totalitarian thought manipulation continue to apply to communication between East and West today. There may be a free-market economy developing in post-communist countries, but we may ask ourselves whether the understanding of terms 'free', 'market', and 'economy' by those who are trying to introduce it, is not still determined by what they learned in the old centrally planned economy. Easily translatable, such notions may create the impression of mutual understanding, while in fact they are traps for foreign economic advisors and financial consultants. Those traps are not set on purpose, but simply result from the fact that neither side is fully aware of the deep divide between the meanings attached to the same notions. It is natural, as we always tend to assume that 'our way of doing things' is the only one, or the right one and since we do not closely examine the meanings of commonly used terminology.

Although the discredited Soviet political system collapsed in Eastern Europe, some of its elements survived. Melich explains this as follows:

> ...lingering patterns of hypocrisy and the difficulties in using language and the media of public communication between the private and public spheres and within the public sphere in general may have been greater than the people themselves were willing to admit.[...] The fact that the language and communicative patterns of the official sphere often dramatically differed from the language used within the private domain, diminished people's ability to engage in a natural public discourse and led to their resignation on its very significance. (Melich 1997, 7)

At a meeting organised by the British Council in Prague in April 1998 and aimed at helping East and West understand each other better, one of the conference organisers, George Schoepflin of the University of London, pointed out that communication could become one of the challenges of the EU's eastward expansion. He stated:

> I would like to emphasise [...] the importance of finding a common language of communication between what I will call at this moment West and East. Post-communist patterns of expression are really very different from those of Western Europe, and it is extremely difficult quite often for the two actually to understand one another. They appear to be understanding one another but in reality they are talking past one another. Secondly, within the EU particular forms of expression have grown up, particular ways of doing things, a particular corporate consciousness has grown up, which is not necessarily entirely known by the 10 countries which are expecting to join the European Union. This meeting will create the personal contacts which will allow some of these problems to be ironed out. (Breffni O'Rourke 1998)

Problems in communication with post-communist countries begin at the level of vocabulary, and only then extend to other areas of language behaviour. F.A. Hayek writes:

> While wisdom is often hidden in the meaning of words, so is error. Naïve interpretations [...] survive and determine our decisions through the words we use. Of particular relevance [...] is the unfortunate fact that many words that we apply to various aspects of the extended order of human co-operation carry misleading connotations of an earlier kind of community. Indeed, many words embodied

> in our language are of such character that, if one habitually employs them, one is led to conclusions not implied by any sober thought about the subject in question, conclusions that also conflict with scientific evidence. (Hayek 1988, 109)

I shall concentrate here on three linguistic and cultural phenomena that I believe to be typical of misunderstanding in contacts with partners in post-communist economies—though to various degrees for various countries of the region. The first is the meaning and function of the word 'social' and the network of expressions to which it is commonly attached. The understanding of this concept in the former Soviet Bloc countries unconsciously affects perception of economic reality and expectations about the role of the state in providing benefits to the population. The second concept is that of 'competition' as opposed to 'co-operation', with the conviction surviving in most countries of the former Soviet Bloc that co-operation is better, morally cleaner and 'socially' more beneficial. The third such semantic area is the discourse about 'money' and financial operations in general, both at the microeconomic (i.e., personal) and macroeconomic level. As it is impossible to discuss economic reforms without reference to financial issues, attitudes about money are of utmost importance and affect understanding of many economic problems.

For Hayek, 'social' is a weasel word. Even the word 'society' is, in his opinion, redundant and misleading as it falsely suggests that very different types of relationships between individuals in different systems could all be brought together under one label (Hayek 1988, 112). Also, he alleges that the word is used to blur the distinction between the government, i.e., the authorities, and the people governed. However, the adjective 'social' is, for him, perhaps the most harmful instance of a weasel word and probably "the most confusing expression in our entire moral and political vocabulary" (Hayek 1988, 114).

While the word 'socialist' became suspect even, or perhaps particularly, in the former communist countries, 'social' lingers on through dozens of expressions. It became a fixed prefix to words such as justice, awareness, institution, policy, democracy, solidarity or work, as if there were any instances of justice or democracy that would not involve people and were happening in a vacuum. The word social gives to these expressions an air of respectability and moral justification. This may go back to the meaning attributed to the word social at the end of the 18th century. In their encyclopedia, published between 1751 and 1772, Diderot and D'Alembert defined the term as, "a word newly introduced in the language to designate those attributes that render a man useful in society, and fit him for human intercourse: 'the social virtues' (quoted after Aron 1968).

Curran (1958, 8), quoted by Hayek (1988, 118), calls the continued usage of social in expressions that simply describe institutions of the state a "semantic fraud", similar to the expression "People's Democracy."

Confusion about the meanings of 'society' and 'social' naturally causes a problem in communication, especially when the transition to Western market economics initially brings more hardship than profit to large sectors of population in Eastern Europe. This may have been particularly visible in Russia, where the last decade of the twentieth century has been ruinous to the country's aspirations to remain a world power, largely due to its dysfunctional and incomplete transition to free market economy. In the introduction to Gustafson's (1999, xii) book on capitalism 'Russian-style', Daniel Yergin notes that "Russians remain deeply ambivalent about this quasi-market system that has brought most of them wrenching change, hardship, and demands for which they had no preparation."

In this context, people's nostalgia for the old style of 'social institutions of the state', 'social safety nets', 'social assistance' for those who did not work, etc. are understandable. However, these sentiments do not allow them to realise that social assistance cannot be taken for granted, and that it was a misperception to believe that it came "at no cost to anybody" (Melich 1997, 6). Melich notes that in communist countries the state was supposed to be the "embodiment of *objective progress* (emphasis added) and knew how to achieve happiness for all" (ibid.). While the state exercised excessive control of every walk of life, through police informants, censorship, etc., it tried to compensate for this penetrating control by providing people with some basic social services to create the illusion of relative wealth and equality.

It is even more difficult for the people affected to accept that their present misfortune is not caused by the transition to market economy, but by the inevitable collapse of the system for which they spent most of their lives working. Unfortunately, the speed and magnitude of the collapse of the Soviet-style centralised economy came as a surprise to both the East and the West, and Central and Eastern Europe were not prepared for the resulting change. There was no time for a linguistic readjustment.

Many people in communist countries expected a positive change almost overnight (which may seem irrational, yet was quite understandable under the circumstances), but the transition brought immediate profit to few and, at least temporarily, hardship to most. Again, financial experts have expected it, but people were not prepared and reacted with hostility not towards the old malfunctioning economy and misleading ideology but towards the emerging market economy. In this situation, 'social institutions' from the previous era were fondly missed and positive sentiments towards, what Poles used to call *państwo opiekuńcze* (tutelar state) were a natural reaction to the existential fear of the unknown (cf. Maaz 1995). A fellow dog walker and local newspaper columnist in my Canadian hometown of Woodstock, Ontario, Bill Bes once pointed out to me that this is somewhat similar to the situation of an obese person who is warned by doctors of cardiovascular problems and put on a diet and exercise regime. Instead of feeling better by rationalizing about the benefits of the current situation that may be his only rescue, such person will likely blame the doctors for his hardship and long for the idle hours of relaxing in front of the TV. Politicians who want to gain popular votes exploit these sentiments of the people and promise them more 'social security' (or just some money, e.g., an extra child supplement or the 13th pension payment) and less uncertainty as such promises are attractive to less entrepreneurial (or less qualified, or older) voters. This is also why the concept of the 'social market economy', introduced by Alfred Mueller-Armack in Germany in opposition to the centrally planned economy, is (mis)interpreted by many as a gentler or more compassionate form of market economy (Zieliński 2001, 43) simply because it uses the word 'social'.

As long as the free-market economy is not properly established, populist politicians may continue to promise what economies cannot deliver. Only a few see this and some openly criticize the political naïveté of people. Maciej Rybiński, a prominent Polish journalist observed in the newspaper *Rzeczpospolita* (9 April 2001, p. A2) on that strange state of public mind:

> Almost half of the Poles believe that, when SLD [a post-communist party called the Alliance of the Democratic Left] takes power, every unemployed person will get a job paid by the state, a briefcase and a desk, and every homeless person will get a flat in an apartment building. Where does this faith come from? Well, from the worldview.

The English word 'worldview', as well as its Polish equivalent *światopogląd*, is calqued from German (*Weltanschauung*). The word was famously used by Wilhelm von Humboldt, German philosopher and linguist, and Prussian Minister of Education. For him language was both a product and a repository of the *Wetlanschauung* of the people who spoke it. As a concept in philosophy, 'worldview' refers to a world perception and the framework of beliefs that act as a filter through which every individual perceives and makes sense of the world. The term made a significant career in the Third Reich, where it practically replaced the word philosophy; 'Philosophy' had acquired negative connotations in public political discourse through its association with many Jewish names and needed to be changed. *Weltanschauung* included the element of 'viewing' and thus replaced thinking with a more instinctive, emotional and often irrational 'on-look'. People were supposed to gain 'natural' understanding of complex problems without analysing them. This, obviously, was very handy from the point of view of propaganda and thought control as it encouraged and promoted switching of the logic and reasoning (for a more detailed analysis of the use of this term in Nazi propaganda cf. Klemperer 2000, 141-147). In communist discourse, on the other hand, the word 'worldview' was often accompanied by the word 'scientific.' In Nazi German, 'scientific worldview' would sound like an oxymoron. In communist Newspeak it signified atheism or Marxism or any 'correct' and 'progressive' point of view. Even if the word 'scientific' or any other 'positive' adjective (e.g., Marxist) was missing, as in the quotation above, the interpretation stayed the same. What the author is saying could be paraphrased: under communism people have learned to expect that the state will provide them with everything for free and they think this will happen again if the communists take over the government. It is no wonder that such promises are popular in a country with high unemployment rate.

One might hope that the emptiness of unwarranted political promises is slowly becoming transparent even to ordinary readers. Another Polish daily, *Gazeta Wyborcza* (11 April 2001, p. 3 of the Sport section), printed the following letter to the editor:

> Since Leszek Miller [the leader of the above mentioned SLD—MS] is an effective politician, when he presented his party's project [...] on physical education, sport, as well as fight against drugs, alcoholism and all the plagues of the young generation of Poles, a heavy stone was heaved from my heart. Unfortunately, it then dropped on my foot. Everyone who can count, even if only with a calculator, knows, that the outlined project [...] is a joke.

This political climate of promising what voters would like to hear and mixing reality with wishful thinking must be taken into account when discussing issues such as reform of the social security system in Eastern Europe or the functioning of financial institutions. The most unfortunate development in recent years is the devaluing of political promises which are becoming worthless propaganda slogans both in Eastern Europe and Western democracies (see Terry Arthur's (2007) examples of various kinds of political 'crap'). This, however, is a topic for another chapter.

When talking about 'competition' as one of the principles of market economy, one needs to be aware of the connotations of the very concept of competition in post-communist societies where this word may evoke negative responses not easily understandable for Western partners. State institutions and countries of the Soviet bloc were supposed to co-operate and not compete with each other. As one product was usually manufactured by one company and often in insufficient quantity, there was not much scope for any meaningful competition anyway. The results of such 'co-operation' or, in other words, 'centrally planned economy', were often disastrous. The reason for these disastrous effects was partly the very elimination of competition from the market and the creation of a state monopoly. However, the state, which controlled the economy, did not refer to its own activities as 'state control', which it was, but as 'planning' or 'co-ordination'—another word whose meaning was shifted to obscure its usage.

"Competition is inevitable where social position is not conferred by heredity," stated Raymond Aron (1968, 43), and his opinion would hardly be contested in the West. Our lives are permeated with competition—from sports to professional careers. If the rules of competition are fair (and this should be part of the definition of the concept of competition), competition may motivate people to do their best.

This does not mean that co-operation is not a valuable form of relationship among people. Co-operation is probably what we would expect from a circle of close friends and colleagues and, indeed, this is precisely the environment where co-operation should prove successful. Experiences of co-ordinating co-operation on a larger scale teach that it is not a suitable ordering principle for larger scale undertakings. Co-operation requires a certain level of consensus of all parties involved about objectives and methods of reaching those objectives. While this may be feasible within a small group of people with common interests, it makes no sense when a larger group of people or several institutions have to deal with new situations and adapt to the unknown. Even high school students tend to protest when told to do group projects as they find it difficult to co-ordinate their schedules in order to find time to meet, even virtually, and work together. And even if they do, students find some members work much harder while others benefit by getting a grade without doing their fair share. If they were to compete against each other, some would excel and others would probably fail. As a failing student creates a problem, this may be the reason why teachers assign group projects in the first place. Hayek (1988: 19) describes competition as a procedure of discovery essential in all kinds of evolution. It is the discovery of optimal, or at least improved and more efficient, ways of dealing with problems.

Centrally planned economies, with their state monopoly on decision making, did not look favourably at the idea of competition. In Polish, even the word *konkurencja* (competition), with its originally exclusively economic connotations, was almost successfully replaced with a term derived from the language of sport, *współzawodnictwo* (sport competition), which was seen as a socialist version of competition based on team work and co-operation. This rather twisted notion resulted from using the same lexical element *współ-* (meaning 'together' or 'with', just like the English 'co-'), which also appears in *współpraca* (co-operation).

The concept of *konkurencja* as equivalent of competition was, in communist ideology, strongly linked with the capitalist economy and associated with exploitation of workers to make produced goods competitive. Thus, even competitive attitudes to one's career would not be looked upon very charitably and in private discourse, competitive colleagues would be labelled as ruthless, greedy and inconsiderate. The word 'ambitious' may have had negative connotations in such work-related contexts. The concept of motivation through competition would not have a lot of appeal to anyone born before 1960. The situation is naturally changing as the new generation of people born and raised after the fall of the system has entered the work force. Yet, they would have still been exposed to the communist way of thinking through their parents' and their teachers' attitudes. It takes a long time to change the world view contained in language.

The distrust of money is not limited to communist and post-communist economies. The love of money is often seen as the root of every evil and the relationship between individuals and money is ambivalent in many cultures. Money is powerful and desirable, but also considered an instrument of manipulation and corruption. Indirect financial transactions took the place of the direct exchange of goods between people and made the very nature of this process more obscure. In communist countries, money lending and the idea of interest on loans or credits were often considered as taking advantage of those in financial need and looked at as dirty business while the stock exchange was often viewed as a kind of casino and discussed in the language of gambling (cf. a very interesting discussion by Terry Arthur 2000). The verb used in communist Polish to describe stock exchange activities of individual share holders was to 'speculate'. It acquired the negative meanings of 'profiteering' or 'gambling', i.e., engaging in possibly profitable but quite likely not very honest or even legal procedures (not necessarily with reference to stock exchange) and could likely land one in prison. The Polish word is likely borrowed from German, possibly from war time and possibly with reference to people who would buy food in villages and smuggle it to cities: German *Spekulant* is someone who makes risky investments. Translations into English include: 'boomer', 'gambler', 'speculator', and 'adventurer'. It may be interesting to note that today, when stock exchange operates in Poland again (and, ironically, is physically located in the former Communist Party's headquarters), the verb to s*peculate* is no longer used for buying and selling of shares and has been replaced by the verb *grać*, which means to 'play' or to 'gamble' and is decidedly less negative.

On top of the ambiguities that are characteristic to discourse about money everywhere, communist economy added its own brand of obscurity. Though money may seem to be central to any economy, money in the Soviet system was not a well-defined concept and it was not easily talked about. Gustafson explains this phenomenon:

> In the Soviet system of central planning, goods were produced and distributed through a combination of planners' orders from above and vigorous bargaining from below. "Money", said Peter Karpov, deputy director of Russia's federal bankruptcy agency, "was like an amusing but insignificant little musical accompaniment." In actual fact, the interesting thing about money in the Soviet system was that its value varied depending on who spent it and

> where. One hundred rubles, in the hands of a well-placed nomenklatura family shopping in one of the closed stores for the Party elite, bought a fortune. In effect, three currencies circulated in the Soviet economy—money, power and connections. The price of any given object was a blend of the three. (Gustafson 1999, 23)

People in communist countries were not earning a lot, but there was also no visible unemployment, which, in turn, may have contributed to rather poor work ethics. As mentioned earlier, an old saying popular in Poland was: "they (i.e., the government) pretend to pay us and we (the workers) pretend to work." Many people felt that there was nothing wrong about doing private business during their official working hours and using the equipment that belonged to the employer for private purposes. Working really hard for little money was often considered naive and foolish, while working hard in your own private business was regarded with a mixture of envy and hostility. Thus, derogatory names such as *prywaciarze* ('privateers' for private business owners) or *badylarze* (derogatory for 'gardeners' derived from *badyl*—'weed', for owners of horticultural businesses) were given to private businessmen in communist Poland and popularized by the communist media. Small scale businessmen and businesswomen were considered to be people who had money, but not necessarily education or sophistication. It is quite likely that these words were invented by communist media, spread through them and were willingly adopted by individual language users because they had already adopted the socialist attitude to wealth and private business enterprise.

Although, privately, possession of money was always desirable, paradoxically, not having money was considered almost virtuous and could be seen as evidence of honesty. Only private business owners (in countries where some private enterprise was allowed, e.g., Poland), people with families abroad (where contacts were allowed), and communist party officials had money. Popular and successful artists, especially actors and writers, whose wealth was considered well deserved, were an exception from the general rule.

As money is central to any market operation, the absence of money from public discourse would indicate that there were no normal market mechanisms in place. The only authentic 'market' operating in most countries of the former Soviet Bloc was 'the black market'. The operations of other institutions based on the flow of money were also obscured. The idea of taxation, for instance, is relatively new in most of Eastern Europe, as—until the collapse of the old system—taxes usually remained a hidden factor. People were paid a salary at the end of a period of work without any indication of what amount, if any, was deducted for taxes, social security, and other purposes. The fact they now know how much tax they pay may appear to some as an additional burden of the market economy. It seemed that the old system had financed public institutions (such as health care and education) without taking taxes from people. This, of course, is a misconception, but it may be more widespread than foreign experts might suspect. The collapse of the old system brought the institution of money, the real currency, back to centre stage of economic life. However, people still need time to learn to see money and talk about it as a normal and objectively measurable part of the economy; this has yet to be achieved. The second PiS government, elected in 2015, further obscured the value of work and the role of financial institutions. It offered more money to people who had children and were in dire need but did so without fiscal responsibility, more to ensure votes than to ensure a healthy economy that could support better living conditions for all.

Poles who emigrated after spending some of their working lives in communist Poland often had great difficulty discussing their salary with their Western employers. A similar situation is happening now with Ukrainian refugees who are applying for jobs in Western countries, jobs often below their qualifications. They are usually not prepared to discuss remuneration questions and agree to what is offered without asking how the pay is determined. In communist Poland, there was very little scope for discussing salary arrangements. It never occurred to me to ask for a raise during my five years of work at Warsaw University and even if I had asked for it, I doubt I would be given one, not because I did not deserve it but because salaries at that level were not negotiable. If everyone makes the same amount of money, there are no secrets.

One other important pair of concepts may be worth mentioning here. I am not sure whether they are typical of Warsaw only but they still have a very normative function there. People, according to ingrained Warsaw standards, fall into one of two categories. Someone is either a *cwaniak*, i.e., a cunning, shrewd, and sly person who comes out on top in any confrontation, or they are a *frajer*, i.e., a helpless victim, a dupe, and a naive fool. In Warsaw, you must never let others think you are a *frajer*, someone others can take advantage of. This would be equal to a social suicide. A lot of rather uncivilized behaviour of Poles, such as jumping the queue, cutting off others in traffic, overtaking other cars on the road, overcharging unsuspecting client, etc. may be attributed to this misplaced belief in the importance of not being seen as a *frajer*. I think I much better fit the *frajer* category and so it is no wonder I so strongly detested and still detest people who were *cwaniaks*. The only person from whom I accept this word as a compliment is my father-in-law. If I make a move in bridge that he considers smart (which does not happen very often) or if I come up with an answer when he does not have one (which does not happen very often either) or when I happen to know a word in English that he is looking for and cannot find, he smiles and calls me *cwaniaczka* (a female form of *cwaniak*). I truly appreciate and relish such moments.

An area where the financial reality has not yet been fully comprehended is the field of education. Many traditional institutions of learning in post-communist countries are still free of charge, and education—from elementary to postgraduate—is seen as an undisputed right rather than a privilege. This leads to a number of beliefs that are not self-evident. Graduate students working on their dissertations in areas of finance, banking, or insurance often feel free to approach companies and ask them for assistance in obtaining data, information or expert advice without any appreciation that the time of a company manager has its price. They assume since their education is free, seeking free assistance from any source available in the country is part of the entitlement. One consulting company manager told me he has at least one graduate student a month approaching his company with requests for information and not a single one addressed the issue of time and compensation. Again, this attitude dates back to communist times when many people felt free to use their time at work (paid by an impersonal state) to engage in their private activities.

Until recently, the assumption that higher education and research should be fully supported by the state came across when researchers from Eastern Europe considered participation in international conferences. If their country's university or government cannot afford to fund them, they often believe their participation should be funded by the conference organizers. If invited, they often expect the host will pay their expenses or waive conference fees, as if those were notional rather than real expenses. Many Eastern Europeans would not consider paying expenses out of their own pocket, which may indeed be impossible for some as salaries in education are still rather low. On the other hand, they would be surprised if a Western colleague did not participate in a conference organized in Eastern Europe for the same reasons. In post-communist countries, there is little understanding of the financial operations of higher education institutions and the reform of this sector of economy will require a significant change in people's attitudes and expectations. Quite honestly, the situation is not different in Canada where many people believe that student fees cover all costs of the university's operation which is not the case.

Communism was not an economic system but rather a system of total political control of everything. As economist Ludwig von Mises (1881-1973) rightly predicted in his 1922 book *Socialism*, communism had no means of economic calculation.

> An economy is a price system. A business must know the costs (or prices) of everything—raw materials, machinery, rental of buildings, labor, inventory, overhead, shipping, and more. In other words, a business must know what it can afford in relation to expected income. Prices are calculated in relation to supply and demand. Under Communism, there was no market to set prices.

> Supply was determined by the government, regardless of demand. Everyone was forced to work, so there was no competition for jobs. The true costs of production were not known. Wages were completely arbitrary, as were prices of goods." (von Mises 1922)

As soon as the communist system in Poland was officially over after the 1989 elections, my husband decided to bring his academic expertise in actuarial science to Poland. Starting in the summer of 1990 and continuing for many years, he, and a group of enthusiasts from all over the world, used all possible sources of funding in order to teach this field of financial mathematics to Polish and other Eastern European students. Teaching the principles of market economy, finance, and professionalism was part of the process of bringing post-communist economies closer to the rest of the Western world. They all observed a number of common problems, characteristic for teaching about market economy in Eastern Europe. These observations may help in understanding why some teaching methods that work well in the West (e.g., workshops or case studies) often fail to produce similarly positive results when applied to teaching financial operations or managerial skills in Eastern Europe. Some issues may go beyond strictly linguistic observations and some may go beyond the regional boundary and apply to certain groups of professionals across the board, especially in countries undergoing economic transformation.

Generally, a detailed categorisation of the group of people who constitute the student body helps in cultural encounters: "Central and Eastern Europeans" is a very broad label and may only be useful for stereotyping, i.e., forming generalised but mostly untrue images of people who belong to a given category. It is always helpful to recognise the more subtle distinctions within a larger group of people, e.g., by country, ethnicity, religion, age, profession, social status, education, or gender. I did not list gender last by accident either. I used to think that in Eastern Europe gender distinction was and is not as important as in some other cultures, although its relative relevance depends on the specific culture as well as the nature of communication. Now, as I am reviewing this manuscript in 2023, I also think that it depends on the government policy at the time. Polish women have become a discriminated-against group (especially in terms of access to prenatal medical care and abortion); a similar phenomenon may also be observed in the US, another country where gender equality is a major political issue.

When teaching groups of managers from financial institutions in Eastern Europe, country and age group are probably the most important factors to consider. The economic situation and the level of economic reform differ in different countries of the region. Some countries have joined the European Union; others are relatively close to the EU membership, while some are still plagued by inflation, corruption, and economic depression. Thus, the same expert advice may be taken as practical and useful information in one place while it will be seen as a speculative theory in another place and may even elicit negative comments. There also seems to be a strong conviction among some post-communist countries that their situation is special and that Western solutions would simply not work there. Although post-communist economy was indeed a new phenomenon in the 1990s, some financial techniques and economic laws are universally applicable, even though special circumstances and country-specific risks have to be considered. This, however, is a point that may have to be made with great care and tact and cannot be assumed to be obvious.

The importance of age groups cannot be overestimated. Age is the factor that distinguishes between those who were educated and gained experience within the communist system and those who were educated after the introduction of market reform. It is crucial to know who the target audience is going to be for any professional training or lecture course. If the audience consists of young people, many of the traps described above will not apply or apply in a very limited way. Young people, especially those who have already been exposed to Western education, do not use doubletalk or Newspeak. If, however, the audience consists of middle aged or senior professionals, they will be the most difficult target group in terms of communication.

First, there are differences in what can be learned by mature adults, how it is learned, and even the degree to which mature adults remain open to such learning at all. The second issue, format of presentation, has been analysed by Maureen Guirdham:

> In regard to formal learning, if, as in many central and eastern European countries, teachers are highly respected and honoured and hierarchies are important, then people may be used to learning from a lecture rather than from the give and take of a discussion. One of the many difficulties experienced by Western academics and others attempting to inculcate Western business education methods in the transition economies has been to make workshops, case studies and other participative learning techniques effective. (Guirdham (1999, 133-134)

It is therefore important to adapt the teaching style to the learning style and expectations characteristic for the target audience. Without correspondence between the two, the teaching process may be a frustrating experience and a waste of time for both sides.

One last factor that needs to be considered here, as indeed in any teaching situation, is the notion of 'face' (as used by Erving Goffman, 1959). For many middle-aged professionals in Eastern Europe, business encounters with Western partners, usually conducted in foreign language, are always associated with an unpleasant degree of uncertainty, anxiety, and thus also the need for self-affirmation in the eyes of the 'foreigners'. One easy way of achieving this is by being critical about the experts' advice, the teaching process, the work done by foreign advisors, etc. One needs to understand that this behaviour by Eastern European partners is often their way of defending their own positions and 'saving face' by threatening the position of the others.

At the end of the Second World War, Victor Klemperer wrote in his book on the Language of the Third Reich that it would be some time before the process of denazification were over. It was so "because it [was]n't only Nazi actions that ha[d] to vanish, but also the Nazi cast of mind, the typical Nazi way of thinking and its breeding-ground: the language of Nazism." (Klemperer 1947/2000, 2)

A comprehensive study on language deterioration under communism is still waiting to be written, but Klemperer's observation fits the period of transition that we are still living through. The communist system may have vanished, but the linguistic habits and the perception of reality by millions of people have been shaped by the communist ideology and it will require both time and conscious effort to change this state of affairs. Developments in Eastern Europe over the last years show this process may involve taking a few steps forward and then a few steps back. Some countries, including Poland, have unfortunately retreated so much that some progress achieved after 1989 may have been wasted. The populist wave has changed the landscape not only in Eastern Europe but also in some countries of Western Europe and the US. One cannot blame PiS or Donald Trump—they simply provided the answer for what people wanted.

There is one additional obstacle to overcome in the fight against the old mindset: while only few people would challenge the view that Nazism was a criminal system (even though this group is growing), there are still millions of people worldwide who believe in communist ideology. We see them parading in Moscow with pictures of Lenin, Stalin, and Putin, and sporting T-shirts with hammer and sickle or the red star. Some people collect communist memorabilia, like the 'baby Lenin' pin, designed as an analogy to depictions of baby Jesus. We also find such supporters in the West, especially among intellectuals, whom Hayek called "professional second-hand dealers in ideas" (Hayek 1998), criticizing the errors of the communist practice, but defending communist ideals. Like many of those who left communist countries behind, I had and still have some degree of what Vesna Goldsworthy calls "an East European allergy to anything that could be described as leftist, which is often the first phase in our westward movement" (2005, 77). I still have not been cured from that allergy by almost 40 years of living abroad. Showing pro-communist sympathies in some countries of the former Soviet block may open communication with some people, but it will likely close doors and end conversations in most situations. People who have lived through the practice of communism will be unlikely to believe the theory.

There is a considerable degree of consensus that the best strategy for peace and prosperity in Europe is to help the emerging economies in Central and Eastern Europe introduce economic reform and a stable market economy. This process began in the 1990s and is well advanced in some countries of the region (though with periodic—I hope—hiccups) while only beginning to take shape in others. As some countries, e.g., Poland, keep swinging from more liberal to more conservative governments, with various degrees of populist rhetoric, it may still be too early to be optimistic about the results of this integration but it is becoming clear that successful communication between the two parts of Europe will be a determining factor in this partnership. For this communication to be successful, both sides must try to understand what divides them, and language patterns are one of the important barriers in mutual understanding. It is also important that communication not be used to assert power but as a means to reach a common goal. The hidden obstacle remains the language itself. Because of the communist misappropriation of words for political purposes, people in Eastern Europe still struggle to find unambiguous language of political and economic thought. The attractiveness of populism is perhaps another phenomenon that has its roots in the totalitarian past of the region and the fact that Central and Eastern European countries do not have enough experience with institutions of a civil society and with democracy in general. And yet, we see populism taking control of Western societies that seemed impervious to such influences. The power of populism must not be underestimated, especially in the era of online information dissemination where everyone can add their two cents to any debate, no matter how ill-informed or hateful.

CHAPTER 11

Empty Promises and the 'Abused Society Syndrome'

The men the American public admire most extravagantly are the most daring liars; the men they detest most violently are those who try to tell them the truth.

Every election is a sort of advance auction of stolen goods,

—H.L. Mencken (1880–1956)

EVER SINCE 1989, the European Union integration of Poland was a distant but definitely a desirable goal for many people of the Solidarność (Solidarity) generation. Poles had a particularly long history of aspirations to "return to Europe" after a period of a forced isolation. It was therefore puzzling that in this arguably most pro-European nation in Eastern Europe, some 80 percent of votes in the 2004 elections to the European Parliament went to political parties openly hostile to the idea of European integration. There is a body of research on the mechanism of what I shall call here populist rhetoric and its attractiveness in both democratic and post-communist societies (NB. Held 1996, Weyland 1999, Meny & Surel 2002; a particular place should also be given to Terry Arthur's 1975 and 2007 books on 'Crap', i.e., the language used by the politicians) and I shall discuss this topic only briefly. What I find particularly disturbing is that despite the collapse of the communist system and decades of relative freedom from any direct oppression, Poles continue to exhibit social behaviours characteristic of communist societies, such as social apathy, low work ethics, high tolerance for criminal activity, alcoholism, etc. I kept struggling to understand these seemingly unrelated phenomena and to find a common explanation for political and social behaviour patterns in societies undergoing transition from an authoritarian system to democracy. As a linguist, I thought that perhaps taking a linguistic look at populism might help me in gaining a better understanding.

The spread of empty promises and all forms of populist rhetoric in public discourse seems to be reaching epidemic proportions worldwide. Whether in political life or in marketing, people are bombarded with promises that were likely never intended to be fulfilled. In political discourse, empty promises are particularly popular during election campaigns. This phenomenon is not limited to specific political agendas or party lines, but seems to be cutting across the wide spectrum of political life, in the West as much as in the East. It is particularly characteristic of the current wave of populism, where politicians are ready to promise anything to get elected. What seems surprising is not that empty promises are being made but rather that so many people still believe them and let the politicians get away without holding them responsible for their words. In post-communist countries people need time to fully get used to politicians having any specific message at all, rather than reciting (or rather reading) from a party script.

'Promise' is one of the so-called performative verbs. In order to perform the action of promising something, one has to utter the words "I promise" or something close to that, hence the notion of performatives. I looked at the performative speech act of promising as it has been used in contemporary public political debates in Poland (based on political speeches and media discourse on recent developments). I also looked at how promises are used by political parties, both those in power and in opposition, and their changing configurations. It was interesting to observe how some of the extreme populist rhetoric resorts to linguistic tools reminiscent of communist and fascist propaganda, but adapted to the new political context of global integration. Initially, I focused on regular promises but it soon became clear that some promises also act as threats.

Populist ideologies and populist politicians often win support by appealing to, or playing to. people's feelings such as fear or insecurity. These anxieties can be transformed, using linguistic tools, into hostility towards those who are perceived as potential threats. In the US, the public hears about terrorists threatening peoples' security or illegal immigrants threatening economic stability; in Poland we have had all kinds of populist propaganda against market reform or European integration that threaten our welfare or our Christian values. The Polish government elected in 2015 uses particular enemy figures: political opposition, women groups, ecologists, teachers, bicycle riders, immigrants from the Middle East, LGBTQ groups, etc. Most recently, people who demand truth about those who helped conceal information about priests molesting children are being vilified. Political discourse of populist groups that engage in this kind of propaganda is characterized by a high frequency of speech acts that take the form of promises but act as 'parasitic threats', i.e., are intended to be interpreted as threats directed at those in the audience who do not support the speaker. I am borrowing the term 'parasitic speech act' from discussions by linguists and philosophers such as Austin, Searle, Derrida, and Halion. I am particularly interested in the linguistic properties of threats attributed to people other than the speaker. It is not unusual for politicians to attribute threats to another party, one whose actual or potential actions could endanger the audience (Stroinska & Cecchetto 2005).

The resulting style of political discourse, as it is seen in Poland, is highly aggressive. Colloquialisms, slang, and vulgarisms are used intentionally in order to give populist politicians more popular appeal. The new political elites that the extreme parties are attempting to promote gain popularity in an environment dominated by anxiety, anger, envy, and fear. In the Western world, first paralyzed by the omnipresent threat of terrorism, then the global economic crisis, and most recently by a global pandemic, it may be instructive to analyze how language can be used to heighten social anxiety.

Populism is a political ideology or rhetorical style that claims the common person is oppressed by some 'elite' or 'special interest group', and that the instruments of power need to be taken away from this self-serving and self-absorbed elite or group and used for the benefit of all the people. A populist reaches out to ordinary people, talking about their economic and social concerns, and appealing to their common sense. An example of this kind of rhetoric was the Conservative Premier of Ontario, Mike Harris' 1995 election promise of the "common sense revolution," with deficit reduction and lower taxes, a promise he actually kept, at least for some time. However, many politicians do not bother to keep their promises. They simply keep making promises that the audience wants to hear. Consequently, populism can be seen as a rhetorical style that can be used to promote a variety of ideologies.

Since political or election promises can be seen as an example of performative speech acts, it might be interesting to see what Speech Act Theory can teach us about empty promises or how we could expand Speech Act Theory to account for election promises. According to Speech Act Theory (Strawson 1964), a successful promise must, among other more technical felicity conditions, be uttered with an intention to be kept. The person making a promise must intend to be seen as willing to fulfill the promise if they can. Obviously, what is being promised must be seen by the person to whom the promise is being made as something desirable and something they would not be receiving in the normal course of action. Thus, a promise of a price hike is not a valid promise because it is not a desirable outcome for the hearer. Neither is a promise of accountability a good one as the voters have the right to assume that those whom they elect would be accountable by definition. For a meaningful promise, the person making a promise must also be able to keep it. There is no point in promising something that is beyond the control or the sphere of influence of the one making the promise.

One does not need to look far to see that most of these conditions do not hold for political promises these days. On occasion, everyone makes promises that turn out to be impossible to keep, but repetition of this behaviour by an individual brands them a liar and untrustworthy. Yet, politicians do just that as a matter of habit but we keep entrusting them, time after time, with our lives and with our possessions. Isn't what the voter really wants is for politicians to do what they say they'll do?

Parasitic Speech Acts are defined as uses of language that are dependent on or derived from the primary uses of language. Thus, if the primary purpose of language is to perform certain conventional speech acts, such as asserting states of affairs, asking questions, or giving orders, parasitic or secondary uses of language are concerned with the performance of indirect communicative acts such as joking, persuasion for the purpose of advertising, poetry writing where language can not be interpreted literally, etc. A parasitic use of language is not unhappy or infelicitous, as Austin labelled it, or a failed use of language but rather a quite-deliberate secondary use of language. A natural question to ask is: do election promises as part of political language constitute the normal use of language or are they parasitic?

Commenting on the presidential candidates for the 2008 election campaign in the US, Michael Kinsley (2008) asserts that American "voters sense correctly that politics is an act" and that it only "becomes more and more of an act" as political campaigns are run more and more professionally. He continues:

> This is one area in which the media and the voters really diverge. Political correspondents respect the professionalism of a well-run campaign and are quickly bored by complaints of artifice. Voters, meanwhile, still take offense and long for sincerity. (Kinsley 2008, 48)

This longing for sincerity explains why most people perceive political discourse as normal language use since politicians, especially those of democratic persuasion, tend to present themselves as ordinary people who are in touch with the electorate. Nevertheless, most political texts are parasitic and fit the categories of theatrical and metaphoric. Just like theatrical discourse, political speeches are framed as opposed to being uttered, which points to their parasitic character. Also, the 'script' uttered by a politician is usually written by someone else, a spin doctor or some other ghostwriter. A political speech writer functions as a kind of a playwright and the politician is often merely a 'speaking body' (just like a cast member in a play). In that political discourse resembles all types of commercial communication, e.g., advertisements, where speakers have no need to identify with the advertised product even if they praise its value. Laura Penny (2005) calls this inflated, insincere speech that is meant to deceive the hearer "bullshit" and observes:

> Another property of commercial speech that leads to bullshit production is that it is not written by the people who have to say or assume responsibility for it. This is also a big problem with most political speech. I am not insisting that everyone draft his own material, though the English teacher in me reckons that anyone who cannot string together a sentence probably shouldn't lead a company or a country. But the number of people working from a script today encourages one to view every public statement as acting, an entire culture emoting like a dinner theatre troupe. Hey, everyone—let's put on a show! This division of rhetorical labor means that the brains who think up the words don't have to say them, and the speakers who give voice to the words don't have to think them. All the better to disconnect them from reality, my dear. (Penny 2005, 12)

As a result, promises made by politicians are practically by default insincere. While Wikipedia might not be the most appropriate source, here, I believe, it is quite instructive to look up the term 'election promise' in that collaborative source of information, edited by the people for the people and thus representative of popular opinions. We read there that an election promise is a promise made to the public by a politician who is trying to win an election. Such promises have long been a central element of elections and remain so today. Election promises are also notable for often being broken once a politician is in office. They are "part of an election platform. (…) They are an essential element in getting people to vote for a candidate. For example, a promise such as to cut taxes or to introduce new social programs may appeal to voters" ("election promises," Wikipedia).

What kind of promise is a promise that is expected to be broken? If it is a promise at all, it is at best an insincere one.

According to the Speech Act Theory, in making an insincere promise, the speaker does not have all the intentions and beliefs they have when making a sincere promise; rather, they only purport to have them (Strawson 1964, 51). Political promises are often insincere promises because they violate the 'essential condition' on promising. This condition states that the speaker intends that the utterance of certain words (i.e. the promise) will place them under an obligation to do the promised action. Also, in sincere promises, the speaker believes it is possible for them to perform the act (Strawson). In political discourse, on the other hand, the speaker knows in the back of their mind that there may be external conditions that will prevent them from fulfilling the promise once they are in office. However, they are not sharing this information with the public.

Also, election promises are usually based on the most optimistic political, economic, and social forecasts for the future (a strong economy, cooperative opposition leaders, and good or at least stabile international situation). Government policies, on the other hand, usually have to plan for the worst possible scenario for the future. They have to be prudent and often take the form of contingency planning. If a politician running for office were to present a plan for the worst-case scenario, their platform would be far less attractive than that of their opponents. Thus, realism about future performance of the economy, etc. would hurt the politician and most likely not help them get elected. Wikipedia (ibid.) adds that a realistic programme for the future "is also difficult to do in ten second news sound bites or thirty second commercials." Therefore, Wikipedia explains, "election promises have been broken for as long as elections have been held and this is likely to continue."

Indeed, there are logical reasons and powerful pressures on politicians who are running for office to make promises which they know they cannot keep. Politicians who tell the truth and do not exaggerate their future ability to deliver on their promises will not appear attractive to the electorate, especially in the political environment that promotes media coverage based on exaggeration.

This can give the exaggerating party an advantage over the truthful one. Government finances are extremely complex and promises are vague enough that the media and public can rarely say for certain that the numbers do not add up. Accordingly, almost all parties continue to promise lower taxes, more social programs, and a balanced budget. I also think that a politician who makes popular promises appears to be in touch with the needs of the electorate. They may not be able or willing to deliver, but the potential voter feels that they at least understand the needs, aspirations, or problems of the common person.

Observing the repetitive nature of the election cycle of broken promises, one would hope that at some point everyone could learn that some things simply do not work in politics or economy. Yet, as Wilhelm Reich observes in his *Mass Psychology of Fascism:*

> …it would not be farfetched to say that it is in the nature of a politician that he does not learn anything from experience… (…) …When dealing with Copernicus, we are ready with the stake. When dealing with a politician, however, a politician who tells a people that the most incredible nonsense is true, who in 1940 holds up to be true precisely the opposite of what he held up to be true in 1939, then millions of people lose all bounds and assert that a miracle has taken place… (Reich 1970, 206)

There are obviously many different types of political promises that are broken as soon as the politician is elected and thus potentially able to keep them. Admittedly, there are situations where perfectly honest and sincere (or so one would hope) promises truly could not be kept for reasons that were either beyond the speaker's control or on ethical grounds. US President Woodrow Wilson promised to keep the USA out of World War I and President Franklin Roosevelt promised in 1940 to keep the US out of World War II. Both promises were later broken, but not due to insincerity or lack of vision. President Herbert Hoover promised in 1928 to end poverty. Likewise, in November 1989, the House of Commons in

Canada unanimously passed a resolution to seek to achieve the goal of eliminating poverty among Canadian children by the year 2000. More than thirty years later, Campaign 2000 to end child and family poverty is still far away from reaching its goals (Campaign 2000 website). It may be debated whether an idealistic goal like this was ever a feasible objective, but it was and remains a noble cause and, like world peace, it may be something that all future generations will continue to strive towards.

Some promises cannot be kept because they are contradictory. An example of a contradictory promise is the recurring election pledge to lower taxes, offer more social programs, and still have a balanced budget. As popular knowledge has it, we cannot eat our cake and have it too: however, when a politician promises all three things during their campaign, many people would rather vote for them than for someone who is forecasting budget cuts only. Politicians and advertisers know that realism and truth do not get anyone elected and do not sell products. Exaggeration, on the other hand, does.

One reason why populist political parties are so successful is that their promises make sense to ordinary people and thus are quite believable. An example of such a promise is the statement repeatedly made by Jarosław Kaczyński, the leader of PiS (Law and Justice), the governing party in Poland in 2005-2007, and then again after 2015. He promised that he would not become Prime Minister, even though it is the normal course of events in a parliamentary democracy. The reason for this promise was understandable for Poles at the time: his twin brother Lech was the country's President. To have both Kaczyński twins serving as President and Prime Minister was considered absurd.

However, by 2006, this reasonable promise was broken and for over a year, Poland was run by almost indistinguishable twin brothers, giving rise to a multitude of political jokes, both in Poland and abroad. Kaczyński's declaration: *"Dla mnie, raz dane słowo, jest święte,"* (for me, a word once given is sacred—J. Kaczyński 10/07/2006) was also considered a joke. Some other reasonable but later-broken promises many voters took seriously because they corresponded to the desires of the Polish society included:

- There will be no coalition with Self-Defence (a populist party that soon after this declaration became part of the Kaczyńskis' ruling coalition).
- We shall withdraw Polish troops from Iraq.
- No former member of the Communist Party will be allowed into the government.

Other promises made by the Kaczyński brothers-lead populist coalition (2005-2007) fall into the category of 'empty promise'. 'Empty promises' are a promise that is either not going to be carried out, or is worthless or meaningless. They only have a chance to be fulfilled if politicians really want to or have the funds and power necessary to keep them. Unfortunately, politicians usually make so many potentially realistic promises that they become impossible to keep just by the virtue of their number. Nevertheless, voters wish to see these promises fulfilled because they are related to issues that are important for them. This is why people tend to believe that these promises are sincere and that politicians who make them truly intend to keep them. Unfortunately, from the populist politician's point of view, these promises are simply an electoral vehicle. As soon as this goal has been reached, promises are either forgotten or moved to a back burner. The following promises, also offered by Law and Justice, fall into that category, in my opinion: "We shall build three million apartments" or "we shall soon lower taxes." In theory, they are achievable and the outcomes would be very welcome from the popular point of view. However, the economy is simply unable to support all that politicians feel free to promise during their election campaigns. In the 2004 provincial election in Ontario, one of the promises made by the Liberal Party was that there would be no new taxes once they came to power. At the same time the Liberals knew—or should have known—that the extent of the deficit incurred by the previous Tory government would prevent them from keeping this promise.

The rationale behind making empty election promises could look like this: make any attractive promises that you think the electorate may want to hear (remember that you will not have to keep them once you are elected); or modify what sounds like a promise by adding a qualifying word such as e.g., could or maybe. This will make your statement or declaration vague enough to give you a safe exit strategy.

This can also apply to business negotiations and the so-called 'bad faith negotiation'. An example might be the promise of future willingness to collaborate or the making of false action plans. An excuse heard from those engaging in bad faith negotiations is that empty promises are what listeners actually want to hear.

When the listener is fixated on getting something, particularly if it is minor, then they may get trapped by the wanting rather than really needing it. The empty promise gives the listener closure for now and enables the negotiation to move on.

This works better for things that will be delivered at an uncertain time in the future. When asked, delivery can be delayed. If pressed, the promiser might actually have to deliver.

For business negotiators, a warning is also offered: As any deceptive method, this holds the danger that it will cause a 'betrayal response'. The recommended repair strategy in business settings, apart from the advice to not get into such situations, is that if you betray someone's trust, it is often best to come clean. Accept responsibility for personal failure and personally apologize. Demonstrate how you will fix failure, and offer compensation. The alternatives to these recovery actions may cost you much more.

It appears that politicians who routinely break election promises are exempted from any need of reparation. They are expected to break some of the promises they make and thus they do not need to worry about the betrayal response from the voters. As long as they can come up with new promises, they have a high chance of getting re-elected.

It seems to me that the populist rhetoric of empty promises is so widespread today that even children understand its mechanism. I recall Ian, my then 12-year-old cousin in Canada telling me about elementary school student council elections and about election speeches candidates had to give. One of the candidates was promising all kinds of activities he would organize if elected and my cousin commented that these were lies. "Just election promises, you know." "Did he get elected?" I asked. My young cousin looked at me surprised and said, "Why would anyone vote for him? Everyone knows what he says isn't true." Indeed, why would anyone vote for him? I guess children have more common sense than adults.

When one listens carefully to what politicians are saying, there are some promises that could be found threatening to those who are not the intended beneficiaries, or who see that the promise is impossible to keep. Dressed as promises, these threats become an instrument for fostering a hostile political atmosphere. This type of political language is particularly common in the discourse of parties that use populist rhetoric based on nationalism or any narrowly defined ideology that forms 'in group' and 'out-group' memberships and the 'us versus them' dichotomy.

An example of such a populist party was the Polish party *Samoobrona* (Self-defence). It was created in 1991 out of the peasants' protests against some difficult economic conditions in agriculture after the 1989 system change. Party leader, Andrzej Lepper rose to power as the 'common man', a peasant, with little or no education. After 1991 he was arrested more than 70 times for illegal peasants' protests that paralyzed highways or railways and later for offensive comments in the parliament. He was often compared to Hitler and Stalin, as well as to the Russian politician Vladimir Zhirinovsky because of his 'nationalism', that is, his open hostility towards the West and his aggressive style. He had the sympathy and electoral support of some peasants and the less-educated and often-unemployed urban population, mostly those who suffered from political and economic reform processes after 1989. His proposed foreign policy was based on Euro-scepticism, anti-globalism, isolationism, xenophobia, and Polish nationalism. Despite the fact that he seemed to only appeal to marginalized social groups, his political organization was first transformed into a trade union of farmers and later into a political party. In June 2005, *Samoobrona's* popular support was between 13 percent and 17 percent, enough to be represented in the Polish Parliament. As the party of the Kaczyński brothers formed a minority government, they had to seek support to form a coalition government and opted for the inclusion of two small populist groups: *Samoobrona* and the League of Polish Families. The argument the twins used was that the other party, the Civic Platform, was not interested in any form of co-operation, something I have no expertise to discuss. In May 2006, Lepper and the leader of the other party, Roman Giertych, became deputy Prime Ministers.

In Poland, after 1989, Liberals perpetuated the myth that "the invisible hand of the market will solve all the problems". The result was unemployment over 30 percent and over 60 percent of people living below acceptable minimum standard of living.

The first solution suggested by Lepper was to guarantee unemployment benefits at the minimum social level to all citizens who, through no fault of their own, did not have a job.

No government after *Samoobrona* (Self-defence) would be able to eliminate jobs because it would hit "Lepper's Reef:" either the government would have to pay unemployment benefits, or it would be blown to bits by the unemployed.

The promise made in the above declaration was phrased as a proposed solution (a promise to do something when elected) and it fits some of the parameters of what Speech Act Theory would see as an 'empty' but 'felicitous promise'. A sympathetic listener would like the speaker to do the act and the speaker knows that. Yet, to anyone with basic understanding of economics it sounds like a recipe for disaster. As such, it functions more as a threat to the country's economic stability than a promise of true universal welfare. However, it certainly sounds attractive to anyone within the group of the unemployed people, disenchanted with political reforms that had robbed them of the job security. I call this kind of promise a 'parasitic speech act'. It is dressed as a promise, but it has to be interpreted as a threat.

Andrzej Lepper committed suicide in 2011. Some people believe he was helped. He can be credited with showing the government that empty promises can translate into public support of those who would not vote for a main-stream platform.

In the 1920s, masses of unemployed workers and many ordinary Germans embittered with sanctions imposed on their country after World War I were attracted to the programme of the NSDAP, the National-Socialist German Workers' Party. Announced by Adolf Hitler in February 1920, it was described as "a political creed, which on the one hand recruits for the movement and on the other is suited to unite and weld together by a commonly recognized obligation those who have been recruited" (Hitler 1943, 458). It proclaimed the common interest before self-interest but listed, at the very top, the following demands that clearly indicate that not everyone was welcome in their organization:

1. We demand the union of all Germans in a Greater Germany on the basis of the right of national self-determination.
2. We demand equality of rights for the German people in its dealings with other nations, and the revocation of the peace treaties of Versailles and Saint-Germain.
3. We demand land and territory (colonies) to feed our people and to settle our surplus population.
4. Only members of the nation may be citizens of the State. Only those of German blood, whatever be their creed, may be members of the nation. Accordingly, no Jew may be a member of the nation.
5. Non-citizens may live in Germany only as guests and must be subject to laws for aliens.

A similarly exclusionist tone can be found in the programme declaration of the All-Polish Youth (*Młodzież Wszechpolska*), a youth faction of the League of Polish Families, at one point part of the Kaczyński brothers' party coalition 2005-07. From their website and in my translation, their declaration reads:

> Identity: We don't come from nowhere. We all are members of a greater community: the Nation. We are Poles; for some it may sound trivial but for us it is the fundamental truth. The foundation of our identity.
>
> Consciousness: In the 21st century, they are telling us, national consciousness is outdated. However, we feel that this is not so. We have to be aware of who we are and where we are heading. Only then can we be truly free.

> Formation: Individual human beings mean nothing. People naturally unite into groups that share a common goal. The All-Polish Youth is an association for young people aware of their identity. Through foundation work, we strive for our generation to remain faithful to what our fathers used to worship.
>
> Join us! (*Młodzież Wszechpolska* website translated by author)

The language used by the All-Polish Youth is vaguely reminiscent of various other nationalistic organizations. They declare a war against liberalism and against a doctrine of unrestricted tolerance and relativism, and proclaim their desire to eliminate from social life all ignominy, lies and dirt. While possibly appealing to some ultra-nationalistic circles, this ideology is perceived as a threat to democratic values. Despite its pledge of allegiance to the Catholic Church, the ideology of the All-Polish Youth is not based on Christian values of love and tolerance, but on exclusion and moral superiority. I leave out the question of presence or absence of any rational message in their programme declarations. When reading this type of text, I have the same sensation as when looking at pictures of Yves Tanguy, French surrealist painter. His landscapes seem to represent something when we first look at them: a city, a building, people scattered in a desert-like setting. When looked at more carefully, whatever we thought was there, dissolves into abstract shapes with no tangible forms.

Populist parties and politicians usually gain popularity in situations where there are threats to stability, security, and social well-being; a situation quite common in many countries of the world at any given time in history. Current security threats, wars, and the danger of religiously motivated terrorism foster ethnic intolerance. Economic instability or lack of employment encourage social conflicts. Shrinking resources and environmental issues, including global health threats, divide countries and regions. Populist demagogy thrives in such contexts. The resulting style of political discourse, as we can observe on a daily basis, is highly aggressive.

Populist politicians often intentionally use colloquialisms, slang, or even vulgarisms in order to achieve more popular mass appeal. They appeal to those who feel marginalized and threatened or to those who feel insecure. They also embolden those who feel disenfranchised and alienated. Politicians promise whatever the audiences want to hear but usually have no intention of keeping their promises. They usually offer simple solutions to complex problems because simple solutions sound agreeable in political speeches. Populists often choose a scapegoat who can be blamed for all problems—a person, a party, an ethnic group, or a social class. It is very sad to watch even intelligent people embrace this rhetoric when they feel that their wellbeing is threatened or when they are persuaded that the values they hold dear are at risk. One other characteristic of populist parties is that they often define themselves as a 'new order' without a political past and without all the political baggage of mistakes, errors, and wrongdoings that the old ruling parties have. As an example, Donald Trump promoted his candidacy for the US presidency by emphasizing the fact that he had no connections to or past work in politics, i.e., no qualifications for the job. Some might call political qualifications 'experience', but spin doctors will tell us that we do not need experience. We need 'change'. My daughter rightly calls it hairdresser's politics: hairdressers often encourage people to change their hair style…

The notion of populism is viewed today as a rather pejorative description. If used to describe a party or individual politicians, it suggests that they are mostly interested in getting the votes and often use rhetoric of nationalism, ethnocentrism, traditionalism, anti-globalism, and xenophobia. However, as an ideology whose focus is on people, populist qualities do not have to represent something negative. There is no doubt that populist qualities can also be attributed to figures like Jesus, who reportedly spoke to the masses and did not exclude anyone. His teachings emphasized the need to be accepting of people from all walks of life and from all ethnic and social backgrounds. He seemed to be particularly supportive of social outcasts and those who were poor and marginalized. He spoke for those who could not speak for themselves. What then makes one populist good and another populist bad? The answer should not simply depend on the position and political affiliation of the voter.

Perhaps the clearest summary of the populist ideology in politics was given by Abraham Lincoln in his 1863 Gettysburg Address, when he advocated for a "government of the people, by the people, for the people." It is probably the most quoted speech in American history and it certainly is not considered manipulative or insincere. A more modern example of what I personally considered positive populism in Poland was the Solidarity movement in the 1980s and the speeches of its leader, Lech Wałęsa. His style, made famous in the 1980s and 90s, was populist, simple, and inclusive. Solidarność (Solidarity) was established as a result of the widespread strikes in August 1980 and later transformed into a federation of independent trade unions. Lech Wałęsa's language was authentic, unscripted, appealing to universal values that united all Poles. Despite some similarity to Andrzej Lepper in terms of his humble background (in 1980, Wałęsa was a 37-year-old electrician at the Gdańsk shipyard), his style always was oriented towards building solidarity within and beyond the post-communist society. In the opening paragraph of his August 31, 1980 address to the fellow shipyard workers at the end of the strike, Wałęsa said:

> My Dear! Kochani! We are returning to work on September 1st. We all know what that date reminds us of, what we think about on that day—we think about our Fatherland, about our national issue, about the common good of the family, whose name is Poland. (Wałęsa 1980)

Even though Wałęsa was talking about national pride and love of his home country, the style was inclusive. There was nothing nationalistic about caring about one's homeland. He talked about the common good of all Poles and not only some 'real' or 'true Poles. He called on everyone to join in building the future Poland through work and not by joining some new 'war on liberalism' or on tolerance. The political elites promoted by the new extreme parties, on the other hand, gain popularity in an environment dominated by anxiety, anger, envy, and fear. And usually by hostility towards some enemy.

Are some of us more likely to believe empty promises? What

makes some people more tolerant of lies? Furthermore, what makes some societies more tolerant of lies? I happened to consider these questions watching political challenges facing Poland after the 2005 election of the Kaczyński government and the subsequent wave of belligerent populist rhetoric. From the perspective of those who, like myself, left the country during the post-Solidarność communist crackdown, carrying with them the ideals of building a civil society, some post-communist developments seemed irrational and shameful. It was not what the Solidarność generation (or the idealists within that group of people who entered the Polish workforce around 1980) was hoping for. It was not what Eastern Europeans were fighting for in 1989. Communism, with the Red Army and its brotherly alliance ready to support it, was no longer an omnipotent threat. Of course, after so many decades of communist rule, which descended upon most of Eastern Europe immediately following an equally cruel Nazi regime, there was no return to normalcy. There was very little normalcy that anyone could remember. Normalcy would have to be created from scratch. Yet, there was an undeniable expectation that things would become better quickly, almost instantly. They did not.

It truly bothered and still bothers me and many of my friends to watch developments in Poland. At times it looked as if people forgot what life was like in communist times: queues, low wages, often meaningless work, lies, hopelessness, alcoholism, and persecution of people who would express opposition to the party line. When I visited Poland after 1989, I would listen to people complaining that everything became available, but there was never enough money to have what one wanted. I knew that many people, especially the elderly, suffered during that period of transformation. The problem was that no one was ready to recognize that problems existed not because economy was being reformed, but rather because it had been mismanaged for so long in the past.

Finally, a seemingly unrelated personal interest in behaviour patterns associated with abuse allowed me to gain some understanding of at least some aspects of the Polish situation. How was it possible, I was asking myself, that some intelligent and talented young people had such low self-esteem or were so incognizant of their social situation to repeatedly involve themselves in harmful relationships, abuse harmful substances, and fail in their careers and personal lives? There seemed to be a parallel between the behaviour of an assault victim and the behaviour of entire populations in countries undergoing transition from communist rule. This similarity is based on an analogy to post-traumatic responses of an abused individual. In her study of brainwashing, Kathleen Taylor (Taylor 2004, 88) notes the similarities between the abuser's behaviour and that of the totalitarian regime, as described by the psychiatrist Robert Lifton in his 1961 book on thought reform in communist China. The similarity between the individual victim of abuse and an abused society is, I believe, a novel insight and allows a better understanding of some social phenomena characteristic for societies in transition from an oppressive system of any political kind. It applies to South Africa after the years of apartheid and to Chile with its military junta experience. It also offers hope that it is possible to help an assaulted society to deal with the effects of social trauma caused by an authoritarian system through various forms of counselling and healing practices.

The research on sexual and violent assault points to certain patterns of behaviour as well as to clusters of health-related problems that the victims may suffer from. Negative health behaviours include lack of exercise, smoking, and alcohol excess (Sheffield et al, 1985). Abuse also causes a plethora of immediate psychological consequences such as: shock, denial, fear, anxiety, withdrawal, guilt, and distrust of others. Chronic psychological effects include: depression, alienation, unhealthy diet-related behaviors (including fasting and overeating), and attempted or completed suicides (Ackard and Neumark-Sztainer 2002; Faravelli et al. 2004; Felitti et al. 1998; Krakow et al. 2002; Ystgaard et al. 2004). Social effects include strained relationships with family, friends, and intimate partners, and marital problems. Some health issues may be both consequences of sexual (or other) violence and factors that increase a person's vulnerability to being victimized again in the future (Brener et al. 1999; Lang et al. 2003), e.g., trading sex for food, money, or other items. The abuse of harmful substances, including smoking cigarettes, drinking alcohol, using drugs or driving after drinking alcohol, are also often associated with abuse (Champion et al. 2004).

While political oppression is not necessarily identical with physical abuse, I believe that authoritarian rule constitutes an abuse of its subjects and the post-traumatic effects of that abuse may hinder transition from authoritarianism to democracy. Just like the abused person may have problems adjusting to normal life, an abused society may seem dysfunctional and irrational even after the abuse has stopped. What is unsettling about the behaviour of victims of abuse, and what is of particular consequence if we extend this analogy to societies, is that these people are vulnerable to suffer repeated assault.

The existing research on assault and its consequences has increased our understanding of factors that make some populations more vulnerable to violence. Vulnerability is a combination of individual, relational, community, and societal factors that increases the likelihood that a person will suffer harm. These factors do not directly cause violence, but contribute to its occurrence making it more likely (Jewkes, Sen, and Garcia-Moreno, 2002; Malamuth 1998). Vulnerability factors for victimization include prior history of violence (for instance witnessing violence towards others, either at home or outside home, e.g., police violence), drug or alcohol use, poverty, strong patriarchal relationship system within family and in other relationships, lack of employment opportunities, lack of institutional support from police and judicial system, general tolerance of crime, and other forms of violence. Even a brief look at Polish public discourse over the last 30 years (i.e., since 1989) shows an increasingly aggressive style of political debates. Polish popular culture is in many ways simply following foreign trends and as such cannot be treated, on its own, as an indication of the social health or malaise, however there is also a marked change in the language used. There is, for instance, a striking, at least for someone from outside, transition to informal address. On television or on the radio, almost everyone in Polish politics and popular culture uses first names, often in the abbreviated form of nicknames. I am not criticizing this practice, just drawing attention to the trend. Advertisements use the second person singular address telling me in no uncertain terms to buy or do something, travel somewhere, etc. This is partly due to Polish grammar. I remember my conversations over food with my good Japanese friend Yasuko who often brought to my attention how pushy I sound to her when I say things like "Yasuko, you must try this" or "Take another piece"... The command-like style of such invitations can be softened by the word "please" or "perhaps".

Polish advertisements skip such softeners and boldly demand: *"Spójrz na swoją fotografię z dzieciństwa, powiedz na głos a następnie uczyń życie, takim jak tylko chcesz!"* ("Look at your childhood photo, say aloud 'be your own boss,' and then make your life whatever you want it to be," from a March 2023 ad for Boss on the Instagram page of Westfield Mokotów shopping centre). I wish life was that simple. Somehow a similar style of ads does not bother me in English, where there is no distinction between informal and formal address. Maybe it is my age or the length of time I have been away from hearing Polish on a daily basis and witnessing it change. Nevertheless, the colloquial style seems to have spread everywhere and with it also not just informal but rude and sometimes even vulgar form of communication.

CHAPTER 12

Polish *Hejt*

SOMETHING STARTED TO CHANGE in Polish public discourse in the 21st century but I am not sure when exactly this change began or what triggered it. I was already living in Canada but spent every summer in Poland. I first thought that it may have started during the first PiS government (2005–07) or maybe in the aftermath of the presidential plane crash in Smoleńsk in 2010. But I think my first shock was the reaction to the publication of the book *Sąsiedzi (Neighbours)* by Jan Tomasz Gross in 2000. The book documented the 1941 murder of 1600 Jewish inhabitants of a small village Jedwabne, near Białystok. The murder was committed by the Polish neighbours of the Jews, the ordinary Poles who, either motivated by antisemitism—present in most of Europe before WWII, not just in Poland, or instigated by Germans, locked up their Jewish neighbours in a barn and set it on fire.

Even though some perpetrators were tried after the war ended, the Jedwabne crime was not widely known in communist Poland and was attributed, in official accounts, to Germans. I first heard about it in 2000 when the publication of Gross's book caused a division among people. My reaction was one of shock and dismay. Like most Poles, I grew up believing that Poles were the victims during WWII. All of a sudden, it turned out that some Poles were also perpetrators. I did not question the historical facts presented by Gross. I did not see why he would be distorting the truth that was terrible enough, no matter how I looked at it. I felt the need to apologize even though there was no one left to apologize to. And yet some people belligerently disputed the motivation behind this publication, denied Polish involvement, and discredited the author. I saw t-shirts saying *Nie przepraszam za Jedwabne*, which could be freely translated as "No apologies for Jedwabne" (literally 'I do not apologize for Jedwabne'). I contemplated getting one and wearing it with the word *No* crossed out. This was the first time when I felt that I parted ways with some people who, until then, I considered likeminded.

Then came the 2005-2007 PiS government. My poor mother could not stand the Kaczyński brothers and, just like my grandmother before her, watched TV and cursed (she never used obscenities and her swear words were usually *a nich ich wszystkich szlag trafi*, which I would translate as either 'let them all be hit by lightning' or 'let them all have a heart attack'. The dictionary suggests 'let them all be damned', which is a good stylistic equivalent but I prefer my interpretations. I feel very sad that mother passed away in 2006, without having seen the end of that era. The year 2010 brought the presidential plane crash at Smoleńsk, a truly tragic accident that was played by PiS as an assassination of President Lech Kaczyński (and over 90 other people who were packed onto the same plane). The tragedy briefly united people but very soon led to another significant chasm within Polish society: there were those who believed the conspiracy theory and blamed the opposition and there were those who blamed the crash on the ill-planned trip to a defunct Belarusian airport in bad weather.

In this context, the All-Polish Youth re-emerged, sporting the Hitler salute (or a similar raised hand gesture) which in Polish context pointed to a surprising lack of both taste and historical knowledge. In 2011, the so-called Independence marches on November 11 (the day Poland regained independence after over a century of partitions and the new National Day after 1989) became a mostly nationalistic parade that ended with street fighting and arrests. Also in 2011, a bit earlier, in the summer, I first heard the word *masakra* (massacre) as a slangy and 'witty' description of something bad. That is a pretty strong word to describe getting a fish with lots of bones at a restaurant or waiting longer than expected for your luggage at the airport. I started to pay attention and saw (in print) the verb 'to massacre (*zmasakrować*) someone in a debate' used a lot. Clearly, it moved from funny slang to public political discourse and it made me immediately think of Victor Klemperer observation of the lives of words in the Third Reich.

Together with Grażyna Drzazga, my former PhD student and now a colleague, we have been watching the surprising developments of Polish political discourse in the public sphere over the last decade or so and observed that it had been changing in an unprecedented way (Stroińska & Drzazga, 2017). To some degree, these changes could simply be a reflection of the populist turn in political discourse across Europe and in North America—vide the 2016 presidential debate in the US. In the Polish context at the time, however, then still marked by what seemed to have been a generally accepted appreciation of tolerance and Christian values, that wave of boorishness was atypical and worrisome. And it was only getting worse.

Political discourse (and political propaganda) regularly makes use of stereotyping for the purpose of singling out individuals or groups as the proverbial 'other' (Waldorn, 2012). Around 2015, the influx of refugees from North Africa and the Middle East to Europe were testing the values and principles declared by Polish society. The rejection of the moral obligation to help those who are less fortunate and the linguistic mechanisms of judging people and putting them into different categories (Kaczyński's famous 'better sorts' and 'worse sorts') are new phenomena that require thorough analysis. Based on our previous research on political propaganda and discourse about minorities (Drzazga et al. 2012), we looked at the use of linguistic means in order to discuss issues of those who are 'different': ethnic, religious, and sexual minorities, as well as political opposition.

We saw a marked shift towards stereotyping. (Hilton & von Hippel 1996, Löschmann & Stroińska 1998). In the refugee crisis, the concepts of ethnicity and religion were intertwined in the media, contributing to the confusion. The language used in public debates of these issues—including parliamentary discussions—was markedly rude and unapologetically offensive. Already in 2016, we believed that this shift was a strong indication of a dangerous change in social attitudes. In the past, such changes led to violent conflicts, e.g., in Kosovo (Stroińska & Popovic, 1999). Using linguistics as a diagnostic tool, we identified specific mechanisms of exploiting language for the purpose of propaganda targeting minorities.

Just like the word 'terrorism' (in the slogan 'war on terrorism') was shortened to 'terror' after 9/11 in the US, the word 'immigrants' suddenly became 'migrants'. The removal of the prefix im-, changed the meaning from 'a person who comes to live permanently in a foreign country', usually due to wars, environmental catastrophes, or for economic reasons, to someone who is on the move, from place to place (either within a country or across national borders) in search of a better life. Usually, such people can return home at any time if they so choose. The deletion of the prefix stripped the unfortunate souls of what used to elicit compassion from others. As 'immigrants', they were fleeing from something bad and seeking a safe place to live. As 'migrants', they were just moving from place to place for no apparent reason, stretching our already overextended welfare and healthcare systems.

In the 2015 parliamentary elections in Poland, PiS presented migrants as the 'other' in order to confront us with the unknown—an unknown culture, unknown expectations, different, possibly dangerous and violent religion—of which majority groups are often afraid. Election slogans, echoed in the Independence marches and nationalistic gatherings talked about the need to defend Poland as a country for Poles (only?). The refugees, especially Muslims, were threatening Polish traditional values, Polish Christian traditions, and everything that Poles held dear. They were represented as an immediate threat, the enemy at the door, even though Poland was not a country of choice for most refugees. Jarosław Kaczyński, the leader of PiS used language reminiscent of Hitler's *Mein Kampf*, talking about refugees as carriers of diseases and dangerous microbes or parasites. And yet, this language was surprisingly effective. Within a short period of time, the attitudes of Poles towards refugees have changed in a dramatic way. In 2014, the report prepared for the UN High Commissioner for Refugees found an overwhelming majority of Poles having positive attitudes. The opening sentence proclaimed that "broadly understood tolerance/respect for other people belong to the values most commonly declared by Poles (95 percent of the respondents pointed out that it is an important human value)" (*Ogólnie rozumiana tolerancja/szacunek do innych ludzi należy do wartości najbardziej powszechnie deklarowanych przez Polaków (95 procent respondentów wskazuje, że jest to ważna wartość ogólnoludzka*) (TNS Hoffman Report 2014, 2). Of the participants, 70 percent had positive attitude towards immigrants and 82 percent had a positive attitude towards refugees (ibid.). The CBOS survey (2021) shows that the number of people opposed to accepting immigrants rose from approximately 20 percent in 2015 (before PiS took over) to 63 percent in 2017, but fell a bit in 2021, to just below 50 percent. In our opinion, PiS achieved this change in attitudes by manipulating people's emotions, using public media, especially television (the main source of information for most people), and having support of the Catholic church, even though one would expect the church to advocate for those who needed assistance.

Fear is one of the strongest emotions, stronger even than hatred. It is also one that can be easily manipulated for quick or short-term political gains. Rick Wilson, an American political strategist pointed out: "Fear is the simplest emotion to tweak in a campaign ad. You associate your opponent with terror, with fear, with crime, with causing pain and uncertainty" (Ball, 2016). According to the *2017 Annual Report of the European Commission against Racism and Intolerance*, "The populist rhetoric has blended into a hatred of non-nationals or minorities; migration and multiculturalism have continued to be presented as a threat to societal cohesion and security." These powerful emotions are conveyed in texts and messages that influence the less critical part of the audience—not just in Poland—who then share them on social media. These worrisome messages should be monitored and special attention should be paid to prevent online trolls and propaganda from dictating the narrative but, despite regulations that aim at prompt removal of hateful content, it seems impossible to accomplish that goal. Designing algorithms to detect hate speech online is an interesting task for a linguist but I am more interested in understanding why so much aggression has accumulated in Poles at a time when Poland was relatively prosperous.

The way we talk about something has far-reaching consequences. The anti-refugee propaganda described those seeking safe haven as carriers of diseases, potential terrorists, and criminals. This opened the way for ordinary people to call them 'barbarians', 'savages', 'social jihad', and many other things that would be inappropriate to quote. We are seeing this phenomenon not only in Poland. People who get the information from the government-controlled media begin to speak the language of the government propaganda and with time adapt their thinking to what they hear on television and—unfortunately, very often also in church. I see educated people repeating absurd conspiracy theories that it would take them less than a minute to fact-check. The use of slang terms, as well as aggressive and vulgar expressions in political and media discourse may indicate that the society's self-esteem is low and that it is receptive to such offensive forms of address. Politicians offend people but then follow up with unrealistic populist promises, reminding me of the well-known cycle of abuse, apologies, and promises that the abuse will never happen again. I consider post-communist societies in Eastern Europe as victims of societal trauma, passed from generation to generation. Just like the victims of traumatic abuse tend to associate with individuals who remind them of their abusers (because this is what they are familiar with), Eastern Europeans perpetuate the cycle of societal abuse by voting for populist parties because they want to believe those promises.

The language of the media is the language of contempt, 'toxic hate speech' shapes a voter's perception of reality and strangely stops them from thinking critically or at least checking the information. The very usage of words such as 'migrant' or 'refugee crisis' not only reflects the change of attitudes, but may also cause a shift in how people react to an underprivileged group and their tragedy.

This negative attitude towards people who—potentially—would want to come to live in Poland is hard to comprehend also because, for generations, it was Poles who sought a better or safer life in other countries. We were the immigrants and refugees. In 1987, when we began our new life in Canada, my husband, who arrived a couple of months earlier to start a job at the University of Western Ontario, volunteered my assistance to the Polish parish priest in

London, Ontario, Father Kamiński. In Edinburgh, the Polish community consisted mostly of the Polish World War II soldiers who fought under the command of General Maczek and stayed in the UK when Poland fell under Soviet control. They were significantly older, even their children were much older than we were. Together with another graduate student, Grzegorz and a post-doc Andrzej, we offered to help clean the Polish chapel, St. Anne's Oratory. That was the kind of help my husband had in mind when he talked to father Kamiński. Father Kamiński said that they had cleaning staff but he was being inundated with letters from refugee camps and said that I could help him in responding to Poles asking him for assistance in getting to Canada. For several months, once or twice a week I spent a few hours trying to organize the process of responding to letters, explaining how the Polish parish could help, etc. At that time, following the communist crackdown in Poland and a huge wave of Polish refugees who filled the refugee camps in Italy, Greece, and other countries, Polish churches were given the right to sponsor people. Father Kamiński's organizational skills were truly amazing and he must have helped hundreds of Poles immigrate to Canada. When I hear my fellow Polish immigrants in Canada complain about this country accepting too many new refugees, I like to remind them how we came to live here.

More recent polls show that the attitudes towards refugees and immigrants in Poland are changing again. A 2021 survey by IBRiS (Sondaż, 2021) shows that the percentage of people who are in favour of accepting refugees is growing. The article opens with the statement: "Politicians stopped playing on the emotions and the attitude of Poles towards refugees.... The majority think that borders should be opened for them" (*Politycy przestali grać na emocjach i zmienił się stosunek Polaków do uchodźców. Większość uważa, że trzeba otworzyć dla nich granice*). According to that survey, at the end of 2021, some 77 percent of Poles supported accepting refugees, a rather dramatic turn from 2017 when approximately 60 percent opposed accepting refugees. This turn was significant as it preceded the sudden wave of refugees from Ukraine following the Russian invasion on February 24, 2022. The unconditional welcome of those fleeing an armed conflict with Russia had been made easier by the fact that Ukrainians and Poles have been living close to each other for centuries, often within one state—even though those states varied throughout history: Poland, Austro-Hungarian Empire, Poland again, Soviet Union, Germany, Ukraine…). Also, over the last several years, there were many Ukrainians working in Poland so they became a natural part of the ethnic landscape. They were also Christians and they were at war with Russia, a country with which Poland has a rather difficult relationship on many occasions in the past.

If one can say that something good could come from this terrible tragedy of Russian invasion, it could be some level of healing of the old wounds between Poland and Ukraine. As people, we are very close. We don't need a translator to understand each other. Our aspirations and dreams are no longer in conflict. When I was young, I remember people from my parents' generation dreaming about returning to Lwów (now Lviv) and other Polish cities that are now outside Polish borders. I am sure similar sentiments were common among those who used to live in German Breslau, today Polish Wrocław. In fact, many people from Lwów were 'repatriated' after the war to Wrocław. I would like to visit Czortków, where my father was born, and Lwów, where he studied, but I do not want the eastern border to move because this would likely have a domino effect with western borders pushed east. No sane person would want this to happen.

While many, if not most Poles actively participated and still participate in helping Ukrainian refugees displaced by the Russian invasion, there are always those who want to score points by spreading negative feelings (made easier by inflation and many economic issues in Poland that are not the result of the war but rather the effects of the years of incompetence of the PiS government) and fear. I hope that the self-preservation instinct and the realization that we are all better off when we stand together with Ukrainians will turn out to be stronger than the toxic rhetoric of the fear mongers.

Since 2015, I have watched the rise of verbal aggression like I have never seen before. Unfortunately, this explosion of hate speech was not limited to Poland but here, I will not attempt any generalizations. The election campaign in 2015 focused its negative propaganda on refugees, trying to scare Poles with visions of a wave of 'infidels' storming the borders. This scare tactic not only worked to give PiS an election victory but it also affected attitudes towards foreigners in general. People were harassed for looking foreign or using foreign languages in public places. I had serious problems trying to wrap my head around this. In my artificially homogeneous homeland—artificially is a euphemism as this uniformity was the result of the mass murder of Polish Jews and the cleansing effect of moving borders—hospitality towards others used to be an unquestionable virtue. Most of us grew up with the tradition of putting an extra plate on the table on Christmas Eve to be able to welcome a lonely traveller; a stranger.

As the wave of immigrants did not materialize, PiS had to find another enemy. And it did. One after the other, various groups found themselves targets of government-promoted hate speech. First there were those classified by Kaczyński as 'the worse sort'. That was still sort of funny and very soon people started making badges and t-shirts that said "I am the worse sort." Then came (in random order) the cyclists (demanding bicycle lanes), teachers (asking for a say in the education reform), Arabian horses (for not doing well under a newly PiS appointed director of the stables in Janów), women wearing fur coats (I cannot remember why), women who thought that they were in charge of their bodies (and protested against changes of the abortion law), feminists (for being feminists), children born through in vitro technology, opposition of all kinds (for being in opposition to PiS), those who were against fascism in the Polish edition (especially a group of brave women who tried to block one of the fascist parades in Warsaw), those who protested against government-controlled television, young doctors who were asking for better wages, those who were unmasking pedophile priests and those who protected them, and, finally, anyone identifying as or standing for LGBTQ+ recognition… I am sure I forgot someone. LGBTQ+ and what PiS calls 'gender ideology' (*ideologia gender*—foreign words, as Victor Klemperer pointed out about the language in the Third Reich and Hitler's word choices in particular, impress people, especially those who do not understand them) have been used as the primary enemy of the 'Polishness' in upcoming parliamentary elections.

Painting someone as an enemy of 'Polishness' (*polskość*, a noun that is very general in its basic meaning, defined by the PWN dictionary online as "concerning Poland and Poles" (*dotyczący Polski, Polaków*) and very specific in its new, nationalistic meaning, narrowed down to those characteristics that are approved by the current government) turned out to be an effective way for building a community of like-minded supporters of the government. I find it surprising that so many people became ardent supporters of the ruling party. Poles normally don't like those who govern them, because of the centuries-long occupation by foreign powers.

The hateful language used to talk about the above enemies or scapegoats follows, as seen in online hate speech found, e.g., in the comments posted by anonymous users online. While the level of hate in public discourse is upsetting, even more troublesome is the disregard for verbal abuse that may quickly become much more than that. Gordon Allport's Scale of Prejudice and Discrimination (1954) shows how aggression escalates. Level 1 in Allport's scale refers to hate speech, i.e., using derogatory language which may cause avoidance of some individuals or groups and which makes those people feel invisible (described as Level 2). This, in turn, may result in discrimination (Level 3) and physical attacks on people and their property (Level 4). The last level (Level 5) is the physical removal of those seen as the out-group: ethnic cleansing and murder.

When we started observing the phenomenon of hate speech in the context of Poland after the government change in 2015 (Stroińska & Drzazga, 2017), we noticed elements of the first and second level of Allport's ladder—antilocution (hate speech) and avoidance (negative attitudes to those who were different). Less than four years later, in 2021, we were already witnessing physical attacks on various ethnic and sexual minorities (Level 4). This keeps escalating, with people beaten up, and some young people driven to suicide because they are being dehumanized by the propaganda and harassed. They are being harassed by ordinary people who feel that the authorities are giving them permission to hate. Daniel Goldhagen describes this process in his 1997 book *Hitler's Willing Executioner: Ordinary*

Germans and the Holocaust. It always starts with dehumanizing the target and this is done by the use of dehumanizing language.

Level 5 on Allport's scale is genocide. We do not see it in Poland but beyond the Polish border in Ukraine, Russian society and Russian troops are being brainwashed to feel that it is okay to kill Ukrainians, because they have been dehumanized by the use of words such as Nazis, *ukropy* (dillweed), and *hoholy* (a Cossack haircut). Some say that ordinary Russians are manipulated by Kremlin propaganda and do not know the truth. I don't believe it. There are ways to tell what is a lie and there are ways to find out the truth. However, it may be safer and easier to pretend and turn away from the uncomfortable reality. Some may be actually profiting from the war, and yet, sooner or later, those who chose to be willfully blind will have to face the truth. Even if they won't be held criminally responsible because they were just the small fish, they may lose family members to this 'military operation' and will likely suffer financial and economic hardship of sanctions, economic downturn, or lack of material comforts — like ordinary Germans did during Hitler's regime. For the bigger fish, however, there will be courts and punishment. Justice is often delayed but it usually catches up with those who feel that laws do not apply to them. I am optimistic enough to believe that I will see it happen in Russia, in Poland, and in all those places where, today, the toxic language of contempt is fostering hate and violence (Stroińska & Drzazga 2020).

If there is anything we have learned from history, it is that we do not learn. It seems that we have learned nothing from the enormous tragedies of the 20th century. In a recent interview, a Polish Holocaust researcher, Barbara Engelking said:

> We know from history that hatred kills. Words kill. When uttered, they transform into aggression, pain, death. They take on the bodies of concrete victims, new and new annihilated lives, again and again. The latest events in the world, but also here at home, confirm that. And yet it is such a simple lesson that we could have learned. But we learn nothing. Evil wins. (Pawlicka 2023)

Professor Engelking was talking about the feeling that the suffering of the victims of the Holocaust was in vain if the world has learned nothing from this unimaginable tragedy. She was speaking in the context of the 80th anniversary of the Warsaw Ghetto uprising in April 1943, a desperate rebellion of people condemned to death only for their ethnicity. The annihilation of the Warsaw Ghetto, the extermination of millions of European Jews, the unimaginable nightmare of the Holocaust—and the world has learned nothing? The suffering of other nations condemned to death by Hitler's regime, including Poles, and young Polish nationalists greet each other with the Hitler salute? Poles and Jews lived as neighbours for centuries, and yet, during the war, many Poles were too afraid or too indifferent to help Jews. Or too greedy to resist benefitting from their demise. Russians and Ukrainians lived as neighbours for centuries too and yet today Russians soldiers obey the orders to bomb civilian targets, kill or kidnap Ukrainian children. Have we really learned nothing from history? Will evil really triumph because we do nothing to stop it?

Evil is not born overnight. Dictatorships may overturn democracies but they cannot last without the little cogs in their wheels, the screws in the giant machine of tyranny doing their work. Each individual human cog has to make a decision—to keep the machine working, to stall it, or to play no part. This choice may not be easy and there are often risks involved in the choices we make. However, there is always a choice. And those choices are easier at the beginning: to cover a swastika on the wall with a spray paint; to tell the janitor that someone put a hateful graffiti on the elevator wall; to report hate speech on the internet website. If people make the choice to stop evil's baby steps, to react to its everyday banality, to say no to a better-paid job that would compromise our integrity, to not laugh at a racist joke, to not participate in badmouthing someone for being different, to simply be decent—maybe the enormous loss of life over the centuries of conflicts would not have been in vain. WWI was supposed to be the war to end all wars. There was supposed to be no poetry after Auschwitz but Theodore Adorno was wrong. There is poetry and it sometimes allows people to express or process what is otherwise unspeakable.

CHAPTER 13

Post Script
The Devil is in the Detail

When I was in Grade 4, nine, perhaps ten years old, I started to take private English lessons, together with my friend Kasia. We became friends because our parents made arrangements for the two of us to learn English together. The teacher, Mr. Kacperski, came to Kasia's apartment and we studied American English, from the books he brought from the US Embassy. The cartoon characters in these books depicted life in small town America in a way that I only began to fully appreciate when I moved to Canada in my early thirties and settled in a small town in Ontario. As part of my parents' plan to make me learn English, my mother brought home some letters from little girls in the USA who responded to a letter from a Polish little girl looking for pen pals. The girl's mother worked together with my mother at the SGGW library, hence the connection. That little Polish girl could not possibly correspond with hundreds of eager American pen pals and gave some of those letters away. I started writing to Sally Axel, a girl my age living in Muscatine, Iowa, and we kept exchanging letters until this correspondence died naturally when we were both in high school. My pen pal Sally also sent me lots of beautiful gifts—plush toys, a Barbie doll, with all kinds of accessories, records with Christmas carols, postcards from Muscatine and from her school trips, a tea towel calendar, a t-shirt, etc. She and her parents were very generous! In the late 1960s, I was the only girl on the block, well the only girl I knew of, with a Barbie! However, even more than by the gifts themselves, I was impressed with things that Sally probably took for granted and did not consider to be gifts. The colourful shiny gift-wrapping paper, for example, was a luxury for me. I still remember a particular package wrapped in blue and green glossy, metallic paper. Such colours did not exist in the late 1960s communist Poland. I used pieces of that paper, carefully straightened, to cover my school exercise books and enjoyed it for months, if not for years. Some of the Barbie dresses came in a pretty box that originally contained greeting cards. I remember the sweet scent of glue on the envelopes from Sally's letters. I remember sniffing it as it smelled like chewing gum or something equally delicious and scarce. Most vividly, I remember a tiny catalogue of accessories for Barbie and Ken and their friends, with all kinds of wonderful things that citizens of my country could only dream about: cars, fridges, picnic baskets, toasters, not to mention a full range of outfits, from swimsuits to evening gowns. In fact, I still have that doll and the accessories it came with. I still have that little catalogue. I even have that postcard box and all of those Barbie dresses, now almost 60 years old. I kept them and did not even allow my daughter, Joanna, to play with that doll when she was little, but she—born and growing up in Canada—had several Barbies of her own. My old doll is a much-treasured possession because of what it once meant to me. What is essential to this anecdote is recognizing the importance of the thoughts I can recall: a country that produces such amazing toys for kids cannot be as bad as they were telling us at school or on TV. A country that cares enough to make wrapping paper so colourful or puts nice scent into glue on envelopes must care about things no one seemed to care about in my country.

Today I may be looking at my first Barbie somewhat differently. I think I understand why Naomi Klein calls Barbie an "archetypal space invader" (Klein 2000) and I am not suggesting that dropping boxes of Barbie dolls in Iraq or Afghanistan would improve the political situation there or significantly change peoples' attitudes towards the United States. Also, the United States is no longer the "gentle giant with no sense of a mission" as Tyrmand referred to it in the 1950s (Tyrmand, 2002). However, for me in 1960s Poland, my

Barbie was without doubt an educational toy that taught me more about political systems of the time than any course on ideology could have ever accomplished.

I lost touch with Sally in high school. Then, in 1996, while I was working in the UK and felt that my life was again at a crossroad, I wanted to connect with her to tell her how grateful I was for her friendship when we were little. I remembered her address in Muscatine and I managed to find out, through some telephone directory information that her brother was still living there. I wrote to Sally to that address but nothing happened. I tried again, a few months or a couple of years later, but to no avail. And then an odd thing happened. A former student of mine came to visit the department. I was in my office and he knocked on my door and asked if I knew who he was. I did. After a nice chat—he was there with his daughter and his aunt—he asked if there was anything he could do for me. He had said earlier that he lived close to the Iowa border, so I asked if he could find Sally for me. I knew he was the kind of person who could do the impossible. And he did. The same evening, he messaged me that Sally was waiting for my phone call.

Her last name was no longer Axel and she no longer lived in Iowa but rather in North Carolina. It was the first time I'd heard her very nice, deep voice. We chatted about our lives, about our families. She and her husband were at that time running a retirement ranch for senior dogs. She asked if I knew what a miniature schnauzer was. I said I do, I had one. Her own schnauzer was Fritz, mine was Snicklefritz! We finally met not long after that, started to exchange messages and it was absolutely amazing to reconnect in such an unbelievable way.

Then we both went through a string of sad events, hers much worse than mine. Her beloved husband suddenly passed away. Alone, she was no longer able to work and look after 12 senior dogs. When they died, she cried but slowly she was down to one or two dogs. And then, an infection caused her to lose her leg. She is now confined to a wheel chair, but, after a period of deep depression, able to do the best she can with her strength and positivity. She volunteers for the humane society, posts about events in her town, takes care of a lovely dachshund Sasha, who was born blind. When I feel down, I think of Sally and if she can do it, so can I. I am so grateful that we found each other after some 40 years.

At the same time as I corresponded with Sally, I also corresponded with a Russian girl from Murmansk. Her name was Natasha. That letter exchange was part of our Russian language instruction at school that started in Grade 5. I regret not putting a greater effort into that correspondence. Perhaps I could have been for the girl from Murmansk a bit like who Sally was to me? At least, I could have offered her some simple pleasures that were not available to her otherwise. While I never asked Sally for anything and was very grateful for the gifts I received (and tried to reciprocate within the limited possibilities of a communist country), the very first letter I had received from Natasha included a request. She asked for something I could not find in my old (pre-war) and outdated Russian dictionary: she asked for a *pisatel'naya ruchka* which turned out to be a writing pen. Of course, I sent her a pen and most likely other things, but I did not put my heart into this friendship. It saddens me to recall this today. I also received one gift from Natasha—a bright orange plastic fox that kept falling apart—the paws and the tail did not fit well with the torso. She most certainly meant well and wanted to be nice, but the toy simply did not work and was poorly made.

These two letter exchanges gave me a lot to ponder at my tender age of 10 or 12. There was definitely a huge difference between the two systems. They produced very different toys. There was no doubt in my mind which toys I liked better and, therefore, which system I considered superior. No propaganda in the entire world could have persuaded me otherwise.

The devil is in the detail. While the official media in Poland and the school system had tried hard to persuade us that the Soviet Union was a paradise and the United States a place of terrible suffering, even as a child I knew that things were not that simple. Why would Natasha have asked me for a pen, in her first letter, if the Soviet Union were a country of plenty? We were told by our Defence Preparation teacher in Grade 8 that the enemy could attack by dropping, from planes, explosive devices disguised as colourful pens. We were not supposed to pick up any foreign-looking objects, however, I am pretty sure, all kids in my class would have done just that, had they seen one on the ground. What bothered me then was a simple question: if our government knew the enemy could try to lure us to pick up a bomb or a landmine that looked like a nice pen, why didn't they make enough pretty pens so that we would have no temptation to pick up something like that from the ground?

I remember from my childhood days feeling an odd kind of appreciation towards foreign tourists who littered the grey landscape of my city with colourful garbage: red Coke cans, cigarette wrappers. I could not explain that feeling but I knew, deep inside, that the world around me was made ugly on purpose or simply because those who decided about its aesthetics did not know any better. I thought that I knew better. First of all, I knew that there was another kind of aesthetics, found in nature, in the old architecture and at the old cemeteries, found in museums and in books. Or even in the colourful wrapping paper and Coke cans, objects designed to look beautiful and please senses. My career dream at the end of high school was to become a graphic designer and design labels and packaging for industrial products. Communist stores were never filled with competing products. Centrally planned economy and state monopoly meant that there was usually one variety of everything and the supply was usually below the demand. There was no need for advertising. Many products, especially food items, had so called 'substitute labels' (*etykiety zastępcze*), usually a piece of thick, yellowish paper with black print stating the name of the product, etc. Sometimes the proper label was not much better. In my imagination, I was designing beautiful and colourful containers and hoped that their aesthetic impact would change social practices. I thought that perhaps people would drink less and in a more civilized way from beautifully designed bottles of alcohol. I admit that this was rather naive and somewhat idealistic. I guess I wanted to design those beautiful product labels for the common good.

I never made it through the portfolio evaluation at the Warsaw Academy of Arts and had to select a different path. I had hoped to switch from German to at least Art History after my first year but the original of my high school diploma was safely locked in the Department of German and I was told that I could not apply for admission to another department without that original piece of paper. So I stayed, switched from German to Linguistics, became a linguist, and embraced the field with all my heart. Still my interest in the role of aesthetics in our daily struggle with totalitarian systems remains.

I finally found an explanation for that feeling of aesthetic discomfort in Zbigniew Herbert's poem "The power of Taste":

> It didn't require great character at all
> our refusal disagreement and resistance
> we had a shred of necessary courage
> but fundamentally it was a matter of taste
> Yes taste
> in which there are fibres of soul and the cartilage of conscience.

Indeed, as Hebert says in his poem: "if we had been better and more attractively tempted", perhaps we would have believed in the ideology that we were told to swallow on a daily basis. It was the ugliness of the communist construction of reality and its "syntax deprived of beauty of the subjunctive" that made some of us, I hope, think critically.

> Our eyes and ears refused obedience
> the princes of our senses proudly chose exile.

The idea that our moral judgments build upon unconscious reflexes and reactions to bad taste or revolting sights has scientific support. A group of researchers at the University of Toronto (Chapman et al. 2009) discovered that the facial grimace accompanying reactions to unfair treatment is basically the same as the one accompanying tasting rotten food or watching disgusting images. The co-author of the study, Adam Anderson, said that our brain had already discovered "a system for rejecting things that are bad for it. Then it co-opted this and attached it to conditions much removed from something tasting or smelling bad" (Keim 2009). Perhaps the power of taste is not just another metaphor. Maybe it can be taken more literally and applied in social life.

There are many people, both in the East and in the West, who still find communist ideals attractive and believe the theory to be right with only practical applications going awry. Those idealists could perhaps take a closer look at communist reality before advocating its introduction to new parts of the world. As someone who made a conscious decision to move away from my home country, I often feel the need to justify my choice. It is an easy assumption that people left communist countries for economic or political reasons. I do not consider any of these truly fitting in my case. I never really suffered economic hardship and I was not involved in politics enough to call myself persecuted. My personal reasons cannot be summed up easily. I guess it was mostly fear. I was not afraid of political persecution. I was not afraid that one day I could turn blind and believe the communist ideology the way Klemperer feared that he might one day succumb to propaganda lies if they surrounded him and if everyone else believed them. I think I was simply afraid that I might be too weak to stay true to my principles if someone were to threaten or coerce me. I wanted to do my PhD. What could I possibly compromise in order to achieve that goal? I wanted to have children. What price would I pay for their safety? Could I be bullied into doing something that would make me look at myself in the mirror with disgust? Quite honestly, I did not want to find out. Maybe it was cowardice. Maybe, after all, I was completely spineless. I simply felt that I did not want to make such choices. I thought that no one had the right to make me make such choices. And I felt that there must be places where such choices did not have to be made.

More than 40 years later, I feel that some of the pressures I was afraid of are human, not political. And those that are political may not exclusively apply to communism. We need to stay true to our inner sense of decency no matter what political system we live in. Life in communist Poland was in many ways easier, more black-and-white, than it is in the free world with more shades of grey. And modern technology along with free access to social media made propaganda much more dangerous. Nevertheless, the simple principle of being able to look at oneself in the mirror without disrespect is still something I believe in. Further more, I still find the concept of the power of taste helpful.

Some 70 years ago, Czesław Miłosz offered his own prescription for breaking with the communist nostalgia and I would like to finish my linguistic observations about my life in the space dominated by propaganda, about totalitarian systems and their language with his wise, even if unorthodox advice. For Miłosz, the aversion to (communist) propaganda proceeded

> not from the functioning of the reasoning mind, but from the revolt of the stomach. A man may persuade himself, by the most logical reasoning, that he will greatly benefit his health by swallowing live frogs; and, thus rationally convinced, he may swallow a first frog, then the second; but at the third his stomach will revolt. (Miłosz 1951/1990, xii-xiii)

I know that there are and there will always be many idealistic people who might believe in improving human nature and many pragmatic people who will believe in anything that justifies the bottom line. I can only wish them the same 'revolt of the stomach' and the 'power of taste', as referred to by Herbert in his poem, when it comes to swallowing the lies of any propaganda.

BIBLIOGRAPHY

Ackard, D.M. and D. Neumark-Sztainer. 2002. "Date violence and date rape among adolescents: associations with disordered eating behaviors and psychological health." *Child Abuse and Neglect*; 26(5):455-73.

Allport, Gordon W. 1954. *The Nature of Prejudice*. Cambridge, MA: Addison-Wesley.

Arendt, Hannah. 1951. *The Origins of Totalitarianism*. New York: Harcourt, Brace and World.

Aron, R. 1968. *Progress and Disillusion: The dialectics of modern society*. London: Pall Mall Press.

Arthur, Terry. 2000. "Is the stock exchange a casino?" *Economic Affairs*. December, 42-45._

Arthur, Terry. 2007. *Crap: A guide to politics*. London: Continuum International Publishing Group.

Arthur, Terry. 1975. *95 per cent is Crap: A plain man's guide to British politics*. Bedford, England: Libertarian Books Limited.

Austin, J. L. 1962. *How to Do Things With Words*. The William James Lectures delivered at Harvard University in 1955. Oxford: Oxford University Press.

Besançon, Alain. 1976. *The Soviet Syndrome*. New York: Harcourt, Brace, Jovanovich.

Booth, Philip & Krzysztof Stroiński. 2006. "Teaching professionalism and the principles of the market economy in post-communist Eastern Europe." In Vittorina Cecchetto & Magda Stroińska (eds.) *The International Classroom: Challenging the Notion*. Frankfurt am main: Peter Lang.

Borowski, Tadeusz. 1967. *This way for the Gas, Ladies and Gentlemen*. Viking, Penguin.

Brener, N.D., P.M. McMahon, C.W. Warren and K.A. Douglas. 1999. "Forced sexual intercourse and associated health-risk behaviors among female college students in the United States." *Journal of Consulting and Clinical Psychology;* 67. 252-9.

Brooks, David. 2008. "The Luxurious Growth," Op-Ed in *The New York Times,* July 15, 2008, accessed online on July 16, 2008 at <http://topics.nytimes.com/top/opinion/editorialsandoped/oped/columnists/davidbrooks/index.html?inline=nyt-per.

Brzezinski, Zbigniew, a quote about Jan Nowak-Jeziorański on Wikiquote.org. Consulted on April 20, 2005 at http://en.wikiquote.org/wiki/Jan_Nowak-Jezioranski.

Champion, H.L., K.L. Foley, R.H. DuRant, R. Hensberry, D. Altman and M. Wolfson. 2004. "Adolescent sexual victimization, use of alcohol and other substances, and other health risk behaviors." *Journal of Adolescent Health.* 35(4). 321-8.

"Empty promises," definition, available on the Changingminds.org website at http://changingminds.org/disciplines/negotiation/tactics/empty_promises.htm.

"Effects of betrayal," definition, available on the Changingminds.org website at http://changingminds.org/explanations/trust/effects_of_betrayal.htm.

Chapman, H. A., Kim, D.A., Susskind, J.M. and Anderson, A.K. 2009. "In Bad Taste: Evidence for the Oral Origins of Moral Disgust." *Science* Vol. 323. no. 5918. 1222 – 1226.

Collin, F. 1997. *Social Reality.* London and New York: Routledge.

Communism: Why it failed? http://www.comptons.com/encyclopedia/ARTICLES/ 0025/00446976_A.html

"Campaign 2000 to End Child and family Poverty in Canada." Available at http://www.campaign2000.ca/ consulted Dec. 6, 2007.
Canovan, Margaret. 1981. *Populism.* New York and London: Harcourt Brace Jovanovich.

CBOS (2021). *Opinia publiczna wobec uchodźców i sytuacji migrantów na granicy z Białorusią* ('Public opinion towards refugees and the situation of migrants at the border with Belorussia'). Research Report 111/2021.Warszawa. Available at: https://www.cbos.pl/SPISKOM.POL/2021/K_111_21.PDF

Cooray, Mark. 1985. "Communism and Democratic Socialism and the creation of a New Man," Available at http://www.ourcivilisation.com/cooray/westdem/chap13.htm. Consulted on May 20, 2006.

Curran, C. 1958. *The Spectator*, JULY 6, page 8

Czcibór-Piotrowski, Andrzej. 1999. *Rzeczy nienasycone*. Warszawa: W.A.B.

Czcibor-Piotrowski, Andrzej. 2001. *Cud w Esfahanie*. Warszawa: W.A.B.

Drzazga, G., Radisevic, I. and Stroińska, M. 2012. "Discourse on minorities and social exclusion in post-communist Poland and Serbia: An exercise in political correctness or a test for tolerance." *Warsaw East European Review*, Vol. II. 115-130.

Drzazga, Grażyna, Stroinska, Magda & Vikki Cecchetto. (2022) "Different words, different worlds: the impact of linguistic labels on societal perception of refugees." *LACUS Forum* 46:3; 14-27.

"Effects of betrayal", definition. Available on the website of ChangingMinds.org online at http://changingminds.org/explanations/trust/effects_of_betrayal.htm.

"Empty promises", definition. Available on the website of ChangingMinds.org online at http://changingminds.org/disciplines/negotiation/tactics/empty_promises.htm.

Gellner, Ernest and Ghita Ionescu, (eds). 1969. *Populism. Its Meanings and National Characteristics*, London: Weidenfeld and Nicolson.

Faravelli, C., A. Giugni, S. Salvatori and V. Ricca. 2004. "Psychopathology after rape." *American Journal of Psychiatry*. 161(8). 1483-5.

Felitti, V.J., R.F. Anda, D. Nordenberg, D.F. Williamson, A.M. Spitz, V. Edwards et al. 1998. "Relationship of childhood abuse and household dysfunction to many of the leading causes of death in adults: the Adverse Childhood Experiences study." *American Journal of Preventive Medicine* 14.245–58.

Fischer-Dueckelmann, Dr. Anna. 1911. *Die Frau als Hausaerztin: ein aerztliches Nachschlagebuch fuer die Frau*, Stuttgart, Sueddeutsches Verlags-Institut

Friszke, Andrzej. 1994/1997. "The March 1968 Protest Movement in Light of Ministry of Interior Reports to the Party Leadership".

INTERMARIUM. Volume 1, Number 1. http://www.columbia.edu/cu/sipa/REGIONAL/ECE/vol1no1/friszke.html. Originally published in Polish in Więź (March 1994).

"Gaidar, Arkady Petrovich." Encyclopedia of Soviet Writers online. Available at http://www.sovlit.com/bios/gaidar.html/.

Gaidar, Egor Timurovich. 1999. Days of defeat and victory. Translated by Jane Ann Miller. Washington, D.C.: University of Washington Press.

Głowiński, Michał. 1990. *Nowomowa po polsku* ('Newspeak in Polish'), Warszawa: PEN.

Głowiński, Michał. 1991. *Marcowe gadanie: komentarze do słów* 1966-1971 ('March Chatter: commentaries on words 1966-1971'), Warszawa: Pomost.

Głowiński, Michał. 1993. *Peereliada: komentarze do slow 1976-1981 ('PRLs Carnival: Some Comments on Words 1976-1981').* Warszawa: PIW.

Głowiński, Michał. 1996. *Mowa w stanie oblężenia*: 1982-1985 ('Language uder Siege: 1982-1985). Warszawa: Open.

Goebbels, Joseph. 1934. Speech delivered at the Party Rally in Nurnberg 1934. Printed in Reichstagung in Nürnberg 1934, Berlin: Vaterländischer Verlag C. A. Weller, 1934. 226-246.

Goffman, Erving. 1959. *The presentation of self in everyday life.* Garden City, N.Y.: Doubleday.

Goldhagen, Daniel. *Hitler's Willing Executioners: Ordinary Germans and the Holocaust.* New York: Vintage Books.

Goldsworthy, Vesna. 2005. *Chernobyl Strawberries.* London: Atlantic Books.

Graczyk, Marcin. 2006. "*Giertych: 'wychowanie patriotyczne do szkół*", *Gazeta Wyborcza*, June 06, 2006. Accessed on April 29, 2009 at http://wyborcza.pl/1,75478,3398318.html.

Gregor, A. James. 2000. *The Faces of Janus: Marxism and Fascism in the Twentieth Century.* New Haven and London: Yale University Press.

Guirdham, M. 1999. *Communicating across Cultures.* London: Macmillan Business.

Gustafson, T. 1999. *Capitalism Russian-style*. Cambridge: Cambridge University Press.

Halion, Kevin. 1989. *Deconstruction and Speech Act Theory: A Defence of the Distinction between Normal and Parasitic Speech Acts*. PhD Dissertation at McMaster University. Available on line at http://www.e-anglais.com/thesis.html.

Hall, Stuart, Chas Critcher, Tony Jefferson, John Clarke and Brian Roberts. 1978. *Policing the Crisis: Mugging, the State, and Law and Order*. London: Macmillan.

Hamilton, Andrew. 2005. "Human dignity and democracy." *Eureka Street, Jesuit Publications*. January/February. http://www.eurekastreet.com.au/articles/0501.html.

Hayek, F.A. 1944. *The Road to Serfdom*. London: Routledge & Kegan Paul.

Hayek, F.A. 1978. *New Studies in Philosophy, Politics, Economics and the History of Ideas*. London, Melbourne and Henley: Routledge & Kegan Paul.

Hayek, F.A. 1988/1998. *The Fatal Conceit: The Errors of Socialism*. Vol. Collected Works of F.A. Hayek, edited by W.W. Bartley III. London: Routledge.

Held, Joseph. 1996. *Populism in Eastern Europe: racism*, nationalism and society. New York: Boulder.

Heller, Mikhail. 1988 *Cogs in the Wheel: The Formation of Soviet Man*. New York: Alfred A. Knopf, Inc.

Hensel, Jana. 2002 Zonenkinder. Berlin: Rowohlt.Hensel, Jana. 2004. *After the Wall*, translated from German by Jefferson Chase. New York: Public Affairs.

Hilton, James L. and von Hippel, William. 1996. "Stereotypes." *Annual Review of Psychology* 47: 237-271.

Hitler, Adolf. 1925. *Mein Kampf*. Verlag Franz Eher Nachf, G.M.B.H.

Hitler, Adolf. 1943/1971. *Mein Kampf*. Boston: Houghton Mifflin Company.

Hunter, Edward. 1950. "Brain-Washing' Tactics Force Chinese into Ranks of Communist Party." *Miami News*, (Sept. 24, 1950), p. 2A.

Huxley, Aldous. 1932/2007. *Brave New World.* London: Vintage.

Jewkes. R., P. Sen and C. Garcia-Moreno. 2002. “Sexual violence.” In: Krug E., L.L. Dahlberg, J.A. Mercy et al., (eds). *World Report on Violence and Health.* Geneva: World Health Organization. 213–239.

Jowett, Garth S. and Victoria O’Donnell. 2006. *Propaganda and Persuasion, 4th edition.* Thousand Oaks, CA: Sage.

Keim, Brandon. 2009. “Immorality a Lot Like Rotten Food.” *Wired* News, February 26, 2009, accessed on May 5, 2009 at http://www.wired.com/wiredscience/2009/02/moraldisgust/.

Kinsley, M. 2008. “Why They Really Run,” *Time* (Canadian Edition), January 14, 2008: 48.

Klamer, A., D.N. McCloskey, and R.M. Solow. 1988. *The Consequences of Economic Rhetoric.* Cambridge: Cambridge University Press.

Klein, Naomi. 2000. *No Logo: Taking Aim at the Brand Bullies.* Toronto: Vintage Canada.

Klemperer, Victor. 1947/2000. *The Language of the Third Reich. LTI: Lingua Tertii Imperii,* translated from German by Martin Brady. London and New Brunswick, N.J.: The Athlone Press.

Koestler, Arthur. 1940. *Darkness at Noon.* London: Jonathan Cape.

Koestler, Arthur. 1955. *The Trail of the Dinosaur and Other Essays.* New York: The MacMillan Company.

Krakow, B., D. Melendrez, L. Johnston, T,D. Warner, J.O. Clark, M. Pacheco et al. 2002. “Sleep-disordered breathing, psychiatric distress, and quality of life impairment in sexual assault survivors.” *Journal of Nervous and Mental Disease* 2002. 442-52.

Kundera, Milan. 1967/2001. *The joke.* New York , NY: Perennial. Aaron Asher Books.

“Lepper’s Reef” (‘Co to jest Rafa Leppera’). 2004. An article published on November 23, 2004 by the Samoobrona Party’s Office.

Levitas, Ruth. 1991. *The Concept of Utopia.* Syracuse, NY: Syracuse University Press.

Lifton, R. J. 1961. *Thought Reform and the Psychology of Totalism: S Study of ‘Brainwashing’ in China.* London: Victor Gollancz.

Löschmann, M. & Stroińska, M. (eds). 1998. *Stereotype im*

Fremdsprachenunterricht, Tübingen: Peter Lang Verlag.

Łysiak, Waldemar. 2000. *Stulecie kłamców*. Chicago, Warszawa: Ex Libris – Polish Book Gallery Inc.

Maaz, H.-J. 1995. *Behind the Wall: The Inner Life of Communist Germany.* New York: Norton.

Majcherek, Janusz A. 2008. "Czas Patriotów" ('Time of the Patriots'), in *Gazeta Wyborcza*, August 8, 2008. Pages 24-25.

Malamuth, N.M. 1998. "The confluence model as an organizing framework for research on sexually aggressive men: risk moderators, imagined aggression, and pornography consumption." In: Geen, R.G. and E. Donnerstein (eds). *Human aggression: theories, research, and implications for social policy.* San Diego: Academic Press. 229–45.

Melich, Jiri S. 1997. "The Post-Communist Mind: Socio-psychological and Cultural Aspects of the Communist Legacy and the Transformation Processes in Eastern Europe." In *Transition in Central and Eastern Europe*, Zeljko Ševic and Glendal Wright (eds). Beograd: YASF- Student Cultural Centre. 20-41.

Mény, Yves and Yves Surel. 2002. "The Constitutive Ambiguity of Populism." In: Mény, Y. and Y. Surel (eds.) *Democracies and the Populist Challenge.* New York: Palgrave.

Miłosz, Czesław. 1951/1990. *The Captive Mind.* New York: Vintage International.

Miodek, Jan (ed.). 1996. *O zagrożeniach i bogactwie Polszczyzny.* Wrocław: Towarzystwo Przyjaciół Polonistyki Wrocławskiej.

Mises von, Alfred. 1922/1981. *Socialism*. Translated from German by J. Kahane. Indianapolis: Liberty Fund.

Neidleman, Jason Andrew. 2001. *The General Will is Citizenship: Inquiries into French Political Thought.* New York: Rowman and Littlefield Publishers Inc.

O'Rourke, B. 1998. "Europe: EU reaches the crossroads with eastward expansion." Available at www.rferl.org/nca/features/1998/04/F.RU.980423133059.html.

Orwell, George. 1945. "Notes on Nationalism." *Polemic*, No 1 - October 1945.

Orwell, George. 1949/1990. *Nineteen Eighty-Four (aka 1984)*. London: Penguin Books.

Orwell, George. 1946/1972. "Politics and the English Language." In *Marxism and Art: Writings in Aesthetics and Criticism*, Berel Lang and Forrest Williams, eds. New York: David McKay Company. Pages 426-37.

Parnas, David Lorge. 1993. "Decoding politicians: A professor in McMaster University's Communications Research Laboratory shows how to find the information in the political speeches." *The Hamilton Spectator*, Hamilton, Ont., Oct 22, 1993, page A.7.

Pawlicka, Aleksandra. 2023. "Prof. Barbara Engelking: Niczego się nie uczymy. Zwycięża zło." *Newsweek*, 21 April 2023. Available at: https://www.newsweek.pl/historia/prof-barbara-engelking-niczego-sie-nie-uczymy-zwycieza-zlo/08xwkhm

Pei, Mario. 1978. *Weasel Words: The art of saying what you don't mean*. New York: Harper & Row.

Penny, Laura. 2005. *Your Call is Important to Us: The Truth about Bullshit*. New York. Crown Publishers.

Piotrowski, Andrzej. 1962. *Prośba o Annę. Opowieść w szesnastu snach*. Warszawa: Wydawnictwo PAX.

Radio Free Europe: The Mission Statement of Radio Free Europe/ Radio Liberty, consulted on April 20, 2005 at http://www.rferl.org/about/organization/mission-statement.asp.

Reich, Wilhelm. 1970. *The Mass Psychology of Fascism*. London: Souvenir Press.

Rogge, O. John. 1959. *Why Men Confess: From the Inquisition to Brainwashing*. New York: Thomas Nelson and Sons. First Edition.

Rousseau, Jean-Jacques. 1782/1985. *The Government of Poland*. Trans. Willmoore Kendall. Indianapolis: Hackett. .

Rousseau, Jean-Jacques. 1762/2003. *On the Social Contract*. Trans. G.D.H. Cole. Dover Publications. Garden City, N.Y. .

Rusch, Claudia. 2003. *Meine freie deutsche Jugend*. Frankfurt am Main: Fischer.

Sapir, Edward. 1929. 'The Status of Linguistics as a Science,' *Language*, 5(4): 207-214.

Searle, John R. 1969. *Speech Acts: An Essay in the Philosophy of Language*. Cambridge: Cambridge University Press.

Sargant, William. 1957. *Battle for the Mind: A Physiology of Conversion and Brainwashing*. London: Heinemann.

Schoepflin, G. 2000. *Nations, Identity, Power: The new politics of Europe*. London: Hurst.

Sheffield, Emilyn A et al. 1985. "Health Status and Leisure Behavior of Sexual Assault Victims: Educational Opportunities for Health and Leisure Professionals". Paper presented at the Annual Meeting of the Southwest Educational Research Association (Austin, TX, January 31-February 2, 1985). Available online at http://eric.ed.gov/

Sigmund, Anna Maria. 2000. *Women of the Third Reich*. Richmond Hill, Ontario: NDE Publishing.

Solzhenitsyn, Aleksandr I. 1973. *The Gulag Archipelago* (1st ed.). Harper & Row.

Stellrecht, Helmut. 1943. *Glauben und Handeln. Ein Bekenntnis der jungen Nation* (Berlin: Zentralverlag der NSDAP., Franz Eher Nachf. English version consulted on line on July 15, 2008 at http://www.calvin.edu/academic/cas/gpa/glauben.htm.

Sondaż: Większość Polaków za przyjmowaniem uchodźców ('Survey: the majority of Poles for accepting refugees'). 2021. *Rzczpospolita* 21.02.2021. Available at: https://www.rp.pl/kraj/art264831-sondaz-wiekszosc-polakow-za-przyjmowaniem-uchodzcow.

Strawson, P. 1964. "Intention and convention in speech acts." *The Philosophical Review* **73**: 439-60, reprinted in Strawson, *Logico-Linguistic Papers*. London: Methuen. 1971.

Strawson, P. 1973. "Austin and 'locutionary meaning.'" In G.Warnock (ed.), *Essays on J. L. Austin*, Oxford: Clarendon Press. 46–68.

Streatfeild, Dominic. 2007. *Brainwash: The Secret History of Mind Control*. New York, N.Y.: St. Martin's Press.

Stroińska, Magda. 1994. "Language that Creates a Social Reality: Linguistic Relativism and the Language of Ideologies", in *Socialist Realism*, Nina Kolesnikoff and Walter Smyrniw (eds). 53-56.

Stroińska, Magda. 1998. "Them and us: on cognitive and pedagogical aspects of the language based stereotyping", in M. Loeschmann and M. Stroińska (eds) *Stereotype im Fremdsprachenunterricht*, Frankfurt am Main: Peter Lang.

Stroińska, M. & P. Popovic. 1999. "Discourse of black and white: linguistic principles of hate speech", in J. Verschueren (ed.) *Language and Ideology: Selected Papers from the 6th International Pragmatics Conference*, IprA v.z.w., Antwerp. 544-557.

Stroińska Magda. 2000. "Forbidden reality: linguistic creation and deconstruction of social reality", in F. Lloyd and C. O'Brien (eds) Secret *Spaces, Forbidden Places*, Oxford: Berghahn Books, 121-132.

Stroińska, Magda. (ed.) 2001. *Relative points of view: Linguistic representations of culture.* Oxford and New York: Berghahn Books.

Stroińska, Magda. 2002. "Language and Totalitarian Regimes", *Journal of Economic Affairs*, 22:2, 23-29.

Stroińska, Magda & Vittorina Cecchetto. 2005. "The rhetoric of threat and insecurity: Speech Act Theory and linguistic mechanisms of populist rhetoric", paper presented at the 2005 International Pragmatics Conference in Riva del Garda, Italy.

Stroińska, M. (2006) "Motivation and anxiety: on the journey to academic success", *The International Classroom: Challenging the notion,* V. Cecchetto and M. Stroińska (eds), Frankfurt/Main: Peter Lang. 111-130.

Stroińska, Magda. 2011. "The linguistic legacy of the communist propaganda in post-communist thought patterns: the case of Poland. In Ernest Andrews (ed) *Legacies of Totalitarian Language in the Discourse Culture of the Post-Totalitarian* Era. Lanham, MD: Lexington, 39-54.

Stroińska, Magda & Grażyna Drzazga. 2017. "Public and private hate speech in Poland." *Warsaw East European Review* VOL VII, 119-134.

Stroińska, Magda & Kate Szymanski. 2017. "Metafora i trauma" (in Polish), *TEXT UND DISKURS* Vol 10; 163-176.

Stroińska, Magda & Vikki Cecchetto. 2019. "Can there be a 'safe haven' for trauma survivors in this social media dominated world?" *TRAMES*, 2019, 23(73/68).

Stroińska, Magda. 2019. "National independence versus societal trauma: can a nation enslaved by its past be independent? *Warsaw East European Review* Vol IX, 27-37.

Stroińska, Magda & Grażyna Drzazga (2020) "Toxic language of contempt: The real purpose of online hate speech." *Warsaw East European Review* VOL X, 79-90.

Taylor, Kathleen. 2004. *Brainwashing: The Science of Thought Control.* Oxford: Oxford University Press.

The American Heritage Dictionary of the English Language. 2003. Fourth Edition. Houghton Mifflin Company.

Thomas, Jenny. 1995. *Meaning in interaction: An introduction to pragmatics.* London: Longman.

TNS Hoffmann. 2014. Stosunek Polaków do uchodźców i osób starających się o przyznanie statusu uchodźcy ('Attidude of Poles towards refugees and persons applying for refugee status'). Kostrzyński, Rafał (editor), Warsaw: UNHCR. Available at https://www.unhcr.org/pl/wp-content/uploads/sites/22/2020/11/Sondaz-UNHCR-2013.pdf

Tyrmand, Leoplold. 2002. *Porachunki osobiste.* Warszawa: Wydawnictwo LTW.

Vonnegut, Jr., Kurt. 1969. *Slaughterhouse-Five or The Children's Crusade.* Delta.

Wacholz, Leon. 1925. *Medycyna sądowa. Na podstawie ustaw obowiązujących na ziemiach polskich.* Warszawa: Gebethner i Wolf.

Waldorn, J. 2012. *The harm in hate speech.* Cambridge, MA: Harvard University Press.

Walton, D. 2000. *Scare Tactics: Arguments That Appeal to Fear and Threats.* Springer Netherlands.

Weyland, Kurt. 1999. "Neoliberal Populism in Latin America and Eastern Europe." *Comparative Politics,* Vol. 31, No. 4. 379-401.

Wittgenstein, Ludwig. 1922. *Tractatus Logico-Philosophicus.* London.

Ystgaard, M., I. Hestetun, M. Loeb and L. Mehlum. 2004. "Is there a specific relationship between childhood sexual and physical abuse and repeated suicidal behavior?" *Child Abuse and Neglect*; 28(8). 863-75.

Zieliński, Michał. 2001. "Słownik wyrazów zbytecznych" ('Dictionary of useless words'), *Wprost*, 22 April 2001. 42-43.

ACKNOWLEDGEMENTS

It is difficult to find a way to thank all those who helped this book to take its final shape, as it took me a lifetime to write it. I shall therefore start at the end and move backwards, from the present to the past.

My most heartfelt thanks go to Dr. Lorene Shyba, the publisher at Durvile & UpRoute Books, for taking on this project, for her encouraging comments, her careful, close reading of the text, and meticulous polishing of my English. Many thanks also to Jillian Bell for her skillful editing of the manuscript and making it more readable.

I also would like to thank Marion Berghahn from Berghahn Books, Oxford for giving me the initial push to write this book. I am sorry that I disappointed her by ending up with a book that was not a strictly academic publication. The world around us has changed so much since 2001 that I simply could not separate my academic perspective from my personal experiences. I am also very grateful to Philip Booth of the Institute of Economic Affairs and now St. Mary's University for inviting me to give a talk on Language and Totalitarian Regimes at IEA in London in 2001, where this whole journey began.

There are very many friends, colleagues, teachers, mentors, and relatives who played a role in shaping my views on language and propaganda. Unfortunately, many of them will not see this book even though they contributed to it in many ways: my brother Andrzej Czcibor-Piotrowski, Zosia Klimaszewska, Peter Szalapaj, Andrzej Mierzejewski, Jim Miller, Vikki Cecchetto, Lieve Spaas, Anna Duszak, my cousins Kelly and Cheryl Warczyglowa, many of my professors from Warsaw University, my academic friends in Warsaw, Edinburgh, at McMaster and in Kingston-upon-Thames. I miss you.

I thank Teresa Dobrzyńska-Janusz for her friendship and mentorship, and for introducing me to Professor Michał Głowiński. I thank Mr. Leszek Chachulski, my French teacher for introducing me to the writings of Victor Klemperer. I learned a lot from my undergraduate and graduate students, in particular Grażyna Drzazga, who became my academic collaborator in the study of propaganda and, more recently, hate speech.

I have a huge debt of gratitude towards Axel Grunwald, whom I met in 1981 and who has been a steadfast supporter of my academic endeavours. He was the first person who allowed me to see Poland through

Western eyes. I am also thankful to Kazimierz Orłoś for many insightful comments and for his amazing books that opened my eyes to how language may get detached from reality.

A very important person in this adventure through the life of language has been my friend Kasia—Kate Szymanski, now a clinical psychologist at Adelphi University. We have been friends for over 60 years, still keep in touch, travel together and even have worked on some joint academic projects. Kasia has not only been my best friend but she also helped me realize how much we have been shaped by the traumas of our parents and the life in communist Poland and many thoughts presented here come from our experiences together.

I would like to give very special thanks to my Parents, Zofia and Eugeniusz, for raising me without lies about history and politics, and for helping me to open doors to all I wanted to know and do. I am sorry that I cannot say this to you in person. Mine was not an ideal home, my Mom worried too much and my Dad passed away before I was old enough to really learn from him. But they both created an environment where I could really grow as a person and they believed that I would be curious. When I was 5, I asked my Father to write something in my *Stammbuch*, a memory book (*pamiętnik*) kids in Poland used to have where friends, family, and other people would write something, or just leave an autograph. He wrote a Latin quote from Ovid: *donec eris felix, multos numerabis amicos; tempora si fuerint nubile, sola eris.* A rough translation would be: "When you are happy, you will have numerous friends. But when times become darker, you will be alone." Who writes something like that to a child unless they want that child to dig deeper?

I would also like to thank my parents in-law for always supporting me and for helping me succeed in my academic career by assisting me with getting over daily life hurdles, not only when my children were little but always. They have been to me like my own parents. Thank you. I am grateful to Kris for going with me half way through life and pushing me to reach for things I would not have attempted without him. I am sad that we got separated in the labyrinth of post-communist transformations but I never regretted choosing the path I chose.

I have written this book mostly for my children, Joanna and Kubuś so that one day they may understand me better, both in terms of my language choices and in terms of my fears and irrational reactions. I hoped that the world they live in will be a better one but I am no longer so sure.

Thank you all, my Friends. You have no idea how much you all mean to me!

MAGDA STROIŃSKA PHD

Magda Stroińska MA (Warsaw), PhD (Edinburgh) has been a Professor of Linguistics and German at McMaster University since 1988. Her major areas of research and publication include sociolinguistics; analysis of discourse, and cross-cultural issues in pragmatics and cognition, in particular linguistic representations of culture; cultural stereotyping; language and politics; propaganda; the issues of identity in exile; aging and bilingualism; translation; interpretation and language brokering; as well as language and psychological trauma. Magda lives in Woodstock, Ontario, Canada.